Odetta. *Christmas Spirituals*. Waterbury, VT: Alcazar Productions, 1988.

Florence Quivar. *Ride On, King Jesus*. Hayes Middlesex, England: EMI Records, 1990.

Derek Lee Ragin, with Moses Hogan and the New World Ensemble. *Ev'ry Time I Feel the Spirit: Spirituals*. Englewood, NJ: Channel Classics, 1991.

Bernice Johnson Reagon, compiler. *Wade in the Water, Vol I: African American Spirituals: The Concert Tradition*. Washington, D.C.: Smithsonian Institution/ Folkways Recordings, 1994.

Bernice Johnson Reagon, compiler. *Wade in the Water, Vol II: African American Congregational Singing*. Washington, D.C.: Smithsonian Institution/Folkways Recordings, 1994.

Paul Robeson. *The Power and the Glory*. New York: Columbia Records, 1991.

Smithsonian Institution. *Been in the Storm So Long: Spirituals, Folk Tales and Children's Games from John's Island, South Carolina*. Washington, D.C.: Smithsonian/Folkways Recordings, 1990.

Jubliant Sykes. *Jubilant*. New York: Sony, 1998.

Linda Tillery and the Cultural Heritage Choir. *Good Time, A Good Time*. Oakland, CA: Tuizer Music, 1995.

Linda Tillery and the Cultural Heritage Choir. *Front Porch Music*. Redway, CA: Earthbeat!, 1997.

Cynthia Willson-Felder. *New Songs of Zion*. Burbank, CA: Warner Bros. Records, Warner Alliance, 1993.

Videos

Kathleen Battle and Jessye Norman. *Spirituals in Concert*. New York: WNET-TV (Produced for Great Performances Series, Jack Venza, Executive Producer), 1993.

Blackside, Inc. (Henry Hampton, Executive Producer). *Eyes on the Prize I: America's Civil Rights Years*. Alexandria, VA: PBS Video, 1986.

Jim Brown. *We Shall Overcome: The Song That Moved a Nation*. San Francisco: California Newsreel, 1989.

Georgia Public Television. (Clate Sanders and Art Rosenbaum, Producers). *Down Yonder: The McIntosh County Shouters*. Athens, GA: University of Georgia Center for Continuing Education, 1988.

KCNC-TV. (Produced by Reynelda Muse and Kevin Hartsfield in collaboration with Arthur Jones and The Spirituals Project). *Balm in Gilead: The Legacy of African American Spirituals*. Denver: KCNC-TV (Channel 4), 1997. Available for educational use only.

Bill Moyers. *Amazing Grace*. Los Angeles: PBS Home Video, 1990.

Bill Moyersl, with Bernice Johnson Reagon. *The Songs are Free*. Cooper Station, NY: Mystic Fire Videos, 1991.

WGBH-TV (Orlando Bagwell, Executive Producer). *Africans in America*. Boston: WGBH, 1998.

WGBH-TV (Orlando Bagwell, Producer-Director). *Roots of Resistance: A Story of the Underground Railroad*. Boston: WGBH-TV, 1990.

Wade in the Water

Wade in the Water

The Wisdom of the Spirituals

Arthur C. Jones

ORBIS BOOKS

Maryknoll, New York 10545

The Catholic Foreign Mission Society of America (Maryknoll) recruits and trains people for overseas missionary service. Through Orbis Books, Maryknoll aims to foster the international dialogue that is essential to mission. The books published, however, reflect the opinions of their authors and are not meant to represent the official position of the society.

To obtain more information about Maryknoll and Orbis Books, please visit our website at www.maryknoll.org.

For more information about the Spirituals and the work of the author contact Arthur C. Jones, Director, The Spirituals Project, 2155 South Race Street, Denver, CO 80208. http://wwwspiritualsproject.org

Manufactured in the United States of America

Library of Congress Cataloging-in-Publication Data

Jones, Arthur C.
    Wade in the water : the wisdom of the spirituals / Arthur C. Jones.
        p.   cm.
    Includes bibliographical references (p.   ) and index.
    ISBN 1-57075-288-5 (pbk.)
    1. Spirituals (Songs)—History and criticism.   2. Afro-Americans—Music—History and criticism.
ML3556.J72   1999
782.25'3—dc21   99-15103
                                                               CIP

To 'Kula, Sékou, Joella
and their twenty-first century peers,
all heirs of the spirit, the struggle and the songs

Contents

Foreword

Vincent Harding

In the course of the last 150 years the vibrant world of those African-American songs called "Spirituals" has been explored and presented to us by a compelling variety of writers from the black community. They have ranged from Frederick Douglass, the fugitive slave turned abolitionist leader and national moral guide, to W. E. B. DuBois, the scholar-philosopher-activist who knew the "sorrow songs" at deep places in his own life; from James Welson Johnson to Bernice Johnson Reagon, both gifted musicians and freedom movement activists; to Howard Thurman and James Cone, religious guides for the nation. These, of course are only a few of the men and women who have been deeply compelled to share with all of us their own transformative wrestlings with the grand resources of their foreparents' creations. In each case, something at the center of their being responded to the insistent beauty and undeniable spiritual genius of these musical products of an enslaved community's struggle with the vital human issues of life and death, hope and despair, slavery and freedom. Something compelled them to share with all Americans their musings on the dark radiance of the songs and the singers.

Now Arthur Jones joins that company of writers, seekers, testifiers, finding himself "suddenly at home" in the presence of the spirituals, discovering in their life a grounding that he had lost, gaining access through their words and music to an "extraordinary healing power." As he addresses us through the pages of *Wade in the Water*, as he sings to us on the accompanying tape, we realize that we are being engaged by a compassionate brother with an unusual, empowering set of gifts. As a result, he is able to offer us a richly textured, remarkably insightful rendering of the spirituals, their original settings, and their possible meanings for us today. Arthur (since we are personal friends, I take the liberty of using his first name here) writes for us as an African-American performing artist who has literally immersed himself in the words, the music, the spirit and the history of these amazing and often undervalued creations of an enslaved people. In addition, he enters them from the perspective of a practicing psychologist who is familiar with the best insights of a Jungian approach to the evolving human spirit. And it is always clear that Arthur is writing as a committed, socially concerned citizen of this nation and this world who, like his enslaved ancestors, is in constant search for "A City Called Heaven," a community rooted and grounded in the continuing struggles for justice, freedom, compassion and hope that we must carry on together in this world.

So when Arthur calls our attention to the ways in which the spirituals testify to "the unlimited possibilities for human transformation," this is not an individualistically oriented vision. Indeed he makes it manifestly clear that he always sees a larger image. For he takes seriously Bernice Johnson Reagon's concern when she says, "I'm not sure if black people can get through the next century without this repertoire." But for him, (as for her) the children of Africa in America must "get through" not only for ourselves, but in order for us to re-claim our role "as moral leaders and agents of transformation of the larger society." (In an important aside, Arthur warns the black community about the danger of losing the spirituals to a single-minded addiction to contemporary gospel music in our churches. For he sees the lyrics of gospel music as far less encouraging to a vision of a renewed society, less engaged than the spirituals in a call to participation in collectively building a new and just social order.)

Among the other gifts that Arthur brings to this work is his obvious openness to the spiritual and musical traditions of Africa. Thus he is able to reflect with us on a number of the ways in which that ancient, ever-present cultural matrix was taken by the enslaved community into the terrible crucible of their experience with North American bondage, and he reminds us of their inspired creation of an African-ized, freedom-oriented version of Christianity. Indeed that African-American religious base is Art's own ultimate ground, and his approach to the spirituals grows out of that setting.

Standing on such a home ground, one that has been shaped by empowering spirit and costly struggles, Arthur invites us all to participate in the world of the spirituals with him. Without any hesitation or apology, he extends a special invitation to those who share with him the African-American ancestry that produced the songs. To us he addresses a bold call to re-claim the spirituals as a great resource in transforming ourselves and this nation. At the same moment,

Arthur declares that the spirituals are available to all persons who are prepared to open themselves to the unsettling, healing power that inhabits these marvelous songs of life. His passionate invitation to all seekers comes partly out of his own generous spirit, a spirit that constantly glows through the written word and is unmistakingly present in his affecting musical presentation of the spirituals. (Since we have all lost so much contact with this music of renewal by this last decade of our century, it was a wise and helpful decision by the publisher to make available to us a tape of Arthur's soulful rendition of a number of the songs he writes about.) But his openness is also shaped by his profound conviction that these songs were created out of "deeply meaningful, archetypally human experiences, relevant not only to the specific circumstances of slavery but also to women and men struggling with issues of justice, freedom, and spiritual wholeness in all times and places."

So his work, written for us all, makes great demands on all of us, whatever our ancestral lineages. Some of us are challenged to seek healing, wisdom, and direction from the people and traditions we have so long rejected and devalued. Some of us are called insistently to take on the painful and enlightened responsibility of moral leadership for a society that so often seems to be dominated by the very people who have long rejected and afflicted us. And eventually Arthur presses all of us to work our way past the morally numbing detritus of modern society and culture to enter again and learn from the world of those enslaved men and women who actually believed in a transformative cosmic reality that extended far beyond what we can see with our eyes, organize with our machines, purchase with our money, or comprehend with our minds.

Introducing us to many fascinating stories, encouraging us to use our imaginations to enter the historical settings where the songs have been most creatively reappropriated, our artist-guide finds many ways to say clearly, "we have to re-claim our songs." And he constantly reminds us that for him the "we" ultimately means all Americans. For he is convinced that the conscious return to the songs and to the circumstances out of which they came can become for us collectively what it has been for him personally, a return to a healing "home," a movement forward to a new level of national maturity, a pilgrimage of renewal through a harsh and often discouraging desert.

When I consider the model he presents, the beauty of his spirit, the gift of his artistry, and the compassionate embrace of his life, it seems to me that his invitation to move from whatever fragile security we now occupy in order to "wade in the water" is at least worthy of our serious consideration. His call seems a risk worth taking, a song worth singing, a journey worth beginning. Perhaps it will be one step toward the discovery or rediscovery of some of our fore-parents. Such an engagement, penetrating all boundaries of time, race, and nationality, such a movement into our deepest spiritual roots, may open the amazing possibility that these singers in the wilderness of slavery could be our guides to new sources of freedom, hope, and accountability. Let us wade in the water and see.

Preface

In some ways the birth of this book seemed serendipitous; it would have not been written except for a series of unexpected experiences. In the fall of 1990 I offered to do a lecture-recital program for the upcoming African American Awareness Month activities at the Denver Museum of Natural History. The title of the program I proposed was "Hidden Meanings in Spirituals," a topic in which I had long been interested, but had not taken time to research. What I later recognized as very preliminary research was enough to prepare me to do a competent job in this first lecture-recital program, which was presented at the Museum in February 1991.

While preparing for that first program on spirituals I found myself thoroughly immersed in the literature in the area. Originally, I had planned the program on spirituals as an interlude in a variety of wide ranging music I wanted to work on and perform, all a part of the work I was doing as a singer after having decided to enter the music world in 1987 (following an extended period during which I had given up my childhood love of singing to focus on developing my career as a clinical psychologist). But in preparing for my program at the Museum, I began to experience a shift in the direction of my intellectual and emotional energies. I began to focus almost exclusively on spirituals. I read about them, sang them, attended concerts and listened to recordings, dreamt about them, and absorbed them thoroughly into my consciousness. It was as if I was suddenly *at home*, having lost my way years before.

As I found myself almost singlemindedly focused on the spirituals, I began to make plans for more lecture-recital programs. Without fail, numerous people thanked me for the programs and especially for the valuable insights about the deeper meanings and functions of the spirituals. Enthusiasm came not only from African Americans, but also from people of varied ethnic and religious backgrounds, confirming my emerging conviction that the music early African Americans created is archetypally relevant to the *human* experience, extending far beyond the folk community of origin. However, I also found,

surprisingly, that a number of people, African Americans and non–
African Americans alike, had very little knowledge of the spirituals.
Not only did they know very little about the historical background
of this body of music, but they were unfamiliar as well with songs I
thought everybody knew, such as "Go Down, Moses," or "Joshua Fit
the Battle of Jericho." This was especially true for people aged thirty-
five and younger.

In my work as a practicing psychologist and teacher of under-
graduate and graduate psychology courses I had specialized for years
in the area of African American mental health, and had published
several articles in the area. But my experience of researching and
performing African American spirituals helped deepen my understanding of African American psychology in ways I could not have
imagined. I began to understand much more fully that the spiritual
songs that originated in slavery are important and accessible survivals
of a culture that has within it elements of extraordinary healing
power. I also began to understand that the spirituals reflect a central
core of African American culture, upon whose foundations almost all
other aspects of our psychological and social history have been built.
Additionally, I began to appreciate the almost unlimited potential of
the spirituals as sources of wisdom and guidance in addressing *current* societal and psychological issues.

Another important personal experience came in the summer of
1991, when I was invited to attend a week-long meeting of African
American spiritual and community leaders from around the country,
organized by the scholar-activist Vincent Harding. The meeting was
convened to continue a discussion that had begun a year earlier (I
had not been present at the first meeting) concerning directions to
pursue as a community that would advance progress toward social
justice, for African Americans as well as other oppressed people. The
spontaneous integration of song and celebration in our meetings
seemed to me providential, fitting synchronistically with my rapidly
deepening understanding of the role of music in the African American experience. I came away feeling not only refreshed but also
warmly and permanently bonded to a community of colleagues and
friends. It seemed to me significant that all of our meetings that week
occurred in a circle, reminiscent of the African ring shout ceremonies
in slavery that gave birth to the spirituals.

Through all of these experiences I began to feel my work as a
singer very much connected to other parts of my life, including especially my work as a psychologist and as a scholar and my expanding

sense of commitment to new areas of community work. I also began to feel connected emotionally to others in the African American tradition, men and women like Roland Hayes, Paul Robeson, Fannie Lou Hamer and Bernice Johnson Reagon, who have experienced the same link between singing and other facets of their lives. It was from this inner reference point that this book was born, along with an urgency to share my thoughts and insights with others. I wanted to communicate something of what I had learned about this tradition of songs, including how early African Americans used them to integrate awareness and action, but also including thoughts about how we might revive that kind of integration in confronting contemporary social and personal issues. I also wanted the book to be accessible to any interested reader, regardless of prior knowledge of the subject. I was especially mindful of the fact, which gained support from questionnaire data I collected during recital programs, that there are many people today who have virtually no understanding of what the spirituals are and why they are important. And for those who are more knowledgeable, I wanted to offer some fresh perspectives on the spirituals, which might spur reflection and dialogue.

In important ways the book that has emerged from these varied experiences is my gift to the African American community and especially to our children. I have begun to share the concern of many in our community that knowledge of the rich tradition of the spirituals is in danger of being lost. My hope is that this book will contribute to our collective effort to keep this tradition alive. However, this book also addresses a larger audience, consisting of anyone open to what I have come to believe are the *universal* applications of the teachings of the spirituals to critical issues of human concern. From this vantage point, the spirituals are a gift to the world, sharing their powerful African American framework of spirituality, morality and effective action with anyone who is willing to listen.

Because the spirituals are in many ways *social action* music, I believe it is a mistake to treat them as simply interesting pieces of history, avoiding the important question of what they have to teach us about the difficult social issues confronting us today. Accordingly, I have included in my discussion some of my own thoughts about the relevance of the spirituals to our late twentieth century and impending twenty-first century concerns, both in the African American community and in American society at large. I am fully aware that in doing this I have taken the risk of alienating some readers who, because they disagree with my extrapolations, will also avoid reading the larger portions of the book that concern themselves with an understanding of the cultural and historical context in which the spirituals developed. My sincere hope is that those who disagree with my applications to contemporary issues will not "throw out the baby with the bath water"; that is, I hope they will focus on the historical and cultural discussion I have provided and take the time to formulate their own ideas about what implications the spirituals have for our lives today.

I have also tried to bring together (from widely disparate sources) pieces of information about the spirituals, which are part of our continuing oral history but about which many people have questions. For example, the idea of coded communication or "hidden meanings" in the spirituals is something many of us have heard about, but most of us have no idea where to go to learn more about it, or we have questions about the extent to which it is really true. In my research I have been frustrated at times about the prospects for integrating the widely varied pieces of such prevalent oral lore, and I have been very excited as it has come together in somewhat of a coherent whole. I am hoping that making this kind of information available under the cover of one book will be helpful to others who have experienced similar frustrations.

I am convinced that it is impossible to gain a full understanding of the spirituals from an examination of song lyrics alone, without hearing (and especially singing) the rhythms and melodies of the songs as well. Accordingly, I have attempted to infuse my discussion of various songs with references to recordings that some readers may want to consult as a supplement to their reading. Unfortunately, the recent technological "advances" in the recording industry have rendered a number of previously available recordings difficult to obtain. However, there also has been a recent increase in the number of recordings of spirituals reissued on compact disc, as well as in the number of new recordings appearing on disc for the first time. Accordingly, I have attempted to direct readers to some of these readily available recordings. I have also tried to utilize, as much as possible, song examples for which written music is readily available in a songbook found in many churches around the country, the *Songs of Zion* collection, published by Abingdon Press.

As mentioned at the outset, it has seemed in some ways that the series of events leading up to the writing of this book were entirely serendipitous. However, deeper reflection leaves me certain that many of the events in my life, including the experiences that have prepared me to write this book, have been guided by a spiritual force much larger than the sum of personal experiences. Therefore, I join with a community of living and ancestral souls, African Americans as well as women and men from myriad cultural traditions, in giving thanks to that guiding spirit, thanks especially for the helpful insights we are able to offer one another, whether in writing, in conversation, or in song.

ARTHUR JONES
Denver, Colorado
January, 1993

Acknowledgments

As with any significant piece of work, there have been many people who have contributed to the development of this book. Although I can't possibly begin to list everyone who has played a part in its conception and evolution, I would like to acknowledge some of the people who have contributed most directly to my work. I want first to acknowledge Anne Jennings, community outreach director at the Denver Museum of Natural History, whose support and encouragement of my initial lecture-recital work on spirituals provided the impetus for all of my later immersion and research in this area. Had Dr. Jennings not been so encouraging at the outset, this book probably would not have been written.

I also want to thank my teachers and colleagues in the music community whose technical and artistic instruction and support prepared me to get to the point where my experience of the spirituals as a *singer* could provide far more insight into their meanings than would ever have been possible if I had approached this area from the exclusive perspective of a scholar or even a dedicated listener. I am particularly grateful to Anne Van Etten, to Richard Boldrey and Polly Liontis, and to the late Charles Lawrie. I am also grateful to Ingrid Thompson, my accompanist, whose own enthusiasm for working in the spirituals repertoire has provided a great source of support and inspiration. I also want to thank my good friend and fellow singer, Marva Lewis, whose encouragement and interest have kept me going at various points along the way. In addition, I want to thank the African American recitalist and opera singer William Warfield, whose willingness to work with me in a series of helpful lessons fulfilled a lifelong dream.

Several people have provided listening ears, ideas, and a great deal of encouragement throughout the entire life of this project. Warren Bellows has been one of those who have been particularly encouraging and supportive and I can't thank him enough. My dear friend Gary Toub has been another person whose ideas and support have been invaluable. Even though Gary and I did not talk at all while I was working on the manuscript for *Wade in the Water*, our regular conversations over a period of more than three years provided significant pieces of the spiritual and psychological foundation on which the book was built.

I also want to thank Vincent Harding, who took time from his impossibly busy schedule to read parts of the manuscript and to offer ideas and encouragement. In addition, Vincent was instrumental in directing me to Robert Ellsberg, editor-in-chief at Orbis Books. Vincent has been a special person in many ways, as a friend, colleague, comrade and informal mentor. He and Rosemarie Harding are two people whose lives of deeply spiritual grounding and accountability are as true to the teachings of the spirituals as anyone's could possibly be. As an extension of the Hardings' marvelous wisdom and spirit, all of the members of our ongoing "Spirit and Struggle" group, sisters and brothers from around the country, have also been in my consciousness constantly throughout the different phases of this project. I can't give enough thanks for the personal examples, support and clarity of thinking all of these members of my extended spiritual family have lent, often unknowingly, to this project.

Robert Ellsberg at Orbis has been extremely supportive and encouraging throughout the life of this project. Working with him has been a great pleasure. I am grateful to Robert for trusting the work of a new author, for suggesting the title of the book, and for gently directing the project to its completion.

Members of my immediate family have been helpful in more ways than I can describe. My young adult sons, 'Kula and Sékou, have not only provided encouragement but also thoughtfully sophisticated conversation and reflection, contributing a great deal to my thinking and writing. Sékou's current focus on issues of religious faith and community service, as a lens through which he views all other life decisions, has provided an example close to home of the fact that there are many dedicated members of younger generations who still believe in the teachings of the creators of the spirituals. 'Kula, who always places community relationships at the top of his list of priorities, has been equally faithful to those teachings. 'Kula was also helpful in assisting me in my attempt to view this work from the perspective of a younger generation, and to become aware of new creative developments that are consistent with the spirit of the ancestors and the songs they created. I can't thank him enough. My pre-school-aged daughter, Joella, has offered the delightful perspective of one who could, through her enthusiastic singing and dancing, help me to understand more fully the magical power of many of the spirituals. And last but certainly not least, Christine Chao, my wife, best friend and colleague, took the time to read every chapter of this book in detail, offering invaluable suggestions and perspectives. For that, and for her consistent love and encouragement, I am highly grateful. I have never lost sight of the fact that I am especially fortunate to be understood and loved by such an extraordinarily wonderful human being.

With me throughout the life of this project has been my personal memory of many who have "crossed over" into the world of the ancestors and who are an important part of the timeless legacy of the spirituals. Particularly special to me are Lois Anderson, Mallie and Dan Bunch, Helen and Billy Costen, Mildred Henderson, Mary Pender, and my father, Ferdinand Jones, Sr. I thank them all for providing important pieces of guidance, wisdom and emotional sustenance, an invaluable part of my ultimate preparation to enter into the stream of the continuing legacy.

Just as *Wade in the Water* was about to go to press I learned that my mother, Esther Jones, had died, unexpectedly. My mother's life-long commitment to her family, reaching down into a new, expanding generation of great grandchildren, was a vibrant affirmation of the messages of love and connectedness that are such an important part of the spirituals tradition. Had she lived, I am confident that she would have seen her reflection in the pages of *Wade in the Water*. The book's publication therefore stands as a tribute to her and her life's work.

Of course, any errors in thinking or perspective contained in this book are entirely mine, and I assume full responsibility for the final synthesis of the many ideas and suggestions offered by all of those who have contributed to and encouraged my work.

Wade in the Water

Chapter 1

"Over My Head I Hear Music in the Air"

African Beginnings

> *Over my head I hear music in the air,*
> *Over my head I hear music in the air,*
> *Over my head I hear music in the air.*
> *There must be a God somewhere.*
> —Traditional African American Spiritual[1]

When Africans came against their will to be enslaved in America, they brought with them a richly textured heritage that included singing and dancing as daily activities, interwoven into everyday routines, expressions of a world view in which communion with the spirits and with tribal sisters and brothers (those living as well as those dead) was not only desirable, but necessary for life, as much as food or water. Although there were certainly major cultural differences among members of the various tribes of African peoples captured for American slavery, the role of music and dance was amazingly similar from tribe to tribe, and these activities were always essential features of the life blood of the people.[2] John Lovell, Jr., author of an inspired, comprehensive study of the origins and development of spirituals, puts it this way:

> To the African, singing and dancing are the breath of the soul. No matter where he goes or what kind of life he is forced to live, these two things he will do; and basically in the African way.... Very few peoples approach the African in the vigor and dynamics of his music.[3]

Clearly, music and dance have always been defining elements of African culture, including the time period of the slave trade. For Africans

1

captured into slavery, music and dance rituals accompanied any number of tribal ceremonies, including ceremonies associated with agricultural rites, ceremonies accompanying royal installations or gatherings, and ceremonies celebrating and re-enacting important historical events. In addition, special music and dance rituals were invoked during preparations for war or to celebrate victory in war, to prepare for hunting expeditions, to celebrate the birth of a child in the community, or to mark various developmental milestones in a child's life, such as the appearance of a first tooth or the beginning of puberty. There were in fact infinite occasions in which music and dance would predominate, celebrating virtually every significant event in the life of a tribe or individual member of the tribe. And while there were various musical instruments employed, group singing was almost always a part of every musical ceremony.[4]

With singing at the center of their music, Africans were highly poetic in the songs they sang. They were prolific in their use of imagery and figures of speech, often employing creative metaphors comically or playfully to comment on the behavior of fellow tribesfolk. Singers would improvise freely, in preview of the music they would later create in America. European visitors were often amazed at the richness and creativity of the singing. Sometimes visitors found themselves the subject of the singing, with leader and chorus composing extemporaneously and singing in typical African call-and-response style. Later, in North America, slave owners would again be ridiculed in poetic, metaphorical call-and-response verses, frequently unaware that they were being made fun of. The template for this kind of "secret" communication through song was clearly laid down in Africa.[5]

To appreciate fully the prominent role of music and dance in African culture one must understand that for Africans, these artistic expressions flow directly from a world view that places a heavy emphasis on intimate connections with divine spiritual forces and with one's fellow tribesfolk. Furthermore, this world view *requires* expression of those connections through the channels of oral communication and physical movement. This is true in daily routines, such as work or play, as well as special occasions, such as the birth of a child or a significant tribal ceremony. In the African experience the spiritual force that runs through all of life is impotent unless it is given direct oral and physical expression. Amiri Baraka, in his insightful discussion of the roots of Black American music, provides an especially vivid portrayal of this holistic and functional character of

African music, contrasting it with the more compartmentalized nature of music as it has evolved in Western culture:

> If we think of African music as regards its intent, we must see that it differed from Western music in that it was a purely *functional* music. .... [There are] some basic types of songs common to West African cultures: songs used by young men to influence young women (courtship, challenge, scorn); songs used by workers to make their tasks easier; songs used by older men to prepare the adolescent boys for manhood, and so on. "Serious" Western music, except for early religious music, has been strictly an "art" music. One would not think of any particular *use* for Haydn's symphonies, except perhaps "the cultivation of the soul." "Serious music" (a term that could only have extra-religious meaning in the West) has never been an integral part of the Westerner's life; no art has been since the Renaissance. .... The discarding of the religious attitude for the "enlightened" concepts of the Renaissance also created the schism between what was art and what was life. It was, and is, inconceivable in the African culture to make a separation between music, dancing, song, the artifact, and a man's life or his worship of the gods. *Expression* issued from life, and *was* beauty.[6]

Baraka's analysis underscores one of the most important ways in which African music differs from music as it functions currently in the West. Even music that appears to the European or American as frivolous, lighthearted or purely entertaining in character is, for the African, always directly connected to a serious and fundamentally spiritual celebration of life in which people in the community affirm regularly their relationship with the forces to which they owe their existence. Just as it is impossible in the African tradition to separate music from other aspects of life, it is also impossible to separate spiritual faith and worship from other parts of life. For example, the common European-American practice of specialized worship, confined to one day of the week and separated from other important life functions, is alien to the traditional African experience. For the African, worship and life are inseparable. The most important way in which this fundamental belief is given expression is through music and dance.[7]

Coming directly from long and firmly established traditions, the women and men captured into slavery from the various tribal nations of western and central Africa were deeply religious peoples, giving expression daily to their religious faith through myriad song and dance rituals. And although the specific content and form of these rituals differed considerably from tribe to tribe, there were two important factors that would contribute to the ability of people from widely diverse tribal backgrounds to form a common identity as they made their transition to the new world. Most obvious was the fact that they were placed in a unifying predicament as involuntary captives of a common enemy. In this respect they were similar to the diverse Native American people who, treated cruelly and identically by European invaders, eventually formed coalitions that previously would have been unimaginable. There is something about a common enemy that evaporates perceived differences dramatically.[8]

The second factor that made it possible for diverse African peoples to assume a common bond as they were captured into slavery was the fact that despite their significant differences, their basic values and myths were quite similar, as was their penchant for expressing these values and life myths in music and dance. Even before capture, such similarities made it possible for otherwise separate peoples to unite in celebrations of dance and song. Historian Sterling Stuckey describes one of these pre-slavery Pan-African gatherings:

> An impressive degree of interethnic contact representing large areas of black Africa, at times took place at such ceremonies in Dahomey. F.E. Forbes, who spent two years in Dahomey and kept a journal of his observations, reports that one such instance of ethnic cross-play involved "groups of females from various parts of Africa, each performing the peculiar dance of her country." When not dancing a dance with elements unique to a given country, they performed dances common to many different countries of Africa: "the ladies would now seize their shields and dance a shield-dance; then a musket, a sword, a bow and arrow dance, in turns." Finally, "they called upon the king to come out and dance with them, and they did not call in vain."[9]

The form taken in these meetings of diverse Africans almost always included "dances common to many different countries in Africa," described by Stuckey as involving a ritual in which the dancers moved in a seemingly monotonous counterclockwise motion, frequently accompanied by musical "shouts," with dancing and singing intensifying incrementally, eventually reaching a point of frenzy, with the participants experiencing moments of emotional and spiritual ecstasy. Inter-ethnic ceremonies were possible because counter-clockwise-movement singing and dancing ceremonies were found in almost all western and central African tribal societies. These ceremonial rituals were associated most often with the occasion of burial of the dead, an event of supreme significance in western and central African culture. Burial was important because African peoples relied heavily on the wisdom of ancestors and the maintenance of a spiritual bond with ancestors as a means of ensuring continuity in the life of the tribe.

The significant role of ancestors in African cultures stems from an even more central unifying factor, the issue of kinship. For African peoples, bonds with immediate, extended and tribal relatives facilitate the survival of the tribe. Typically, there is a complex system of kinship bonds, including various classifications of ancestors, ranging from those remembered by many in the tribe to those remembered by none (but recorded in oral history). In addition, there is communication with children in the tribe who are yet unborn. As psychologist Wade Nobles explains, traditional African kinship systems

> stretched laterally (horizontally) in every direction as well as vertically. Hence, each member of the tribe was related not only to the tribal ancestors (both living-dead and spirits) but also to all those still unborn. In addition, each was a brother or sister, father or mother, grandmother or grandfather, cousin or brother-in-law, uncle or aunt, or some relation to everybody else.[10]

Thus, women and men who came to America to serve as slaves were also a people whose sense of themselves was intensely communal. Each person felt, as the East African scholar John Mbiti would say, that "I am because we are; and because we are, therefore, I am."[11] Cultural commonalities prepared each person to unite with others from foreign tribes to form a new "we," bonded together in a Pan-African spirit to resist, at every turn, the unjust condition of involuntary servitude.[12] And while there was at one time a lively debate about the extent to which the cruel conditions of slavery obliterated their values, traditions and sensibilities, it is now unquestionably clear that African philosophies and traditions remained strong throughout slavery, especially with regard to the most robust of cultural traits, the tendency to express self through music and dance.[13]

The immediate problem for Africans coming together in bondage was the problem of language. Not yet fluent in the language of their captors or spiritually ready to adopt that language as their own, enslaved Africans required a new linguistic medium to communicate their commitments to each other and to the spirits. Fortunately, their past histories provided such a medium. Just as West Africans before slavery had come together in counterclockwise-movement dance rituals to worship the gods and commune with each other, ethnically diverse Africans in America now employed the same ritual in forming their new tribal identity as African Americans. The result was a ceremony eventually known as the ring shout.[14] At first, the verbal utterances that came out of these ceremonies were simply emotional shouts and moans, in which music and rhythm were more important than words, since participants came from such diverse language backgrounds. Eventually, the shouts and moans developed into the songs that are now called spirituals. Lydia Parrish, author of an important book on the song traditions of African peoples of the Georgia Sea Islands, describes this evolution:

> Those who have traveled in Africa, and have seen native dancing, are convinced that the shout of the American Negro is nothing more than a survival of an African tribal dance, and that the accompanying chants in their form and melody are quite as typical of Africa as the dance itself. It is recognized, of course, that the words of the Old Testament have been substituted by the Negro for those of his native land. When the slaves grew more familiar with the English language, they evolved the more complicated religious songs that are now popularly called spirituals.[15]

As Parrish notes, the content of the songs that evolved from the ring shout eventually came to include material drawn from the Bibles of the singers' captors, and especially from stories of the Old Testament. When people talk about spirituals, they are usually referring to these songs, created in slavery and containing themes from Jewish and Christian religious traditions. This is the usage of the term *spiritual* that is employed in the current book. It is important to understand that spirituals are not the same as gospel music, a twentieth-century composed art form that evolved from the spirituals tradition.[16]

A common misconception of the nature of the evolution of the spirituals is that enslaved Africans, once acculturated in the new land,

abandoned their own traditions (usually thought of, by those igno-
rant of the backgrounds, as heathen) and became "civilized" via the
adoption of the Christian religion of their slave masters. In this view
the spiritual songs the slaves created reflected not only a new religious belief system but also, in some more extreme versions of this
view, an imitation of the white hymns and spiritual songs of the slave
holders.[17] It is important that we correct these misconceptions in
order to have clear the perspective that is the foundation for the
major points of discussion in this book.

First, we must understand that the enslaved Africans who created
the spirituals were not Christian, in the sense of instant conversion
to a new religion. The large-scale adoption of Christianity by African
Americans did not actually occur until close to the end of slavery and
the beginning of the emancipation period. The conversion process
was gradual, and the result was a creative blend of African traditions
and Christianity, creating a new, transformed religion different in
form and substance from the religion of the slave holder. In fact,
many of the enslaved people during the time of the slave trade held
tightly to traditional religious beliefs and practices, renewed and
strengthened by the continual arrival of new captives from western
and central Africa. This strengthened the African core of the new
religious orientation that gradually emerged.[18] What was true
throughout the period of development of the new African American
religious folk music was that many of the newly arrived Africans
recognized in Christian doctrine the presence of principles that, *if
they were actually lived*, would be thoroughly consistent with their own
traditional belief system, emphasizing love of fellow humans, commitment to justice, and the ultimate rule of divine will. However,
newly arrived Africans were also very much aware of the hypocrisy
of slave masters, whose active participation in slavery was in itself
fundamentally contradictory to the beliefs they espoused in Sunday
church services. One of the most well known of spirituals comments
on this contradiction:

> *I got a robe,*
> *You got a robe,*
> *All God's children got a robe.*
> *When I get to Heaven gonna put on my robe,*
> *Gonna shout all over God's Heaven, Heaven, Heaven!*
> *Everybody talkin' 'bout Heaven ain't going there,*
> *Heaven, Heaven.*
> *Gonna shout all over God's Heaven!*[19]

Unbeknownst to slave holders, who thought songs like this to be playful and frivolous, the slave composer of this song used poetic subtlety to poke fun at the hypocrisy of the uncomprehending outsider, rejoicing in the confident knowledge that the final judgment of the divine ruler would prevail. The detached feeling of the lyrics clearly reveals a songwriter who was not about to identify with a religion so easily contradicted by the behavior of its most devout believers. The adoption of this and similar songs by the larger folk community of enslaved Africans reflects the fact that this now unknown songwriter was successful in communicating the collective spirit of the African American community. A song like this, sung joyfully and rhythmically, with dancing and joyful celebration, affirmed the African belief in a divine spirit at work in the daily lives of the people, who are "all God's children," smiled on and ensured of the approval of God in heaven. The Christian slave master, extreme in his hypocrisy, was clearly excluded from this divine community, since "everybody talkin' 'bout Heaven ain't going there." As Lovell notes,

> The slave adopted the symbols of the Christian religion but not the hypocritical practices. He recalled that Christianity had introduced the slave traffic; that, as Linda Brent said, there was a great difference between religion and Christianity; that, as Matlock proves, Christianity in the South was founded in regions where the people were too poor to keep slaves. In many areas he accepted Christianity but only on his terms; he did not accept the white man's broken and bespattered Christianity. . . . It is true that many slaves, by learning to read and other devices, learned about the Bible, Old Testament and New. And having learned, they taught their fellows. *But the Bible acquired in this fashion was less religious doctrine and more the kind of pithy story the African had been used to for centuries* (emphasis added).[20]

Rather than a new religion, Christianity and its tradition of storytelling (especially in the Old Testament) represented primarily for enslaved people a rich source of material, readily available to Africans from diverse preslavery backgrounds, for use in continuing in the new world the African tradition of song and dance, with storytelling and poetry at the center of the singing. Coming out of the ring shout, the spirituals represented one major body of new *African American* songs.

In an important sense *spirituals,* a term used commonly today by Americans of African as well as European descent, is a misnomer, reflective of our collective ignorance of African traditions. As we have seen, all music in the African tradition is spiritual, even when accompanying activities are seen from a European-American perspective as secular. Africans in America during the slave period continued their tradition of singing to accompany work and other daily activities, never separating in their intentions work or other secular songs from specifically religious songs.[21] In a sense, then, all folksongs composed by African Americans during slavery were spirituals, since music and spirituality are so intimately linked in the African oral tradition. However, the term *spiritual* is so entrenched and widespread that I have continued to use it specifically to refer to folksongs composed in slavery whose content was manifestly religious or philosophical, frequently containing material drawn from the Bible. Songs of this nature constitute the majority of African American folksongs.[22] One factor supporting the classification "spirituals" for this body of songs is the powerful religious symbolism they frequently employ, a factor that has contributed to their survival and widespread appeal. As Lovell has noted, the symbols of Christianity were consistent with the poetic needs of the early African American folk composer:

If a slave, even a religious slave, seeks an outlet for expression, he wants and needs a system capable of direct language and undercurrent symbolism at the same time. Nothing fits this better than the Christian religion. It has a firm base in traditionalism. But it strikes out in two other directions, a much better and radically different life on earth and a supremely better and revolutionary life in a world beyond the grave. Since poets are helpless without symbolism and since slave poets find symbolism indispensable (as self-protection and prevention of the destruction of their creative product, if for no other reasons), the Christian religion was made to order for the slave poet we are studying. He seized upon it and put it to as good use as poets anywhere have done.[23]

Again, however, it is important to separate this use of Christian symbolism from the idea that most enslaved African Americans were Christian in the sense of wholesale adoption of the religion of their captors; they were not.

Not only is the nature of early African American spirituality and its reflection in songs misunderstood, but the role of music and dance in African culture generally is often misconstrued by outside observers. For example, the still prevalent view of enslaved Africans as "happy go lucky" because of their constant resort to music and dance is based on the failure to understand the cultural roots of these early African American cultural activities. In fact, the whole tradition of minstrel songs and their pejorative imitation of early African American music stemmed from ignorance of the basic nature and function of slave songs, which, as we have discussed, were rooted firmly in African traditions, with intensely religious foundations. These pervasively negative and stereotypic portrayals of African American music, especially singing, have probably contributed to the misunderstanding of the nature of spirituals, even in the African American community.[24]

Smugly aware of the failure of outsiders to understand their intentions, enslaved Africans established as a first priority the use of songs as a means of combating the potentially destructive internal psychological damage that could be inflicted by the experience of prolonged enslavement. If we understand this music correctly, as a continuation of the African oral tradition in which a community of singers and dancers derives personal and spiritual power from participation in their art, then we realize that enslaved Africans in America were beginning to fashion for daily use a potent method of maintaining spiritual and self-integrity in the midst of injustice and suffering. Contrary to popular belief, this was not escapism. Rather, it was an extension of African communal and spiritual power gained through oral and body expression.

It is natural and predictable that Africans taken unwillingly into bondage would employ that which was most familiar to them: the strengthening of tribal, kinship and spiritual bonds through the power of music and dance. This was the same power that would appear, a century after emancipation, in the freedom movement led by the Rev. Martin Luther King, Jr., and his African American tribesfolk. In that movement the transformation of souls and laws would be accompanied by thousands of singing warriors, literally marching (dancing) their way through the streets of the Jim Crow South.[25] The fact that a thoroughly effective movement for freedom based on African American cultural foundations could be waged as recently as the 1960s supports the idea that the cultural legacy of early Africans continues today, maintained through the oral tradition. However, we have a tendency to forget about these cultural anchors. Periodically we have to be reminded of their continuing power, as by the brilliant scholar-artist-activist Paul Robeson:

> The *power of spirit* that our people have is intangible, but it is a great force that must be unleashed in the struggles of today. A spirit of steadfast determination, exaltation in the face of trials — it is the very soul of our people that has been formed through the long and weary years of our march toward freedom. It is the deathless spirit of the great ones who have led our people in the past — Douglass, Tubman and all the others — and of the millions who kept "a-inching along." That spirit lives in our people's songs — in the sublime grandeur of "Deep River," in the driving power of "Jacob's Ladder," in the militancy of "Joshua Fit the Battle of Jericho," and in the poignant beauty of all of our spirituals.[26]

Robeson's timeless reflections indicate his understanding of the functions of music as it evolved in the continuing spirit of enslaved Africans in America, extending into struggles for freedom even after the formal institution of slavery was abolished — and still relevant to "the struggles of today." As the practice of the ring shout continued among those enslaved on Southern plantations, often in secret meetings late at night or early in the morning, the obvious focus of the singers and dancers was the salient experience of oppression represented by the institution of slavery. The immediate concern was spiritual and psychological survival, beginning with the basic determination that however their role was defined externally, they would never identify with those external definitions; rather, they would persist in their knowledge of themselves as spiritually complete human beings. In the words of one of the songs they created, they would maintain their "right to the tree of life" and periodically they would reaffirm that determination as they sang, in secret meetings, "Before I'd be a slave I'd be buried in my grave." Outsiders would refer to African American tribesfolk as slaves, but they themselves would never accept this designation.[27]

The nature of the holocaust of slavery is sometimes suppressed in our collective consciousness, but the memory of that experience is important psychologically, not only to prevent its recurrence, but also to understand the roots of the current dilemmas that face us. The most basic outcome of that holocaust, similar to a later tragedy that would accrue to Jews in World War II, was genocide, by the thousands. Wyatt Tee Walker, citing music historian John Rublowsky, calls our attention to the unbelievable numbers of deaths over the period of the slave trade (approximately 1619–1865):

> By conservative estimate, upward of fourteen million Africans were imported into the Atlantic slave trade. For every African that reached these shores alive, four died in the machinery of slavery at one end or the other of the traffic or in the dreadful Middle Passage. That's at least sixty million people lost from West Africa in less than four hundred years—genocide on a scale unmatched in recorded history.[28]

For those who did survive, the experience was bleak. The visions of docile, childlike servants that are maintained, enigmatically, in our cultural consciousness are serious distortions of the actual reality, which has been communicated to us by African Americans who experienced firsthand the cruelty of slavery. Aside from the constant task of maintaining one's psychological and spiritual dignity, daily experiences of physical brutality were more the norm than the exception, as illustrated in a testimony from the child of a survivor:

> One day while my mammy was washing her back my sister noticed ugly disfiguring scars on it. Inquiring about them, we found, much to our amazement, that they were Mammy's relics of the now gone, if not forgotten, slave days. This was her first reference to her "misery days" that she had made in my presence. Of course we all thought she was telling us a big story and we made fun of her. With eyes flashing, she stopped bathing, dried her back and reached for the smelly ol' black whip that hung behind the kitchen door. Bidding us to strip down to our waists, my little mammy with the boney bent-over back, struck each of us as hard as ever she could with that black-snake whip. Each stroke of the whip drew blood from our backs. "Now," she said to us, "you have a taste of slavery days."[29]

There are few periods in the history of human civilization that match the stark cruelty experienced by African victims of the American holocaust.[30] This experience pushed cultural adaptation strategies to their ultimate limits; the ring shout and the songs that came out of it would be challenged to sustain the normal spiritual and emotional life of their participants while also fostering an extraordinary level of human adaptation in which singers and dancers could attain a sense of personal and collective sanity in an absurdly insane environment. In response to this critical challenge, the African heritage of life-sustaining song and dance combined with the oppressive conditions of slavery to forge a body of new *African American* songs of exceptional power and depth, sung in connection with the rhythmic body movements of the ring shout and eventually known as Negro spirituals. These uniquely moving songs took African cultural forms to their highest level, providing the backdrop in America for more than three hundred years of African survival, spiritual sustenance and effective resistance.[31] Later, with the help of the Fisk Jubilee Singers and other pioneering African American concert artists, the archetypal power of these songs would be revealed, as women and men in contexts far removed historically and geographically from American slavery would discover that spirituals have a seemingly magical ability to speak to universal issues of the human spirit.[32]

When we understand correctly the immensely significant role of the oral tradition in African and African American experience, we realize that these songs communicate a great deal of wisdom and guidance concerning personal and social issues. Because some of us are not accustomed to regarding music in this way, it is easy to forget or neglect these cultural treasures. It is often difficult even for African Americans to make the necessary shift in perspective that permits us to understand fully the value of the music of our ancestors, which properly experienced provides an important component of our education as enlightened human beings. As the historian Carter G. Woodson would say, our "mis-education" makes it difficult for us to value and understand the notion that a body of folksongs could serve as a source of information concerning informed and productive contemporary living.[33] Many of us have understood these issues intuitively; we have demonstrated that understanding in the spheres of our lives that are still heavily under African influence, as in the worship experience of the African American church or in daily social intercourse within the protected barriers of the African American community, where our physically expressive, musically rhythmic instincts flourish.[34] However, the racism that permeates American society makes it difficult for *any* of us to view African American cultural contributions clearly.[35]

The great poet James Weldon Johnson, in the introduction to the second volume of a landmark collection of spirituals, describes the broad range of life experience on which the spirituals comment and inform us:

Although the Spirituals in a general classification fall under the heading "religious songs," all of them are by no means religious in a narrow or special sense. All of them are by no means songs of worship, though having a religious origin in usage. In the Spirituals the Negro did express his religious hopes and fears, his faith and his doubts. In them he also expressed his theological and ethical views, and sounded his exhortations and warnings. Songs of this character constitute the bulk of the Spirituals. But in a large proportion of the songs the Negro passed over the strict limits of religion and covered nearly the whole range of group experiences—the notable omission being sex. In many of the Spirituals the Negro gave wide play to his imagination; he dreamed his dreams and declared his visions; he uttered his despair and prophesied his victories; he also spoke the group wisdom and expressed the group philosophy of life. Indeed, the Spirituals taken as a whole contain a record and a revelation of the deeper thoughts and experiences of the Negro in this country for a period beginning three hundred years ago and covering two and a half centuries. If you wish to know what they are you will find them written more plainly in these songs than in any pages of history.[36]

Johnson is revealing in his statement his understanding that the oral tradition among early Africans was a powerful conveyer of information and world view, equivalent in substance to great written works in the European tradition. He also helps to underscore the idea that the spiritual aspect of these African American songs is much broader in scope than the range of religious or spiritual concerns as they are thought of and experienced in the majority cultural frame of reference.

When we immerse ourselves in the world of the spirituals, divorcing ourselves from the distorted projections of the larger culture, we are also reminded that an understanding of the messages contained in these songs requires that we attend to the nuances of music, rhythm and body movement that form the heart of African (American) sensibility; that sensibility permeates all aspects of African American life. To comprehend the teachings of a Martin Luther King, Jr., for example, reading of written transcripts of his speeches is severely inadequate. One must listen to a recording, or better, view a film or videotape to come close to a complete understanding. Even a video recording is inadequate in comparison with a live experience of the event. This is because the rhythmic-musical aspects of an African American message are at least as important as the words used. The message comes out of a gestalt of the words and the musicality of the communicator. Even when a "speech" is involved, music is still present in the rhythmic cadences and varied pitches of the speaker. Similarly, the "message" of the spirituals, which form the ancestral basis for these cultural strands, cannot be gleaned simply from the words; adequate understanding requires attention to the content of the poetry combined with the emotional experience of the music and rhythms of the song.[37]

When we approach study of the spirituals from this perspective, we appreciate more fully the comments of James Weldon Johnson concerning the wide aspects of life on which the spirituals comment and teach. However, in contrast to the larger culture, which instructs us that understanding begins with thought and logic and flows eventually into values and emotions, the spiritual song (as well as all of the African American cultural forms evolved from it) functions in the opposite way; it begins with feeling and emotion and eventually utilizes that channel to provide direction concerning issues of logic and intellect. This is an approach to knowledge that is characteristic of the African experience, both on the African continent and in America.[38] Paul Robeson, unquestionably one of the intellectual giants of the twentieth century, commented on this, illustrating the predominance in his personal life of an African approach to knowledge: "I, as an African, feel things rather than comprehend them." Continuing, he explained further that sound, and specifically music, was the major sensory channel through which he experienced those feelings. The African oral tradition, Robeson said, produced "great talkers, great orators, and where writing was unknown, folktales and oral tradition kept the ears rather than the eyes sharpened. I am the same. . . . I hear my way through the world."[39] In this context one appreciates Robeson's love and understanding of the African American folk song as the foundation of the oral tradition as it has evolved in America:

Yes, I heard my people singing! — in the glow of parlor coalstove and on summer porches sweet with lilac air, from choir loft and Sunday morning pews — and my soul was filled with their harmonies. Then, too, I heard these songs in the very sermons of my father, for in the Negro's speech *there is much of the phrasing and rhythms of the folk-song* (emphasis added).[40]

The teachings that emerge as we experience early African American music in the way that Robeson describes are particularly relevant to the issues of oppression that have necessarily been of concern to African Americans throughout our history in America. However, the wisdom communicated by the spirituals extends as well to universal matters of human life that transcend their specific cultural context of origin. As such, the spirituals have a great deal to say to all Americans, regardless of ethnic or cultural roots.

Our discussion in the remaining chapters is directed to the specific lessons to be learned, lessons which have implications for the personal and social issues that face us as we anticipate the arrival of the twenty-first century. Adequate understanding of these lessons requires that we use all of our faculties, leading with the channels of sensation and feeling. Those who are not accustomed to approaching information in this way will have to adjust their normal approach. However, they will find that such an adjustment will be well worth their effort, and will prepare them to understand how it was that the great scholar-activist W.E.B. Du Bois could say, confidently, that

> Little of beauty has America given to the world save the rude grandeur God himself stamped on her bosom; the human spirit in this new world has expressed itself in vigor and ingenuity rather than in beauty. And so by fateful chance the Negro folk-song — the rhythmic cry of the slave — stands to-day not simply as the sole American music, but as the most beautiful expression of human experience born this side of the seas. It has been neglected, it has been, and is, half despised, and above all it has been persistently mistaken and misunderstood; but notwithstanding, it still remains as the singular spiritual heritage of the nation and the greatest gift of the Negro people.[41]

∽

It is March 18, 1990. Opera divas Kathleen Battle and Jessye Norman are beginning their New York Carnegie Hall recital, devoted entirely to spirituals. They open with a rousing rendition of "Great Gittin' Up Mornin'," with full orchestra and chorus, followed by Norman's rendition of "Sinner, Please Don't Let This Harvest Pass." As the applause diminishes and becomes silence, the great jazz flutist Hubert Laws floats into the air the first notes of "Over My Head." The music seems indeed to drift over our heads. Kathleen Battle then joins harpist Nancy Allen in a duet, dancing her lovely, lyrical soprano voice alongside supporting chords from Allen's harp:

Over my head I hear music in the air,
Over my head I hear music in the air,
Over my head I hear music in the air.
There must be a God somewhere.

We understand immediately that with such incredibly beautiful music present, there must indeed be a God, *somewhere*. We are ready for our journey into the world of the African American spiritual.[42]

~ Chapter 2 ~

"Sometimes I Feel Like a Motherless Child"

Suffering and Transformation

On one of these sale days, I saw a mother lead seven children to the auction block. She knew that some of them would be taken from her; but they took all. The children were sold to a slave-trader, and their mother was bought by a man in her own town. Before night her children were all far away. She begged the trader to tell her where he intended to take them; this he refused to do. How could he, when he knew he would sell them, one by one, wherever he could command the highest price? I met that mother in the street, and her wild haggard face lives to-day in my mind. She wrung her hands in anguish, and exclaimed, "Gone! all gone! Why don't God kill me?" I had no words wherewith to comfort her. Instances of this kind are of daily, yea, of hourly occurrence.

—Harriet Jacobs, escaped slave[1]

Sometimes I feel like a motherless child,
Sometimes I feel like a motherless child,
Sometimes I feel like a motherless child,
A long ways from home,
A long ways from home.
A long ways from home,
A long ways from home.

Sometimes I feel like I'm almost gone,
Sometimes I feel like I'm almost gone,
Sometimes I feel like I'm almost gone,

18

A long ways from home,
A long ways from home.
A long ways from home,
A long ways from home.
                    —Traditional African American Spiritual[2]

The fact that children born in slavery were so frequently torn from their mothers and families made the personal grief of the "motherless child" alarmingly familiar during the period of American slavery. The experience of the "motherless child," sadly ever present, provided a frame of reference from which one might describe the severity of one's inner sufferings. Even one who had never been physically separated from mother could sing, during particularly trying times, "Sometimes, I feel *like* a motherless child," assured that others in the community would understand intimately the precise level of pain associated with the difficult life experiences to which the singer referred. To announce, in song, that a life event made one feel "like a motherless child" was to equate the pain associated with that event with the extreme torment occasioned by the "daily, yea, hourly" occurrence of mother-child separation.[3]

Harriet Jacobs, an ex-slave, wrote extensively about her experiences, leaving an eloquent literary statement for posterity. However, most Africans in America had neither the freedom nor the necessary literary skills to offer their perspectives in writing. Drawing on the African oral tradition, they left their legacy in song. Arguably, "Sometimes I Feel Like a Motherless Child" is the most important of the songs they passed on to us; it is probably not coincidental that it is one of a handful of African American folksongs that has survived sufficiently well to make itself known even to those with little or no familiarity with specific songs in the spirituals tradition.[4]

The ability of the enslaved community to embrace a song that lamented the anguish of the motherless child revealed, among other things, the precious way in which that community regarded children and families, continuing the long-established African tradition that emphasized the pricelessness of kinship bonds. Conversely, the singers of "Motherless Child" also announced their shock in witnessing the emergence in the "new world" of a culture which demonstrated, early in its history, that the goal of economic advancement and prosperity was more important than the protection and nourishment of children. The blues-like expression of "Motherless Child" was in fact a foreshadowing of the long-term consequences of such tragically misplaced priorities in the beginning construction of American "progress," reflecting these early African American singers' understanding that of all the damages inflicted by slavery, the blatant disregard of the psychological and physical welfare of children was the most odious. In announcing their lament so boldly, enslaved Africans also demonstrated their understanding that a society that neglects and abuses children is guaranteed trouble, since children embody hopes for the future survival and continuation of any viable community.

Of course, slave holders regarded such blatant mistreatment of African children as inconsequential, since enslaved people were viewed as property, functioning merely to serve the economic needs of property owners. In this mental framework, the welfare of slave holders' families was thought to be protected and removed from the daily business of the auction block. However, those enslaved in this arrangement recognized that the abuse of the children of the enslaved African was not as disconnected from the psychological welfare of the slave holder's family as he so blithely assumed. Harriet Jacobs continues:

I can testify, from my own experience and observation, that slavery is a curse to the whites as well as to the blacks. It makes the white fathers cruel and sensual, the sons violent and licentious; it contaminates the daughters, and makes the wives wretched. And as for the colored race, it needs an abler pen than mine to describe the extremity of their sufferings, the depth of their degradation.

Yet few slaveholders seem to be aware of the wide-spread moral ruin occasioned by this wicked system. Their talk is of blighted crops—not of the blight on their children's souls.[5]

Jacobs revealed in her profound statements her understanding of the intimate connection between the oppression of the victim and the reciprocal oppression, often unconscious, of the victimizer, who must himself succumb to moral and psychological deterioration in order to participate so actively in the inhumane treatment of innocent people.[6] The lament of "Motherless Child," with its poignant words and haunting melody, echoed the eloquent literary statements of writers like Jacobs, expressing the immediate pain of Africans in America *as well as* the unconscious misery inflicted on the children and families of the oppressors.

The singing of "Motherless Child" and similar songs was one of the few tools Africans in slavery had available for emotional conso-lation. In this respect, the African oral tradition seemed made to order for a people in bondage, offering a channel for emotional expression as a first step in the healing of deep psychological and spiritual wounds. The symbol of the motherless child was an apt representa-tion of feelings about a wide variety of abuses, including the rape of slave women, the extreme physical abuse of women and men (some-times reaching the point of murder), the disregard of all intimate relationships, and the extreme injustice accompanying the very fact of lifelong involuntary servitude. Indeed, this all reminded those in bondage that the site of present existence was quite "a long ways from home."[7]

Clearly the lament of the "motherless child" expressed the extreme limits of a painful despair, an emotion which was quite familiar to those who inhabited the slave quarters. Other songs went beyond the specific imagery of the motherless child to express directly the profound suffering of generations of people in slavery. Consider, for example,

> *I'm troubled in mind,*
> *If Jesus don't help me I surely will die.*[8]

or,

> *The blind man stood on the road and cried,*
> *Oh, the blind man stood on the road and cried,*
> *Crying, oh my Lord, save-a me.*
> *The blind man stood on the road and cried.*[9]

In the singing of such songs, enslaved Africans began to construct out of their cultural roots an advanced, effective psychological method, one that might well be employed in the modern-day par-allels of their experience, reflected in such current terminology as *post-traumatic stress*.[10] At the heart of the method was the understand-ing that the experience of emotionally expressive singing is transfor-mative, as noted by the theologian-philosopher Howard Thurman:

> This is the discovery made by the slave that finds its expression in song—a complete and final refusal to be stopped. The spirit broods over all the stubborn and recalcitrant aspects of experi-ence, until they begin slowly but inevitably to take the shape of

one's deep desiring. There is a bottomless resourcefulness in man that ultimately enables him to transform "the spear of frustration into a shaft of light." Under such a circumstance even one's deepest distress becomes so sanctified that a vast illumination points the way to the land one seeks. . . . "The Blind Man stood on the road and cried" — the answer came in the cry itself. What a panorama of the ultimate dignity of the human spirit.[11]

The nature of the transformation referred to by Thurman was one that provided nourishment for weary souls, folks who too frequently felt and were motherless, fatherless or childless. The music available to assist in their transformation was ever present, "in the air," providing sustenance for the human spirit. Such music granted participating listeners and singers access to the *knowledge* (not simply belief) that whatever suffering they endured, there was an overarching spirit present that would eventually set things right. Thus, they would sing, "Over my head I hear music in the air. . . . There *must* be a God somewhere!" As Vincent Harding has put it, "Has this not always been one of the great strengths of our people, to face the storm without flinching, but then to see hope at its center: 'Nobody knows the trouble I seen. . . . Glory, Hallelujah.' "[12]

The transformation ensuing from singing also involved the enslaved African's physical being; the inner spiritual transformation was accompanied by corresponding changes in the body. Historian-activist-singer Bernice Johnson Reagon, in one of her many workshops on the tradition of African American folk music, commented on this multifaceted transformation process and the importance of continuing the process in our current communities:

> Songs are a way to get to singing, though singing is what you're aiming for. And the singing is running sound through your body. You cannot sing a song and not change your condition. . . . I am talking about a culture that thinks it is important to exercise this part of your being. The part of your being that is tampered with when you run this sound through your body is a part of you that our culture thinks should be developed and cultivated, that you should be familiar with, that you should be able to get to as often as possible, and that if it is not developed, you are underdeveloped as a human being! If you go through your life and you don't meet this part of yourself, somehow the culture has failed you.[13]

In her work, Reagon implores us to continue to teach about this transformation process, aware that those of us who do not learn about it are underdeveloped as human beings. She, as we all should be, is saddened by the fact that such teaching is unavailable to many of our children. However, children born into slavery did not have to be taught, consciously, about this process. The music and the participating musicians were present from the moment of birth, and the evidence of the singers' transformation was available for the developing child to witness; the learning process was automatic. In fact, new songs were being created continually out of daily experience. As talented members of the community composed new songs, those songs that reflected and expressed the collective experience of the community most effectively were adopted and owned by the group. The identities of the original composers of these songs were usually forgotten, and aptly so, since these composers were simply conduits for the expression of the collective thoughts and feelings of the community.[14] James Miller McKim, in his travels, described his conversation with a member of the slave community about the way in which new songs came into being:

> I asked one of these blacks—one of the most intelligent I had met—where they got these songs. "Dey make em, sah." "How do they make them?" After a pause, evidently casting about for an explanation, he said, "I'll tell you; it's dis way. My master call me up and order me a short peck of corn and a hundred lash. My friends see it and is sorry for me. When dey come to de praise meeting dat night dey sing about it. Some's very good singers and know how; and dey work it in, work it in, you know; till dey get it right; and dat's de way."[15]

As new songs emerged, there was ample material from which to draw for the transformation process, as the above anecdote illustrates. The singing that surfaced was cathartic and therapeutic.[16] We have much to learn from these wise composers and singers, for many of them were able to transcend an experience of extreme degradation, emerging from it as spiritually, morally and emotionally evolved human beings. The fact that there were also many emotional and physical casualties is not shocking; the fact that there were so many who emerged from their suffering to live on psychological and spiritual "higher ground" *is*.[17] Their ability to utilize the transforming power of music, as Reagon has illustrated, had a great deal to do with such an exceptional record of spiritual and emotional evolution.[18]

Aside from the basic act of singing and "running sound through the body," the transformation associated with the singing of spirituals was also assisted by the powerful symbolism of the song lyrics. As Howard Thurman has indicated, the richness of the symbolism of slave songs, drawn from the varied sources of the Bible, nature and personal experience, was particularly well suited for the process of transcending suffering and creating meaningful life, just when it seemed that such creation was impossible.[19] However, the power of the specific symbolism of "Motherless Child" and similar songs of grief and suffering was only partially effective as the basis for the transformation process. At times, such songs helped to relieve pain, but only, as ex-slave and abolitionist Frederick Douglass put it, "as an aching heart is relieved by its tears."[20] The process of transformation required not only emotional release and catharsis, but also the opportunity for the incorporation of symbols of hope and renewal. Many of the spirituals served both purposes, providing singers with a medium for the periodic expression of sorrows while at the same time offering a channel for the experience of hope. The emotional reality of both sides of the continuum, suffering and hope, was necessary for the construction of a genuine and stable psychological protection from the horrors of the slave experience.

As they were exposed to the dominant religion, Christianity, Africans in America gradually began a new syncretistic tradition that combined elements of both African and Christian religious practices and ideas.[21] Appropriately, the symbols of hope they employed in this new tradition included the images of the Baby Jesus and Mother Mary. In accessing the healing power of such symbols, the community of early African American singers continued a tradition that had long been established on the African continent and was strikingly similar to methods of depth psychology that would later be "discovered" by the Swiss psychiatrist Carl Jung. People immersed in this tradition knew that symbols, embraced in earnest and nurtured in the soul, have a powerful ability to promote healing, personal fortitude and emotional growth.[22] Consider, for example, one of the songs they created and embraced:

> *Mary had a baby, my Lord.*
> *Mary had a baby, my Lord.*
> *Oh, Mary had a baby, Mary had a baby, Mary had a baby,*
> *My Lord.*

What did she name him, my Lord?
What did she name him, my Lord?
Oh, what did she name him, what did she name him,
What did she name him, my Lord?

She named him King Jesus, my Lord.
She named him King Jesus, my Lord.
She named him King Jesus, she named him King Jesus,
She named him King Jesus,
My Lord!

In this song, rich in symbolism, Mary is introduced casually, as if she were simply one of many women in the community. In fact, the image of Mary as an intimate friend and "sister" is found throughout the repertoire of Christmas spirituals. In all of these songs, the birth of Mary's child, like all births in the African community, is heralded and cherished. The importance of the birth is reflected in the repeated announcement of the birth event. In this particular song the melody line underscores that importance. Rising in pitch with the first two recitations of "Mary had a baby," the melody line climaxes on the third repetition of the phrase; as a result we experience a heightened awareness of the special significance of this birth event. The melody line then descends in pitch, finally ending with "my Lord" at the end of each phrase. With this progression of phrases of increasingly descending pitch, we are assisted in our emotional understanding of the sadness which is also present, a sadness ensuing from the oppressive outer circumstances of the birth, reflective of the external conditions in which children in slavery are born.

Although Mary is an ordinary woman, the selection of "king" to describe her child, Jesus, calls our attention to the fact that this is no ordinary birth; rather, this mother-son relationship has the special significance and protection of royalty. Thus the familiar Christmas story is told in a form that has particular relevance to the life circumstances of a people with such painful "motherless child" experiences. In owning and singing this song, the community provides a conduit for the transformation of wounded spirits into an experience of hope. At the same time, the community is able to maintain sight of current realities. That sense of awareness of distressing present realities is stressed even more in another version of "Mary Had a Baby":

Mary had a baby,
Yes, Lord.

Mary had a baby,
Yes, my Lord.
Mary had a baby,
Yes, Lord,
The people keep a-comin' and the train done gone.

What did she name Him?
Yes, Lord
She named him King Jesus,
Yes, my Lord.
Wonderful Counselor,
Yes, Lord,
The people keep a-comin' and the train done gone.[23]

In this version, the phrases "Yes, Lord" and "Yes, my lord" are accented, expressing the irony of the situation in which the mother gives birth to a special child while chances for escape from oppression continue to elude the community, which has been ever hopeful that the underground railroad will make itself available, *today* if not sooner.[24] Sadly, "the people keep a-comin' and the train done gone," reflects the shattered hopes of people who have gathered together (physically and emotionally) in hope of changing their circumstances, only to be disappointed by the continued illusion of actual freedom. Psychologically, this is a particularly powerful song, providing both the hope embodied in the symbolism of the Christmas story and the firm grounding in the reality of current circumstances. The tension between these opposite energies of hope and despair must have provided secure motivational grounding for the outer struggle for freedom, beginning in slavery and continuing into the twentieth century.[25]

Perhaps the most effective symbolization of the Christmas story and its conflicting images of hope, fear and sadness is contained in the archetypally important song, "Sister Mary Had-a But One Child":

Sister Mary had-a but one child,
Born in Bethlehem.
And-a every time-a that baby cried,
She'd-a rocked him in a weary land,
She'd-a rocked him in a weary land.

Oh, three wise men to Jerusalem came.
They traveled very far.

They said, "Where is he, born King of the Jews,
For we have a-seen his star."

King Herod's heart was troubled,
He marveled but his face was grim.
He said, "Tell me where the Child may be found,
I'll go and worship him."

An angel appeared to Joseph,
And gave him-a this-a command:
Arise ye, take-a your wife and child,
Go flee into Egypt land.

For yonder comes old Herod,
A wicked man and bold.
He's slayin' all the children,
From six to eight days old,
From six to eight days old.

Sister Mary had-a but one child,
Born in Bethlehem.
And-a every time-a that baby cried,
She'd-a rocked him in a weary land,
She'd-a rocked him in a weary land.[26]

In this song the complete Christmas story is told, with the full range of emotion and meaning relevant to the experience of slavery. As we experience the song's words and melody, we find ourselves feeling certain that this song must have been composed by a woman or group of women, persons with the actual experience of giving birth to children and being confronted repeatedly with the ironic prospect of rocking and comforting those cherished children "in a weary land" where they might be wrenched away from their mothers at any time. In hearing this song, we understand immediately the need to cherish every moment available for precious parenting. The hope provided in those moments, and in the song's message, provides at least some protection from the devastating emotional impact of actual experiences, experiences like the ones reported by Charity Bowery, enslaved in North Carolina in the early nineteenth century:

Sixteen children I've had, first and last; and twelve I've nursed for my mistress. I always set my heart upon buying freedom for some of my children. . . . But mistress McKinley wouldn't let me have my children. One after another—one after another—she sold 'em away from me. Oh, how *many* times that woman broke my heart![27]

Charity Bowery's testimony, typical of the personal accounts of African women in bondage, calls out directly for spiritual allegiance with Sister Mary, whose love and whose fear for her child are of equal magnitude to those of enslaved women. The symbolic story of Sister Mary's triumph over the evil forces in her environment provides an opening for the emergence of hope in circumstances where hope would otherwise be impossible.

In another testimony we see a direct parallel to the situation of Sister Mary and Jesus, hiding secretly in a manger and awaiting word of the imminent danger posed by Herod and his compatriots:

Aunt Kitty, Uncle Ben and Isaac Jones had all told me of the woman who hid with her children in the woods. . . . She had been cruelly treated and run away with her children—seeking shelter under the ground. There another child was born to her. . . . Here mother and children lived in precarious freedom.[28]

The mother and children described in this incident were eventually captured, an outcome frequently experienced by fugitive slaves. In almost all other respects, however, their situation was almost identical to that of "Sister Mary" and her child. When they heard the Mary story, women like this must have gravitated immediately to its deepest meaning, the hope that had to be kept alive that they could "flee into Egypt land." In this hope African mothers could somehow dim the painful sounds of their crying children, children to whom they could not give enough to eat, could not be with as much as they wished, and to whom all of their care, all of their nurturing, had to be administered "in a weary land." This was a land where the children's tragic destinies were always frighteningly imminent; Herod, the slave holder or slave trader, was always just a few steps away.

This song also has another layer of meaning. The fact that Herod "marveled," despite his grim face, indicates that, at least unconsciously, Herod recognizes the preciousness of this child, much as the slave holder at some level is aware that African children, like his own, are special. And Sister Mary, who "had-a but one child," is certainly aware of the preciousness of this birth. With only one child,

Mary had to be particularly vigilant and protective, honoring any and all warnings about potential harm to her baby. In her love, she "rocked him," ever aware of their life together in a weary land. Like Mary, all mothers in slavery experienced the same sense of critical urgency in caring for their children.

To appreciate fully the powerful emotional impact of this song, we must also be aware of the gently soothing, syncopated 2/4 background rhythm, providing a progressively deepening sensation of loving, protective rocking in the ironic context of conspicuously oppressive surroundings.[29] In a song like this, complete possibilities for transformation present themselves, in the two-edged symbolism, in the effective poetry, in the enchanting melody, and in the underlying pulsating rhythms. To sing this song and to make it part of one's spiritual and physical being is to provide oneself with an optimal shield against the internalization of outward conditions of oppression. Further, it offers an enduring sense of hope in spite of current realities. To accuse singers of songs like this of escapism is to fail to recognize the ability of the human spirit to provide inner protection and realistic awareness concurrently.

The symbolism of the Jesus story and its message of better times ahead were explored most fully in songs about Jesus' death and the opportunity provided to singers to identify with a life in which suffering offered the promise of redemption and salvation. The most famous of these songs is "Were You There?," one of the most emotionally powerful of the spirituals:

> *Were you there when they crucified my Lord?*
> *Were you there when they crucified my Lord?*
> *Oh, sometimes it causes me to tremble, tremble, tremble.*
> *Were you there when they crucified my Lord?*

In successive verses the singer asks:

> *Were you there when they nailed him to the cross?*
> *Were you there when they pierced him in the side?*
> *Were you there when the sun refused to shine?*
> *Were you there when they laid him in the tomb?*

ending each time with:

> *Oh, sometimes it causes me to tremble, tremble, tremble.*
> *Were you there when they crucified my Lord?*[30]

In their actual life experiences, enslaved Africans must have recognized the parallels between the crucifixion of Jesus and the hangings, whippings and other violent abuses experienced by members of their own community, as illustrated in the following testimony:

> I remember one old slave, who was the most abused man I ever *did* see. His master had knocked and kicked him about till he had hardly a sound joint in his body. ... His face was all smashed up, and his right leg was broken to pieces. One day, when his master was mad with him for something, he made him mount a wild horse that nobody could ride; and the horse threw him, and fell on him, and crushed his leg. ... When he got old and a cripple ... his master ... meant to drown him; and I believe he would, if the neighbors hadn't come and saved him. If he had (tried to resist) they'd hung him. Slaves hadn't much chance when the white folks want to get 'em hung. ... And as for a whipping, a slave don't get whipped according to his crime, but according to the ambition of the master.[31]

Those experiencing or witnessing events such as those described in this testimony must certainly have seen in the personage of Jesus a man to whom they could feel connected intimately, and whose experience, like their own, caused them "to tremble."

Again, full appreciation of the message of "Were You There?" requires attention to both the melody and words sung simultaneously; anyone who has heard or sung this spiritual understands at once its exceptional communicative power. The archetypal immediacy of the melody line and chorus ("Oh, sometimes it causes me to tremble, tremble, tremble; were you there when they crucified my Lord?"), repeated over and over, guides us into the spiritual recesses of our souls; and the symbolism of crucifixion, so similar in physical and emotional impact to the daily life of people in slavery, assists the singer and listener in understanding the suffering that was present in that experience. It also provides us with a glimpse of a transformative process in which singers could experience hope that their present suffering was not the end of the story. Just as the Bible tells the story of a Jesus who died to save humanity, so the suffering of the slave has meaning for life in the present and the future. James Cone has commented on this essential meaning in the symbolism of "Were You There?" and similar spirituals:

Because black slaves knew the significance of the pain and the shame of Jesus' death on the cross, they found themselves by his side. ... Through the blood of slavery, black slaves transcended the limitations of space and time. Jesus' time became their time, and they encountered a new historical existence.[32]

With this kind of perspective arising out of the symbolism of the life and death of Jesus, one can understand how the community of Africans in bondage chose in another, now famous spiritual to highlight one additional aspect of the crucifixion story:

> *They crucified my Lord,*
> *And He never said a mumbalin' word.*
> *They crucified my Lord,*
> *And He never said a mumbalin' word;*
> *Not a word, not a word, not a word!*
>
> *They pierced Him in the side . . .*
> *The blood came streamin' down . . .*
> *He hung His head and died . . .*
> *And he never said a mumbalin' word;*
> *Not a word, not a word, not a word!*[33]

In this song we are again struck by the immensely transforming power of simple words and phrases, sung to the tune of an inspired, repetitive melody line, once more leading us progressively into the inner reaches of the spirit, deepening that inner journey with each repetition.[34] This time we encounter the identification of the oppressed with the stoicism of Jesus. The story, strictly taken, is altered, of course; Jesus is reported in the Bible to have uttered at least a few words.[35] This illustrates the fact that the theology revealed in the spirituals is not fundamentalist religion; rather, the core symbolism, as it speaks to the life of an oppressed people, is embraced and utilized as material for songs. In this particular case, the most important symbolism is embodied in Jesus the stoic, paralleling the ability of African people to endure stoically the physical and emotional agony of slavery. They could be beaten, raped, sold away from family, forced to "breed," and finally killed at the whim of their oppressors; the abuse they experienced was a crucifixion every bit as real as the one suffered by Jesus. Although they could not control the outward circumstances of their abuse, they could control very definitely the extent to which they acknowledged their pain. To be silent was one powerful form of resistance. Their ability to endure, stoically, such extreme conditions was buttressed by their knowledge that "trouble don't last alway":

> *I'm so glad trouble don't last alway,*
> *I'm so glad trouble don't last alway,*
> *I'm so glad trouble don't last alway,*
> *Oh my Lord, oh my Lord, what shall I do?*[36]

This, in turn, could give rise to their ability to stay the course, expressed in many of their songs. For example:

> *I ain't got weary yet,*
> *I ain't got weary yet,*
> *I been in the wilderness a mighty long time,*
> *And I ain't got weary yet.*
>
> *I been praying like Silas,*
> *I been preaching like Paul . . .*
>
> *I been walking with the Savior,*
> *I been walking with the Lord,*
> *I been in the wilderness a mighty long time,*
> *And I ain't got weary yet.*[37]

All of these spirituals teach us, more effectively than any other means imaginable, the unlimited possibilities for human transformation and the manner in which the transformation process is aided and supported by the power of song and symbol. We can only imagine what it was like to be in the presence of such music, sung in secret meetings all night, over and over, accompanied by the ecstatic dancing of the ring shout or simply sung expressively in African style, creating in the process a sense of meaning when the very idea of meaning would seem to be absurd. The music by itself is sufficiently powerful; singing in the original setting of communal dance and celebration must certainly have been accompanied by a unique feeling of power.[38] We can gain perhaps a small glimpse of the integration of dancing, "shouting" and singing in another version of the Christmas story, a spiritual entitled "Shout for Joy." Here, a spiritual, through the added power of the ring shout, transformed the despair

and powerlessness of the enslaved community into an invincible personage, watched over by angels and named "Mighty Counselor,
Prince of Peace." Here, Africans in slavery also remembered their own
royal roots:

> *O, Lord, shout for joy! (sung four times),*
> *Mary had a Baby, shout for joy! (sung twice),*
> *Born in a stable, shout for joy! (sung twice),*
> *They laid Him in a manger, shout for joy! (sung twice),*
> *They named Him King Jesus, shout for joy! (sung twice).*

> *He was the Prince of Peace,*
> *A Mighty Counselor,*
> *The King of Kings,*
> *That Christmas, in the morning.*

> *Shepherds came to see Him, shout for joy!*
> *Wise men brought Him presents, shout for joy!*
> *King Herod tried to find Him, shout for joy!*
> *They went away to Egypt, shout for joy!*
> *Mary rode a donkey, shout for joy!*
> *Joseph walked beside her, shout for joy!*
> *Angels watching over, shout for joy!*

> *O, Lord, shout for joy! (sung four times),*
> *He was the Prince of Peace,*
> *A Mighty Counselor,*
> *The King of Kings,*
> *O, Lord, shout for joy!!!*

Singing and absorbing into our senses a song like this, powerful in
its melodic and rhythmic impact, we experience an invitation into
the ring shout and we imagine ourselves dancing in a circle, in a
steady, counterclockwise motion, feeling connected to a larger community of children, mothers and fathers. We again feel ourselves
centered in the inner healing reserves of our souls, aided by the
gently repetitive African rhythms, by the vivid symbolism of a
divinely exalted and protected family, and by the centuries-old pattern of entrance into the world of the spirits that accompanies travel
(dancing) in a counterclockwise direction, gesturing toward the left.[39]
I know of no method of meditation or therapy that could have a

more potent impact on the human spirit. We have to marvel at the ability of the ancestors to provide themselves and us, if we are open to it, such effective channels for emotional and spiritual healing.

The transformation process that emerges from such musical and spiritual immersion produces an enduring confidence that present suffering does in fact have meaning, that life is ultimately ruled by divine forces and that those forces (not slave holders, not slaves) will have the final word on issues of justice and freedom. Confidently, the sufferer knows that troubles will cease: "Oh, by an' by, by an' by, I'm gonna lay down this heavy load."[40] This transformed person also feels assured of having "a home in-a dat rock," no longer motherless or homeless.[41] There is no doubt that, contrary to the flawed judgment and perceptions of the slave holder, the transformed person has "a right to the tree of life."

As we marvel at the ability of the ancestors to reap for themselves such abundant spiritual harvest out of a weary and barren landscape, we have to ask ourselves what we might learn from their songs, their singing and their transformation. When viewed and experienced correctly, the body of spirituals on the theme of suffering and transformation is a witness to a community of women and men with a profound consciousness and self-understanding, a superior level of assertion and responsibility, and a great capacity for emotional transcendence. But perhaps most important, these songs also stand as an historical record of the reality of their oppression, unparalleled in the history of human civilization.

The piece of American history recorded in songs of suffering and transformation provides a sharp corrective to the written documents, which have omitted this fundamental piece of the American past. For many, this corrective is disturbing, much at odds with the preferred view of America as champion of the oppressed and land of the free. However, this more accurate picture, if faced squarely, has the potential itself to be emotionally transformative, particularly in a society with such a long history of denying its ugly, shadow side.

As every beginning psychotherapist learns, a person unable to acknowledge and confront misdirected or unresolved issues in early childhood is guaranteed serious emotional consequences at some later point in life. That basic fact of individual experience is equally applicable to the life of a society. Mainstream America, as yet unable (unwilling?) to confront the pathological aspects of its early history, is certain to suffer negative long-term repercussions. In fact, there are signs that the effects of centuries of denial in America have already begun to take hold, in the cyclical explosions of the urban centers, in the proliferation of the homeless, in the spread of illicit drug use, in the escalation of crimes of violence. And given its early history of abuse of African children, there is a special irony in the current national crisis of child abuse and neglect.[42] These developments all seem capped by a widespread inner malaise, curious in its reflection of an economically prosperous people whose financial security has not yet provided any stable sense of satisfaction or contentment.[43] In responding to a series of acute internal crises, the policies of the American government are lacking in any clear direction; rather, America's leadership seems to be groping to maintain, somehow, a position of dominance in the world, continuing to avoid confrontation of its chronic domestic ills. These are serious sufferings, much in need of the opportunities for understanding and emotional encounter offered by African American songs of suffering and transformation.

These songs offer particularly important comfort and learning to those of us who have already confronted the nightmare of America's childhood past. Some of us, living and traveling in America's twentieth-century African communities, have long seen fully the complete historical record. We have also seen the continuation in our time of the American legacy of oppression, against us and against other sisters and brothers of color. Although some formidable legal barriers to our freedom have been eliminated, the cancer of racism and hatred continues to grow. We find ourselves curious, given what we see, that our meager efforts in recent years to hold America accountable for its reckless past have been greeted with accusations of "reverse discrimination." We have not seen any sign of change in patterns of power in private, governmental and educational sectors, yet the accusations continue. Token gestures of having a few of us "sit by the door," feigning importance and power, do not diminish our awareness of the continuing nightmare reflected in our life in America.

For many of our clearest-visioned sisters and brothers, the songs of our ancestors have always lingered in the air, providing a seemingly boundless fountain of transformative spiritual sustenance to combat the persistent stubbornness of America's stance toward African peoples. However, the last few decades have witnessed the softening and sometimes silencing of these ancestral songs. In fact, there are children born in our community today who don't hear the songs at all, songs that have made up a large part of the foundation of our survival as a people. When these songs are present in the air, a "cloud of witnesses" from the past leaps out at us, reminding us that there are many who have come before us who have suffered even more difficult crises but have nonetheless emerged emotionally and spiritually whole. However, at various times in our history we have internalized the misrepresentations of our songs imposed on us from the outside and we have somehow concluded that we no longer need those songs. Some of us have complained that the songs embarrass us. We have to learn, again, to recognize the distortions contained in such misrepresentations; we have to reclaim our songs, freeing the air again for their comforting and transformative presence.

Our serious predicament as Africans in America requires that we find a way to seek advice from the elders, those living as well as those dead. In fact, we can feel the urgency of that need taking hold at this very minute, as some of us decide that it is time to have a talk with the ancestors. As we gather together, entering into the realm of the spirits, we see the face of our brother Howard Thurman, still teaching and preaching from his pulpit in the land of the living-dead.

⌒

Brother Thurman calls to us to come together in a circle around him. As he often did when he lived among us, he signals as well to others from outside our circle to join in our communal reflections. He indicates that anyone open to the teachings of the African American ancestors is welcome. We feel encouraged as we see other sisters and brothers, brown, red, yellow and white, joining with us, eager, as we are, to learn from one of the strongest and wisest of our ancestral souls. As we all settle down, anxious to hear from Brother Thurman, he directs our attention, surprisingly, to one of the living elders, August Wilson. Brother Wilson greets us briefly and then introduces us to another elder, named Bynum. We find ourselves momentarily confused, wondering where this is all leading. But then Bynum begins speaking. Inaudible at first, Bynum's voice becomes louder and clearer as we continue to listen. We can now see his face clearly. After speaking to us briefly, he turns to talk with another man, whose face is also now visible. Brother Thurman instructs us to listen carefully:

> Now, I can look at you, Mr. Loomis, and see a man who done forgot his song. Forgot how to sing it. A fellow forget that and he forget who he is. Forget how he's supposed to mark down life. Now, I used to travel all up and down this road and that . . . looking here and there. Searching. Just like you, Mr. Loomis.

I didn't know what I was searching for. The only thing I knew was something was keeping me dissatisfied. Something wasn't making my heart smooth and easy. Then one day my daddy gave me a song. That song had a weight to it that was hard to handle. That song was hard to carry. I fought against it. Didn't want to accept that song. I tried to find my daddy to give him back the song. But I found out it wasn't his song. It was my song. It had come from way deep inside me. I looked long back in memory and gathered up pieces and snatches of things to make that song. I was making it up out of myself. And that song helped me on the road. Made it smooth to where my footsteps didn't bite back at me. All the time that song getting bigger and bigger. That song growing with each step of the road. It got so I used all of myself up in the making of that song. Then I was the song in search of itself. That song rattling in my throat and I'm looking for it. See, Mr. Loomis, when a man forgets his song he goes off in search of it . . . till he find out he's got it with him all the time.

As we continue to listen to the dialogue between these two elders, we notice that the figure of Loomis is beginning to change; he is becoming us, all of us together, seeking to understand exactly what it is that Bynum is trying to teach.

We are now aware of the collective voice of the ancestors, singing to each of us in the sound chambers of our individual spirits. As we begin to hear the melodies and words of the songs within us, we find ourselves preparing to join in the singing, gesturing to our children, who are waiting in another corner of the room. As the children enter the inner circle, we begin singing. Our sound grows in intensity and we are now one large chorus, chanting in multiple rhythms and harmonies: "Sometimes I feel like a motherless child . . . I'm troubled in mind . . . Were you there when they crucified my Lord?" The sound of our music continues to expand, finally filling the room; we are moving together in a circle, counterclockwise, singing, dancing and shouting! We sing one song after another; we feel our individual spirits intermingling. It is a chilling, ecstatic experience.

In time, our singing dims, but the ancestors continue to speak. The voice of one of the elder sisters, a woman named Harriet Tubman, is particularly clear. She is beginning a sermon. After some preliminary reflections, she launches into the heart of her text. She implores us to remember that in the battle for survival and spiritual sustenance,

the ancestors always knew that any song that expressed and transformed their sorrows would have to be followed by songs that
informed and assisted their confrontation of the external structures
of their oppression. In directing us to this fact, Sister Tubman is
reminding us that the process of individual and collective transformation includes the necessity to *fight* as well as to *pray*. She is exhort-
ing us to understand that our powerful songs of suffering and
transformation represent only a small portion of the music in the air
available to us. Sister Tubman is *preaching* now, encouraged by our
collective "Amens!" She is singing, "Go Down, Moses." Just as she is
absolutely certain that she has our complete attention, her voice dims
and her face fades. She is gone.[44]

∽

It is now May 27, 1990. The eight performers known as the Harlem
Spiritual Ensemble, founded in 1986 by Francois Clemmons and Louis
Smart, are performing a concert at St. Andrew's Episcopal Church in
New York City. As the only professional group in the world dedicated
exclusively to performing spirituals, they are particularly enthusiastic
about continuing the legacy of religious folksong left by African
Americans in bondage. The ensemble's performance style incorpo-
rates nineteenth-century African American dialect as well as the use
of conga drums to accentuate the underlying African rhythms of the
music.

Appropriately, the singers open their program with "Motherless
Chile." They hum in unison the beginning melody line, a cappella.
They end their humming by singing, also in unison, "a long way
from home"; we sense the many levels of meaning contained in that
poetically significant phrase. In the background we can almost hear
the painful lament of the ancestors, although we have but a small
glimpse of their suffering. Even so, the feelings and sensibilities that
are communicated so poignantly are of great help to us, assisting in
our understanding of the necessity of the ancestors' active involvement in the long struggle to secure their freedom, and ours. Affirming
our understanding, the beat of the congas announces the transition
to the next song on the program, "Go Down, Moses," reflecting the
direct link between the inner suffering and transformation of "Motherless Chile," and the ongoing campaign to dismantle the institutions
of racism and oppression, expressed and preserved in songs of struggle and resistance.[45]

∽ Chapter 3 ∽

"Joshua Fit the Battle of Jericho"

Struggle and Resistance

Remember Americans, that we must and shall be free, and enlightened as you are, will you wait until we shall, under God, obtain our liberty by the crushing arm of power? Will it not be dreadful for you? I speak Americans for your good. We must and shall be free I say, in spite of you. You may do your best to keep us in wretchedness and misery, to enrich you and your children, but God will deliver us from under you.
—David Walker[1]

> *Joshua fit the Battle of Jericho, Jericho, Jericho.*
> *Joshua fit the Battle of Jericho,*
> *And the walls come tumbling down!*
>
> *You may talk about your King of Gideon,*
> *You may talk about your man of Saul,*
> *But there's none like good ole Joshua,*
> *At the Battle of Jericho.*
>
> *Up to the walls of Jericho,*
> *He marched with-a spear in hand.*
> *Go blow them ram horns, Joshua cried,*
> *'Cause the battle am-a in my hands.*
>
> *Then the lam ram sheep horns begin to blow,*
> *The trumpets begin to sound.*
> *Joshua commanded the children to shout,*
> *And the walls come tumbling down, that morning!*

Joshua fit the Battle of Jericho, Jericho, Jericho.
Joshua fit the Battle of Jericho,
And the walls come tumbling down!
—Traditional African American Spiritual[2]

From the beginning of their enslavement Africans forced away from their homes to labor in the unmerciful service of Europeans in America were aware of the contradictions inherent in a society so ardently committed to the ideals of Christian brotherhood and freedom, yet so enthusiastically involved in the fundamentally inhumane and immoral institution of slavery. But however confused their captors might have been about the issue of freedom, those held in captivity were absolutely clear that their human right to freedom was being violated. They also knew that they themselves would have to secure their freedom, since their captors had managed miraculously to exclude persons of color (black as well as red) from membership in the human race.

Beginning on the slave ships, African captives began their active struggle for freedom, expressed variably in the forms of revolt, escape and suicide. Consistent with African traditions, they punctuated their actions with songs. Even those who threw themselves overboard into the ocean, committing suicide in preference to a lifetime of captivity, did so to the accompaniment of "songs of triumph," as Vincent Harding has reported:

> Once again, the history of slaves was inadequate to capture the meaning of black struggle. It could not bear the terrible significance of such "songs of triumph," sung in magnificent unity by those Africans on the deck and those moving in the depths of the water. In European eyes these singers could only be "ignorant creatures" whose lives were to be forever blotted from the pages of the world's real history. Even in our own time more recent versions of conventional wisdom would relegate such black action to the category of unfortunate, ineffectual escapism, or limited passive resistance at best. Contrary to such opinions, both the songs and the singers remain embedded in the black freedom movement in America.[3]

Harding's remarks also serve to remind us how often the African American freedom struggle has been misunderstood and underestimated in its intentions and in the scope of its power. He has shown us, convincingly, that the signs of active struggle were present from the onset of African captivity, flowing like a river toward the ultimate, certain goal of complete freedom and justice.[4] During the slave period, Africans in America framed the issue of freedom in active terms; they knew that they would have to be their own agents of liberty. At the same time they retained complete faith in the endorsement and guidance of spiritual forces larger than themselves. In their African-derived frame of reference, there was no contradiction between this absolute faith in the divine and the concomitant assumption of responsibility for personal and collective action. As the scholar Molefi Kete Asante has shown, the African principle known as *ma'at* renders the operation of divine forces as centered within each individual person; the evidence supports the idea that this basic African world view remained active as the African experience was transplanted in America.[5] Thus the African American freedom fighter David Walker could announce boldly to the American rulers, "God will deliver us from under you," communicating the collective will of the people to engage in struggles for freedom, in multiple arenas, confidently assured of the support and inspiration of the spirit of God as it was experienced within the individual and community.

Throughout slavery the freedom struggle would take a variety of forms: arson, insurrection, murder, escape, written and oral exhortation, calls for African emigration, suicide, or simply the iron will to survive. Those held captive would draw their inspiration from a supportive community of outlying runaways, from free Africans, or from the freedom victories of other colonized Africans in the Western Hemisphere.[6] Combining their faith and their hopes, those still held captive composed and embraced rhythmic, joyful songs, bursting with the anticipation of freedom. For example, in one of the most famous of their songs, they sang jubilantly,

> *Didn't my Lord deliver Daniel, deliver Daniel, deliver Daniel?*
> *Didn't my Lord deliver Daniel,*
> *And why not-a every man?*
>
> *He delivered Daniel from the lion's den,*
> *Jonah from the belly of the whale,*
> *And the Hebrew children from the fiery furnace,*
> *And why not-a every man?*[7]

In such songs it is clear that the affirmative answers to the questions had no need to be stated; they were *assumed*. The singers *knew* they would be delivered. As David Walker and countless other warriors for freedom affirmed, "We must and shall be free," a sentiment bolstered by the spirited, confident rhythms of their songs. They also knew that they, like Daniel in the lion's den, David fighting Goliath, or Moses leading his people across the Red Sea, would be active participants in the delivery process.

Symbolically, the stories of the Old Testament held particularly special meaning. In their African-derived spiritual cosmology, the captives constructed a life-consciousness that included ready connections to figures of the ancient past. The stories of the Hebrew children became their stories. In their spiritual imagination they lived and breathed the experiences of such biblical heroes as David, Daniel, Moses and Joshua, all engaged actively in divinely inspired battles for freedom. These stories served as a major source of material for spirituals, underscoring the fact that Africans in slavery not only desired freedom, but identified most strongly with figures who were actively involved and ultimately victorious in their biblically documented freedom struggles. Cut off by slavery from connections to biological ancestors, they improvised on biblical material to create spiritual equivalents. Enslaved Africans recognized in the scriptures something very special; in the African tradition it was not difficult to connect this spiritual resource to the everyday tasks facing them. It was irrelevant to them that their European captors had so deftly managed to disconnect their lives from their supposed religious beliefs. To the Africans in America, the stories of the Bible had obvious meaning, very much connected to the reality of their struggles as a community.[8]

In one of the most illuminating discussions of the large body of spirituals with Old Testament themes, historian Lawrence Levine has described the way in which the unique theological perspective of enslaved Africans influenced their choices of biblical material and the way these choices emerged in the songs. Levine argues that

> these songs state as clearly as anything the manner in which the sacred world of the slaves was able to fuse the precedents of the past, the conditions of the present, and the promise of the future in one connected reality. In this respect there was always a latent and symbolic element of protest in the slave's religious songs which frequently became overt and explicit.[9]

Levine's important research supports strongly the notion that songs based on Old Testament stories were not simply a source of comfort and identification; they were in fact spiritual vehicles by means of which enslaved Africans transported themselves into the actual experience of the Israelites in bondage, utilizing biblical accounts of ultimate victory to sustain their parallel visions of victory in America. This ability of the captives to utilize the past to transform present reality as well as stake out clear visions for the future was strikingly similar to the traditional use of ancestral wisdom in the West African philosophical and religious framework. In this framework the distinctions among past, present and future, so prevalent in the European experience, are virtually nonexistent.[10]

The ability of enslaved Africans to draw so effectively on the wisdom of Old Testament stories produced songs which provided an additional source of personal and social transformation, extending beyond emotional comfort and protection into the larger, critically important arena of active social protest and change. The songs issuing from this transformative process are powerful testimony to a collective wisdom from which we can learn a great deal if we are able to understand and acknowledge its unique power.

Levine's insightful discussion also helps raise the issue of latent and "double" meanings in the spirituals, especially those with Old Testament themes, but also relevant to many spirituals utilizing the central New Testament figure of Jesus. Frederick Douglass was among those who called our attention to this important issue when he wrote,

A keen observer might have detected in our repeated singing ot

> "O Canaan, sweet Canaan,
> I am bound for the land of Canaan,"

something more than a hope of reaching heaven. We meant to reach the *north* — and the north was our Canaan.

> "I thought I heard them say,
> There were lions in the way,
> I don't expect to stay
>   Much longer here.
> Run to Jesus — shun the danger —
> I don't expect to stay
>   Much longer here,"

was a favorite air, and had a double meaning. In the lips of
some, it meant the expectation of a speedy summons to a
world of spirits; but in the lips of *our* company, it simply
meant a speedy pilgrimage toward a free state, and deliver-
ance from all the evils and dangers of slavery.[11]

There is considerable evidence that spirituals were in fact often
used in the way described by Douglass, as secret codes of communication for feelings and plans about escape, revolt and protest. Two
of the songs most frequently mentioned in this regard are the familiar
spirituals "Go Down, Moses" and "Steal Away":

When Israel was in Egypt land,
Let my people go;
Oppressed so hard they could not stand,
Let my people go.

"Thus saith the Lord," bold Moses said,
Let my people go;
If not, I'll smite your first-born dead,
Let my people go.

Go down, Moses,
Way down in Egypt land.
Tell ole Pharaoh,
Let my people go![12]

∽

Steal away, steal away, steal away to Jesus!
Steal away, steal away home,
I ain't got long to stay here!

My Lord calls me,
He calls me by the thunder;
The trumpet sounds within-a my soul,
I ain't got long to stay here![13]

Harriet Tubman was said to have used "Go Down, Moses" as a signal
to call candidates for escape to freedom in her clandestine Underground Railroad, and in fact was frequently referred to by her com-

patriots as Moses. Nat Turner, in his insurrection in Southampton County, Virginia, in 1831, is said to have used "Steal Away" as a signal to his co-conspirators to gather together, the time of which was signaled by signs from God, sounding "within-a my soul." Some, in fact, believe Nat Turner to be the composer of that song. The historical circumstances also support the possibility that "Go Down, Moses" may have been composed and utilized in the course of the planned revolt of Denmark Vesey in Charleston, South Carolina, in 1822.[14]

Although it is impossible to determine with any certainty the dates of composition of any specific songs, there is no question that spirituals and other songs were used frequently for secret communication among fellow captives or between captives and people in the free community working to facilitate escape or revolt. For example, it is difficult to recognize anything but secret communication in a song used in celebration of Nat Turner's Virginia rebellion:

> *You mought be a Carroll from Carrollton,*
> *Arrive here night afo' Lawd made creation,*
>> *But you can't keep the world from moverin' around*
>> *And* not turn her *back from the gaining ground* (emphasis
>> added).

This song, described by Russell Ames, makes fun of the aristocratic Carroll family; that meaning is easy to detect. In the chorus, however, the phrase "not turn her" is reported to have been a disguised reference to Nat Turner. The chorus, sung over and over, affirmed the resolve of the community to persist in its pursuit of revolution, a resolve encouraged by the courageous actions of Nat Turner and his rebel band.[15]

Some songs even served as maps, pointing the way to routes leading to freedom and safety. The most well known of these songs is "Follow the Drinking Gourd," which directed runaway slaves to keep traveling in the direction of the Big Dipper:

> *Follow the drinkin' gourd!*
> *Follow the drinkin' gourd,*
> *For the old man is a-waitin' for to carry you to freedom,*
> *If you follow the drinkin' gourd.*
> *When the sun comes back and the first quail calls,*
> *Follow the drinkin' gourd,*

For the old man is a-waitin' for to carry you to freedom,
If you follow the drinkin' gourd.[16]

Short of announcing imminent plans for revolt or escape, many songs called participants to secret meetings or worship. Miles Mark Fisher, for example, has made some interesting observations about the spiritual "Let Us Break Bread Together," familiar to many of us now as a communion hymn. In the usual version of this song, the following words appear:

> *Let us break bread (drink wine, praise God) together on our knees*
> *(repeated once).*
> *When I fall on my knees,* with my face to the rising sun,
> *Oh, Lord, have mercy on me!* (emphasis added).[17]

Fisher, pointing to the curious words, "with my face to the rising sun," notes that it is very likely that the song in its original setting "relates hardly at all to holy communion, which does not necessarily require early morning administration or a devotee who faces east." Rather, Fisher argues, it was employed as a signal song calling enslaved Africans to secret meetings.[18] Undoubtedly, there were many instances of this kind of secret communication through song, in circumstances falling short of outright insurrection or physical flight. Some of the secret meetings simply occurred for the purpose of worship, an activity which was itself threatening to many slave holders, who recognized, more than they wished to admit, the very close relationship between religion among Africans and their tendency to become engaged in active resistance to slavery.[19]

Clearly, enslaved Africans employed spirituals and other folksongs as secret coded communications, announcing plans for escape, revolt and clandestine meetings, or cheering on comrades in battle. However, it would be a mistake to conclude that such secret communication was the only purpose served by most spirituals, or that needs for secret communication provided the primary motivation for their creation. Songs like "Follow the Drinking Gourd" may well have served the primary purpose of facilitating safe escape for fugitives. And clearly the "not turn her" song was composed for the purpose of secret communication, boosting morale and providing a channel for ridicule of those in power, giving impetus to further acts of courage. Nevertheless, it is likely that in the great majority of cases the employment of spirituals instrumentally for political purposes was an improvisation on an already existing art form rather than the primary purpose of their initial composition.

It is notable that "Follow the Drinking Gourd" and similar songs have experienced relatively little active life beyond the historical circumstance of slavery. It is likely that there were many such songs utilized for secret communication, but for the most part those songs have not survived for us to examine them. Deeply religious spirituals, such as "Go Down, Moses," continue, more than 130 years after "emancipation," to capture the interest and attention of people around the world.[20] Of course, one reason for the survival of these spirituals over more esoteric songs is that the secret nature of certain songs precluded their being revealed to collectors and observers, for obvious reasons. It is impossible to determine the extent to which this phenomenon was at work in their disappearance in the oral history repertoire. Notwithstanding, I believe that one additional reason why many of the spirituals have survived is because the original inspirations behind their creation derived from deeply meaningful, archetypally human experiences, relevant not only to the specific circumstance of slavery but also to women and men struggling with issues of justice, freedom and spiritual wholeness in all times and all places. In some respects, I find myself agreeing with Harold Courlander, who wrote,

> If songs of the type of "Steal Away to Jesus" and "Go Down, Moses" are to be considered conscious disguises for political, temporal meanings, a large part of the religious repertoire must be placed in the same category. . . . A large number of spirituals and anthems were worded so that they could have a disguised meaning; but it is not safe to assume (or even take the word of persons who were born in slavery) that they were created as anything else but religious songs.[21]

Courlander's position, however, reflects only part of a highly complex picture. While we can concur with him that the primary motivation for the composition of most spirituals was religious, we also have to remind ourselves that "religious" in the African tradition is much broader in scope and function than it is in the European/American experience. As we have seen, Africans in America were able to extend themselves backward and forward in history, utilizing biblical accounts of past events to relate to both current realities and expectations of future events. This ability was a direct function of an African world view, which validated the continuing spiritual impact of important ancestral figures.

In their transformative use of the religion of their captors, enslaved Africans were able to embrace the heroic world of Old and New Testament biblical figures, bringing those figures into the spiritually active ancestral background of their experience in America and bolstering their resolve and persistence in their struggle for freedom. In an experiential sense they were reliving the actual experience of the Israelites, including the inspired leadership of a Joshua or a Moses. The songs that emerged from that inner experience often served as a means to communicate present plans and aspirations, while at the same time expressing deeply spiritual connections to events and people from the ancient past. The understanding that ensued between the Africans involved in this process was "secret," in large part a function of the failure of those outside the African community to understand the complex religious phenomenology of the singers.[22] Thus, a leader on the eve of a planned insurrection might well have involved her co-conspirators in singing, "See that band all dressed in red; it looks like the band that Moses led; God's a-gonna trouble the water!," knowing that all members of the group would understand this as affirmation of their spirited anticipation of imminent freedom and as confirmation of their valued role as leaders of "the band" of freedom fighters.[23]

The ability of Africans in bondage to utilize biblical material functionally, as an integral feature of their daily spiritual and community life, is also related to their facility with improvisation, which is another prominent feature of the African tradition. Not only were early African Americans able to improvise on biblical material to make it relevant to their own needs, but they were able as well to employ material from various songs and biblical stories in infinite combinations and permutations, continually creating new versions of already existing songs. This reflected their spontaneous ability to improvise in a manner consistent with the needs of specific circumstances. Such improvisation extended to melody lines as well, although this was not as extensive as the improvisation of words. Improvisation in spirituals was a preview of later African American musical developments, such as jazz, where improvisation would in fact be central to the very definition of the art form. Clearly, the written transcriptions of melodies and words of spirituals that are familiar to us now are simply approximations of the most frequently favored versions of the songs, recorded in print by collectors and arrangers and popularized by concert performers in the period following the end of legalized slavery. In the time of their composition, spirituals were sung and utilized in numerous forms and contexts, with new versions appearing continually to fit the demands of particular situations. With this understanding it is easy for us to see that a song composed primarily as an expression of religious commitment and faith could in fact be utilized in a particular situation to communicate a specific clandestine plan. It is very likely that this occurred on many occasions.[24]

Another factor which needs to be taken into account in understanding the nature of spirituals as secret communication is the general issue of mask and symbol, relevant to all folk music, but particularly pertinent in the case of African American spirituals, where the issue of secrecy was of obvious significance. Any song with any potential to be viewed as a threat to the status quo posed multiple dangers to the survival of Africans in the community. In his comprehensive study of the history and functions of the African American spiritual, John Lovell has provided an extensive discussion of the way in which spirituals, by their very nature as folksongs, emerged in such a way that their primary meanings would be understood only to those in the folk community of origin, Africans in slavery. This natural characteristic of all folksongs was accentuated by the urgent needs for secrecy. This, combined with the long-established African tradition of utilizing mask and irony in their songs, produced a body of music that could readily be utilized when needed as a basis for secret communication, and it is clear that Africans in America exploited this ready resource at every available opportunity. This ability to utilize songs in this way is not at all in conflict with the idea that they were often composed primarily as an expression of deep religious feelings and beliefs. In fact, the two purposes are quite complementary and consistent with the African tradition of utilizing spiritually significant singing for functional purposes (see Chapter 1).[25]

The use of mask and symbol is still prevalent in the African American community; a personal experience illustrates the way the process operates. As a child growing up in New York City, there were many occasions in which my peer group would employ private language to communicate group feelings and thoughts, changing that language once the outer community began to sense these private meanings. I remember vividly a specific experience, which occurred when I was in high school and which illustrates the way we employed mask and symbol in our community. An article in one of the national news magazines had reported that the boxer Muhammad Ali (known then as Cassius Clay) had appropriated the word *foxes* to describe the many pretty women surrounding him at every public event. My male peer group and I chuckled at the obvious ignorance of whites, who were unaware of a term we had long used to describe attractive females. But we also felt encouraged that our private communications were so well protected; members of the majority community seemed totally oblivious to the nuances of our communication, unless those underlying meanings somehow came to their attention in the form of language used in their presence by black celebrities.

The knowledge of our ability to be so successful in our efforts to converse privately was a boost to our collective self-esteem and immensely helpful in our attempts to communicate with each other about experiences of racism (or about any topic we wished to conceal from outsiders). We could hold long conversations in public places, secure in our knowledge that those outside of our African American circle would understand very little of what we said, despite the fact that we were speaking their language. *We did not create this style of communication simply for the sake of secrecy; it was a style naturally flowing out of the musically expressive poetry of the African American cultural experience.* However, we were also grateful that we could utilize our communication for covert purposes when we so desired. Without knowing it, we were experiencing the operation of mask and symbol in a way very similar to how that process operated in the songs of our ancestors.

An example of a song composed for one purpose, but used secretly for other, masked purposes is the familiar spiritual "Wade in the Water." This song was created to accompany the rite of baptism, but Harriet Tubman used it to communicate to fugitives escaping to the North that they should be sure to "wade in the water" in order to throw bloodhounds off their scent. An improvised version of this song when it was used for this purpose was:

> *Jordan's water is chilly and cold,*
> *God's going to trouble the water,*
> *It chills the body but lifts the soul,*
> *God's going to trouble the water.*
>
> *Wade in the water,*
> *Wade in the water, children.*
> *Wade in the water.*

If you get there before I do,
God's going to trouble the water,
Tell all of my friends I'm comin' too ...

Tubman's and others' improvisations on already existing spirituals, employing them clandestinely in the multilayered struggle for freedom, were repeated at many times and places.[26]

To summarize, it is clear that the natural operation of mask and symbol, the prevalence of improvisation and the existence of a complex African-derived theological system all combined to create conditions that supported the use of spirituals in the secret service of the ongoing struggle for freedom, while also providing a medium for the expression of fervently religious commitments and convictions. In this context spirituals served different specific purposes at various times and places, an extension of the African tradition of singing to serve everyday functional purposes. There was no fixed meaning for any particular song; meanings were variable and fluid. At the same time, the archetypally spiritual dimension of many of the songs made them relevant to the human experience of oppression, wherever and whenever in the world it might appear. The spiritual and improvisational genius of Africans in American slavery seems to have had a timeless and infectious impact; people worldwide who have "caught the bug" have found the needed inspiration to persist in their geographically and culturally diverse efforts to eliminate the external sources of their oppression.[27]

One of the most important motivational factors in sustaining the seemingly endless struggle to end slavery was the presence of countless leaders whose individual acts of courage served as inspirations to the larger community. Most of those individuals remain nameless, but the memory of leaders whose names are familiar to us still invokes strong feelings of pride and hope. During slavery, word of the deeds of freedom fighters like Nat Turner, Denmark Vesey, Gabriel Prosser, Harriet Tubman, Sojourner Truth, David Walker, Henry Highland Garnet and Thomas Van Rensselaer spread rapidly throughout the African community, supporting and encouraging similar plans on the part of fellow compatriots.[28]

It is not surprising that many of the important songs of the struggle utilized biblical stories of victorious freedom fighters, providing an easy parallel to African leaders in America and forecasting similar successes. A song like "Joshua Fit the Battle of Jericho," for example, could honor the actions of any number of "Joshuas" in the African community who led their people in battle in many different "Jerichos." It could also be used as biblical support for planned battles. For example, in his meetings with co-conspirators in Charleston, South Carolina, Denmark Vesey preached from the Bible, using verses from the Book of Joshua to draw parallels between the biblical story of Joshua and the plans for insurrection in Charleston.[29] The singing of "Joshua Fit the Battle of Jericho" might well have accompanied Vesey's preaching. Of course, we have no way of determining with any certainty the circumstances in which "Joshua" was composed, or all the settings in which it was sung. However, from what we know of enslaved Africans' use of spirituals of this type, we can extrapolate safely that this song was employed on many levels in the encouragement and strengthening of the long-fought struggle. John Lovell has supported such a notion in his comments about "Joshua":

> The walls of Jericho are symbolic of a long-standing tradition which kept the ex-slaves out of Canaan, their promised land. If ... the revolutionary implications had not been inherent in the subject matter, the slave poet would certainly have passed over Joshua and his prize battle as a dramatic theme. ... Step by step the poet follows Joshua. (1) "Up to de walls of Jericho, He marched with spear in han'," (2) " 'Go blow dem ram horns,' Joshua cried, 'Kase de battle am in my hand.' " (3) "Joshua commanded de chillen to shout, An' de walls come tumblin' down."
>
> Only the most naive reader misses the point that what Joshua did can be done again and again, wherever wrong and evil are to be overthrown ... Once the walls are down, the ex-slaves walk into the capital of Canaan, free men in a free land.[30]

Lovell's interpretation underscores the infinite possibilities of the Joshua story to support actions already committed and to predict and encourage future victories. No wonder that the Joshua story was employed improvisationally in the ring shout, providing opportunities for participants to act out the Battle of Jericho, thereby deepening the emotional impact of the singing. Levine recounts the story of a group of white Quaker students who had the opportunity to witness such a happening at an African American camp meeting in 1818. Levine also explains the psychological and spiritual significance of this and similar events:

They watched in fascination and bewilderment as the black worshippers moved slowly around and around in a circle chanting:

> We're traveling to Immanuel's land,
> Glory! Halle-lu-jah.

Occasionally the dancers paused to blow a tin horn. The meaning of the ceremony gradually dawned upon one of the white youths: he was watching "Joshua's chosen men marching around the walls of Jericho, blowing the rams' horns and shouting, until the walls fell." The students were witnessing the slaves' "ring shout"—that counterclockwise, shuffling dance which frequently lasted long into the night. The shout often became a medium through which the ecstatic dancers were transformed into actual participants in historic actions: Joshua's army marching around the walls of Jericho, the children of Israel following Moses out of Egypt.[31]

In Levine's description and explanation we can see how the singing of songs recounting the Joshua story was on many occasions much more than simply an expression of religious faith and also more than simply a vehicle for masked communication. Of course, it is probable that on some occasions the singing also served these and other specific purposes, outside the circle of the ring shout. On all of these occasions, however, the symbol of the Battle of Jericho must certainly have provided a powerful affirmation and reflection of the experience of Africans in bondage and an important channel of assistance in a struggle which had the clear long-term aim of dismantling the institution of slavery. In their imagination the tired warriors captured that event as a time in which they would rejoice that the walls of slavery had finally "come tumblin' down!" This, in turn, motivated them to continue in their active effort to fulfill their prophecy.

The list of spirituals featuring Old Testament heroes is unending. Often the song composers employed imaginative poetic imagery to embellish the vision of freedom. "Little David play on your harp," "Ezekiel saw the wheel," "Samson was a witness," all of the heroic figures of the Old Testament were "lifted up" and celebrated, their victories serving as divine documentation of the ultimate victories awaiting those still in bondage in Pharaoh's America. However, the most powerful figure the African American sojourners embraced was represented in the central New Testament character, Jesus. Although

Jesus appears more often in spirituals as expressive of the inner life of the singers (see Chapters 2 and 4), he also serves in some songs as a companion or leader in battle, similar to the Old Testament heroes. As James Cone has pointed out, the combined attributes of divinity and humanity made Jesus a figure larger than life, readily available to the soldiers in the struggle, in experiential rather than abstract terms:

> Jesus was not the subject of theological questioning. He was perceived in the reality of the black experience, and black slaves affirmed both his *divinity* and *humanity* without debating the philosophical question, "How can God become man?" . . . Jesus was an experience, a historical presence in motion, liberating and moving the people in freedom.[32]

As the warriors welcomed Jesus into their lives, not only was the biblical story of his birth, death and resurrection important for inner transformation, but his role as a current, loyal companion and leader in battle was equally, if not more significant. One of the most majestic musical affirmations of Jesus' leadership was expressed in "Ride On, King Jesus!"

> *Ride on, King Jesus,*
> *No man can-a hinder me;*
> *Ride on, King Jesus,*
> *No man can-a hinder me!*
>
> *I was young when I begun,*
> *No man can-a hinder me;*
> *But now my race is almost done;*
> *No man can-a hinder me!*[33]

In this song, we can feel the resolve of generations of African Americans who have used it to bolster their persistent ride on the road to freedom. With its lively and spirited rhythms, we sense that the ancestral composer of this song intended its power to be experienced in the personally and socially transformative circle of the ring shout, strengthening even further the mounting resistance to decades (centuries) of slavery. In singing and dancing this song, we can be sure that each participant felt, with complete determination, "No man can-a hinder me!"[34]

Some songs reflect the frustrations of a struggle that is persistent but slow in its results. For example, one rhythmically upbeat spiritual exhorts members of the community to "keep a-inching along, like a poor inch worm; Jesus will come by and by. . . . We must watch as well as pray; Jesus will come by and by."[35] This spiritual is often interpreted as a song anticipating death and the eventual second coming of Christ. That meaning may well have been intended in some contexts. However, careful analysis leads us to see its additional role as a song descriptive of the slow but certain road to freedom, replete with multiple tensions and contradictions. In its steady, upbeat rhythm it communicates optimism and the expectation of victory. However, the lyrics also call the singer into reality; the road to freedom is long and tedious, often leaving the traveler feeling like "a poor inch worm." Progress is steady, nonetheless, and "Jesus will come by and by." One implication is that Jesus, who conquered death, can certainly handle the time it takes to conquer slavery, and his companions can draw strength from his example and his certain appearance to confirm the end of the drawn-out battle. The ambiguity of the phrase "we must watch as well as pray" leaves open lively possibilities for the song's use as a masked signal of opportunities for escape or rebellion, where "Jesus" might well appear in the form of a Harriet Tubman, a Nat Turner, or any number of future leaders in the struggle. People in the community had to be vigilant and ready to act quickly on the opportunities which became available to them.[36]

Of all the symbols employed in the spirituals affirming present, past and future victories over the institution of slavery, the image of heaven is one of the most ubiquitous. "Goin' home," "riding up in the chariot," "crossing over Jordan," "going over there," and similar metaphorical references to "the promised land" appear in dozens of spirituals. For many singers these images referred to concrete places on earth. As John Lovell has commented, "The slave needed a home. His poetry invented one—heav'm. Although the poet used afterlife terminology, he was not necessarily talking about a home after death. This emphasis is on the idea of home and the idea of the slave at last having and reaching his home."[37] On hundreds of occasions the desire to go "home" led to individual and collective plans to flee from plantation bondage. Often the songs used were composed on the spot, as by Harriet Tubman the evening before her escape:

Good bye, I'm going to leave you,
Good bye, I'll meet you in the kingdom.

Tubman sang this song jubilantly, confident of her plans for escape. And she sang similar songs in front of her master, who was totally unaware of her intentions until she had actually escaped.[38]

The common misconception of the spirituals as primarily other-worldly in focus simply does not stand up under the evidence. One important part of the picture not usually discussed has been pointed out by John Lovell, who has reminded us that the majority of the African people serving in slavery were young women and men, concerned primarily, as are young people everywhere, with life in the present. It is difficult to conceive of them as preoccupied with "crossing over" into a promised land of life after death. A picture which better fits the evidence is that of a vigorously strong young community (necessary for the grueling work of slavery) determined to secure some kind of a meaningful life on earth, preferably outside of slavery.[39] Frequently, the songs associated with their determination employed poetic imagery depicting an anticipated or imagined "heaven" or applauding the successful "crossing over" into "heaven" by friends or family members. Sometimes when they received word, as from a relative who had arrived in Africa during the period of African repatriation of freed slaves, they might announce in song, "I heard from heaven today," referring to Africa, or to whatever final destination applied. For example, they might have sung,

> *Oh, Peter, go ring-a them bells,*
> *Peter, go ring-a them bells,*
> *Peter, go ring-a them bells,*
> *I heard from heaven today!*[40]

The "heaven" of the spirituals, when used in this "present world" manner, was not simply a fantasy, indicating a passive waiting for freedom, although it certainly was used at times as an internal image to combat the excruciating realities of everyday life. Much of the time the image was an active motivator to action, at times inciting captives into violent acts of revolution. On these occasions many Africans found, in James Cone's words, "the courage and the power to take up arms against slave masters and mistresses."[41] Some of their songs reflected this courage, as in the following:

> *Marching up the heavenly road,*
> *I'm bound to fight until I die.*
> *O fare you well friends, fare you well foes,*

Marching up the heavenly road,
I leave you all my eyes to close,
Marching up the heavenly road.[42]

We can easily picture the singers of this song as active members of Nat Turner's band, or as participants in any of the hundreds of slave rebellions that occurred when Africans in America decided they could no longer accept abuse or witness the mistreatment of friends or family members. Singing this song, the singers successfully masked their rage with the manifest image of death, safely deceiving the slave holder into believing that his docile and passive slaves were again dreaming of heaven but thankfully loyal in the present to his unrelenting demands for service. Skillfully, the singers affirmed their inner loyalty to a legitimate, heavenly master, but also announced their determination to take up arms against the earthly master. Eventually, the determined resolve of the singers was heard in a more openly bold song, one which finally escaped the emotional limitations of mask and symbol when it was evident that the singers could no longer contain themselves:

Oh, freedom!
Oh, freedom!
Oh, freedom over me!
And before I'd be a slave,
I'll be buried in my grave,
And go home to my Lord and be free![43]

Here, another layer of meaning was added. The singer would certainly not sit around, passively waiting for death, but would fight for freedom. If unsuccessful, then death was certainly preferable to bondage. The singers must have been aware of the parallel to Patrick Henry's "Give me liberty or give me death!"—a phrase the majority community experienced as relevant only to white libertarians. The transforming power of "Oh, Freedom," composed around the time of the official announcement of "emancipation," carried it into African American community gatherings in the 1880s, into the collection of Hampton Institute songs in 1909, into the African American freedom movement of the 1960s, and into justice and freedom movements around the world, in places the original composer could not have imagined. As was true of many other spirituals, this was an inspired song, with deeply archetypal meanings and applications.[44]

Of course, none of these songs had any fixed meanings but were available "in the air" to any African person needing them for any specific purposes. In the mainstream of the African tradition the songs were highly functional; they could be improvised or utilized in various ways. Bernice Johnson Reagon reminds us again of this decidedly African context when she asks us to remember that

> all of those words, "crossing over," "in the morning," "when I rise," all of those words, all of those phrases, could be applied to any practical, everyday situation, talking about changing your life. It had to be a change as drastic as death. The songs are free, and they have the meaning placed in them by the singers. So you can't say every song that has "Canaan" means Canada (or) every song that has "crossing over Jordan" means after I die. It means Canada if it *meant* Canada. It means "crossing over Jordan when I die" if that's what it *means*. It just as clearly can be a resistance song as it can be this internal nurturing of the soul![45]

Reagon is also calling our attention to the perennial tension in the African American experience between the need for action and the need for "internal nurturing of the soul." Any effective change involves both, and the presence of both kinds of transformation, inner and outer, has always been critical to the success of any of our efforts at social change. The use of spirituals for both purposes reflects that two-edged need.

After official slavery ended, the struggle for freedom would become much more ambiguous, with the specific aims being far less clear. The combination of inner spiritual fortitude and outer activism would not only be helpful but necessary. As early as 1847 Frederick Douglass, writing in his newspaper *North Star*, would envision the larger arena of the freedom struggle, including the need to attack the vicious racism of the "free" North:

> We solemnly dedicate the *North Star* to the cause of our long oppressed and plundered countrymen. . . . It shall fearlessly assert your rights, faithfully proclaim your wrongs and earnestly demand for you instant and evenhanded justice. Giving no quarter to slavery at the South, it will hold no truce with oppressors at the North. . . . Every effort to injure or degrade you or your cause . . . shall find in it a constant, unswerving and inflexible foe.

We shall energetically assail the ramparts of Slavery and Prejudice, be they composed of church or state, or seek the destruction of every refuge of lies, under which tyranny may aim to conceal and protect itself.[46]

Douglass had already sketched out the complex nature of the continuing fight, taking in North and South, church and state, personal as well as institutional forms of racism. The task would be alarmingly complex. In anticipation of that complexity, two kinds of battle energies, reflective of two major lines of present and future attack, could be seen in the varieties of spirituals being sung. On the one hand, one could hear the bold, confrontational approach represented in "Joshua Fit the Battle of Jericho," and could perhaps imagine the future strategies of a Malcolm X. On the other hand, the focused nonviolent resistance strategy of a Martin Luther King, Jr., might be heard in a spiritual like "Study War No More":

> *Gonna lay down my sword and shield,*
> *Down by the riverside,*
> *Down by the riverside,*
> *Down by the riverside;*
> *Gonna lay down my sword and shield,*
> *Down by the riverside,*
> *I ain't gonna study war no more.*[47]

The two approaches would both be necessary, as complements to each other, in order for the final victory to be attained. A century and a quarter into the ambiguous phase of the freedom struggle, James Cone would direct our attention to these seemingly conflicting energies in his brilliant work on the lives of Malcolm and Martin. Cone would demonstrate effectively that these two important heirs of the struggle needed and learned from each other more than they knew, and the struggle benefitted immensely from their dual, complementary contributions.[48] Those different but equally necessary contributions could be seen in the struggle at any point in its history, taking the form of different faces and heroes, but present throughout.

As Douglass's comments seemed to predict, the end of official slavery did not actually usher in any true freedom for African Americans; instead, they were thrust into an extended battle to secure that freedom, a battle for which they were thoroughly unprepared. The goals were now much more difficult to define. It would be too risky to pin hopes for freedom on any concrete goal, for that strategy had not succeeded when they had equated freedom with the concrete aim of ending slavery. So, what would the focus be?

New Harriet Tubmans and Nat Turners would emerge, with names like W.E.B. Du Bois, Booker T. Washington, Ida B. Wells, Marcus Garvey, James Weldon Johnson, Zora Neale Hurston, Paul Robeson, and many others, women and men, heirs of the struggles of generations of African ancestors in America. Some, like Paul Robeson, would recognize the critical role of the African cultural legacy, expressed most centrally in the spirituals. Others, like Marcus Garvey, Langston Hughes, Zora Neale Hurston and their Harlem Renaissance associates, would forge new forms and functions for African American artistic expression. They too recognized the central role of the aesthetic in any form of African American resistance. It was also now clear that despite the valiant struggle of the ancestors to maintain their spiritual and psychological dignity as African people, there had been psychological casualties, expressed in a form psychologist Na'im Akbar described as "chains and images of psychological slavery," bringing with it troubling problems of self-deprecation and ignorance. As the struggle continued, it was predictable that it would eventually come to a head, exploding in the form of a focused phase of radical agitation, flowing through the two divergent channels represented by the leaders Martin Luther King, Jr., and Malcolm X.[49]

On the Southern front of the war, Martin's soldiers ushered the legacy of song into the second half of the twentieth century. Their decision to channel the heart of their movement through the African conduit of musical expression clearly enhanced their effectiveness. Bernice Johnson Reagon, present even then on the front lines, revived the old spiritual, improvising its words into a new set of lyrics: "Over my head, I see freedom in the air" rang out from the chorus of singers who accompanied her as they marched together in Albany, Georgia. In response, "tears that had long been clotted in dry throats gushed forth when another neighbor raised his hand at meeting to tell he'd been down to the court house to register and next week all his family was going to be there."[50]

In other cities of the Southern branch of the movement, similar transformations occurred. Members of the Congress of Racial Equality improvised on the old spiritual "How Do You Feel?" in the various places where they brought Martin's nonviolent resistance strategy to bear on institutions throughout the South. Another adaptation produced "We Shall Not Be Moved," which could be heard from a group of Talladega College students protesting police brutality in the community around their campus. Their resistance song proved so effective that it appeared at almost all subsequent battles of the movement, extending even into the North. In Mississippi the charismatic singer-activist Fannie Lou Hamer collaborated with Carlton Reese to rework the old spiritual "Go Tell It on the Mountain." After a speech by the inspirational leader Ella Baker at the State Convention of the Mississippi Democratic Convention, the powerful words and melody of this transformed spiritual could be heard loud and clear, announcing to anyone within hearing that a new world was in the making: "Go tell it on the mountain, to let my people go!"[51]

For Martin's nonviolent soldiers the goals were, at least in the beginning, very clear; they sought to end legal segregation and to establish the right to vote for disenfranchised African Americans. This clear focus may explain in part why the freedom workers were so organized and why they so naturally stepped into the stream of folk-song left by the ancestors. For Malcolm, the Northern general, the ambiguity which had been forecast a century earlier by Douglass was more salient than it was for Martin. Arguably, the legal barriers in the North were less significant, but the diffuse and widespread impact of racism was nonetheless equal, if not in fact more devastating (as Martin would later discover in his Northern campaign). Malcolm's task was in this respect more difficult. (We face similar issues today as we prepare for the twenty-first century.)

Malcolm and his colleagues in the Nation of Islam were astute in recognizing that as much as battling external oppression, the movement also required that an attack be launched on self-hatred and self-ignorance. Malcolm, spiritually anchored and brilliant in his knowledge of his people, made important inroads in these internal African American community battlefields.[52] But paradoxically his agenda, ripe for the role of African-derived song, failed to capitalize on this cultural tradition. As much as Malcolm had evolved with respect to his African consciousness, he failed to recognize the extent to which the spirituals tradition was a direct extension of the African legacy. When he and the Nation of Islam disassociated themselves from Christianity (for very good reasons), they threw out the proverbial baby with the bath water, failing to see that in the best of the African American "Christian" tradition there is a religious and musical legacy far divergent in form and substance from the religion of the oppressors.

We can only speculate on the extent to which Malcolm's impact would have been magnified by the inclusion of a central aesthetic element in the Northern movement. As awareness of Malcolm's contribution is now gaining ground, it may be young rap artists and others in the artistic community who are the key players, who are sufficiently conversant with both the political and aesthetic dimensions of the African American experience to serve as leaders in maximizing the impact of Malcolm's important nationalistic visions. It will be exciting to see what new creative, functionally African artistic forms will emerge.

∽

It is December 29, 1945. Paul Robeson and his brilliant piano accompanist, Lawrence Brown, are performing one of the many concerts of spirituals and folksongs that they have presented to New York audiences. Brown, a collaborator of brothers James Weldon Johnson and J. Rosamond Johnson in their landmark collection of spirituals published in 1925, had met Robeson in England in 1922. Three years later, after a chance contact in Harlem, they decided to plan the first professional solo concert devoted entirely to spirituals. Robeson, whose father was a slave, is strong in his awareness of spirituals and their functions as sources of internal grounding and motivators of external action; he was therefore instantly at home in this repertoire.

Having worked together now for twenty years, Robeson and Brown are totally comfortable with each other. Brown frequently joins Robeson in vocal duets, where he serves as both accompanist and co-singer. Tonight, after performing much of their standard repertoire, including "By and By," "Sometimes I Feel Like a Motherless Child," "Go Down, Moses" and "Balm in Gilead," Robeson and Brown begin a creative rendition of "Joshua Fit De Battle of Jericho," sung to an unusually fast tempo. The two men sing together; Brown simultaneously provides a rhythmically percussive accompaniment on piano. Both singers alternate singing the lead, with the other providing vocal echoes and accents. The African rhythms leap out in bold relief, and our usual sensation of marching associated with this song is transformed into the feeling of a joyful dance, paralleling the inner transformation which must have occurred frequently as Africans in bondage sang this song. The vision of victory at Jericho is clear. Like the ancestors, we find ourselves actual witnesses to the final blow. With the Jericho campaign now completed, we are now ready for new, more complex battles, and it will be helpful for us to be reminded of the spiritual transformation the ancestors experienced as they continued to compose songs out of the raw material of the oppressors' religion. Their continuing spiritual evolution augmented their internal reserves, providing needed energy for the long fight ahead, a fight now re-emerging in our time.[53]

~ Chapter 4 ~

"City Called Heaven"

A Working, Everyday Spirituality

Now, at this supposedly "secular" moment in our modernity, there is much evidence that we have begun to learn, again, that we cannot properly understand ourselves or others without some sense of the world of the numinous, that world which drives, defines, and shapes us, which frightens or repels us, and which feeds our deepest needs.

— Vincent Harding[1]

I am a poor pilgrim of sorrow,
I'm tossed in this wide world alone.
No hope have I for tomorrow;
I've started to make Heaven my home.

Sometimes I am tossed and driven, Lord,
Sometimes I don't know where to roam.
I've heard of a city called Heaven;
I've started to make it my home.

— Traditional African American Spiritual[2]

As time progressed, it became clear to most Africans in the United States that they would be destined to reside in North America, separated permanently from their homeland. Some small numbers would escape to Africa through the efforts of the American Colonization Society. However, the work of the Colonization Society was viewed with suspicion by many Africans in bondage, who perceived accurately that the actions of members of the Society frequently revealed more about their own fears than any genuine concern for African American people. That is, the efforts of the Colonization Society often represented the interests of groups desperate to remove from the country a community of "free" Negroes who were living testimony to the contradictions inherent in a system of slavery based on race. In addition, the presence of these emancipated blacks was seen as a threat to the prevailing order because of their frequent roles as leaders in the design of plans for insurrection. The Colonization Society was therefore anxious to see them repatriated to Africa. In reaction, Africans in America defended their right to pursue their dreams of a meaningful life in America; they felt that they, as much as anybody (or perhaps more than anybody, considering their enormous contribution in the form of labor and toil), had a right to live as free people in America. For this and other reasons, their struggles as a people would take place primarily in the land of their enslavement, within the frame of their new identity as African Americans.[3]

It was inevitable that Africans in bondage would find a way to continue, somehow, their deeply ingrained Pan-African tradition of integrating spiritual consciousness into everyday life. The historical record indicates that they succeeded admirably in this goal; their religious consciousness remained high and thoroughly integrated into their daily struggles. As our knowledge increases about the evolution of religion in the enslaved community, we are discovering that early black American religion was infused with strong elements of a core African cosmological and experiential perspective, even stronger than previously thought.[4] The songs associated with religious experience during slavery must therefore be viewed in that light. Historian Sterling Stuckey has underscored this point:

> Too often spirituals are studied apart from their natural, ceremonial context. . . . Abstracted from slave ritual performance . . . they appear to be under Christian influence to a disproportionate extent. Though the impact of Christianity on them is obvious and considerable, the spirituals take on an altogether new coloration when one looks at slave religion on the plantations where most slaves were found and where African religion, contrary to the accepted scholarly wisdom, was practiced.[5]

One striking example of a song that takes on new meanings when understood from the perspective outlined by Stuckey is the familiar spiritual, "Wade in the Water":

> *Wade in the water,*
> *Wade in the water, children,*

Wade in the water,
God's a-gonna trouble the water![6]

In commenting on different versions of this song, observers have long
noted that it was sung in encouragement and celebration of the spirit
of Africans in bondage as they participated in the Christian rite of
baptism by immersion.[7] However, these "Christian" baptismal ceremonies frequently served as a mask for a more traditional West African religious ceremony in which a tall cross, driven by a deacon into
the river bottom, served as a bridge facilitating communication
between the worlds of the living and the dead. In addition, the cross
placed in the water in this manner also symbolized the four corners
of the earth and the four winds of heaven. When the cross was utilized in this way by enslaved African worshipers,

> it was as if the sun in its orbit was mirrored, revealing the full-
> ness of the Bakongo religion. And since those who lived a good
> life might experience rebirth in generations of grandchildren,
> the cycle of death and rebirth could hardly have been more
> suggestive than through the staff-cross—a symbol of communal
> renewal.[8]

Thus, the symbol of the cross and the song, "Wade in the Water,"
very often communicated meanings among worshipers that were
very different from those attributed by outsiders unaware of the continued influence of African religious ideas and practices. Retaining
important pieces of their traditional cosmology, enslaved Africans
continued the African rite of communication with the ancestors,
deepening in turn their relationships with the divine forces overseeing the worlds of both the living and the dead. This is but one example of many such traditional religious ceremonies persisting in the
community of enslaved Africans:

> Christianity provided a protective exterior beneath which more
> complex, less familiar (to outsiders) religious principles and
> practices were operative. The very features of Christianity pecu-
> liar to slaves were often outward manifestations of deeper Afri-
> can religious concerns, products of a religious outlook toward
> which the master class might otherwise be hostile. By operating
> under the cover of Christianity, vital aspects of Africanity, which
> some considered eccentric in movement, sound and symbolism,

could more easily be practiced openly. Slaves therefore had readily available the prospect of practicing, without being scorned, essential features of African faith together with those of the new faith.[9]

Given this cultural context it is easy to understand why Christianity, even in its Africanized form, was slow to take hold in the community of Africans enslaved in America. Aside from the strong resistance to conversion in the enslaved community, many slave holders, who feared the association between religion in the slave quarters and the emergence of plans for rebellion, provided an additional barrier to conversion by forbidding their captives to engage in any form of religious worship. (This prohibition did not prevent the convening of secret worship services, but it certainly did encourage the salience of African forms of worship.) The reticence of African worshipers to adopt Christianity was bolstered further by their refusal to identify with a religion that was so frequently employed to rationalize the perpetuation of slavery. Moreover, many Africans in bondage were aware that the most piously Christian slave holders were also the cruelest with respect to their treatment of slaves. For example, one woman who had been enslaved in Maryland offered the following observations in an interview conducted in 1863:

> Those who were Christians & held slaves were the hardest masters. . . . Now everybody that has got common sense knows that Sunday is a day of rest. And if you do the least thing in the world that they don't like, they will mark it down against you, and Monday you have got to take a whipping. Now, the card-player & the horse-racer won't be there to trouble you. They will eat their breakfast in the morning and feed their dogs, & then be off, & you won't see them again till night. *I would rather be with a card-player or sportsman, by half, than a Christian* (emphasis added).[10]

For people in bondage, African religious beliefs and practices were significantly more substantive, experientially as well as ethically and morally, than the hypocritical religion practiced by their oppressors. One illustration of their determination to resist accommodation to a new religion is reflected in an interesting legend passed down among the Gullah people of Solomon Legare Island, gleaned by theologian Will Coleman from the testimony of ex-slave Phyllis Green:

There is a legend that summarizes the ambivalence some African American slaves felt toward both the religion and lifestyle of their masters. . . . According to this legend, they came directly from Africa; they were not second-or-third-generation African Americans. The legend . . . implies that they brought their religion and way of life with them and would not allow their own belief system to be modified by their new surroundings. In other words, they did not "adjust." . . . When it was time for them to demonstrate their willingness to participate in the system that had enslaved them, they pretended to accommodate the slave driver. But instead, they transformed themselves into air-borne beings and flew home to freedom. By noon they still could be seen flying over the Atlantic Ocean. By sunset, only their voices could be heard. "Dem gone home."[11]

The presence of this legend and its survival for several generations in the Gullah community reflect the tenacity and courage of a people grounded firmly in their heritage and unwilling to be "broken." By keeping alive the story of ancestors imbued with supernatural powers, who had returned to the homeland, they maintained a strong psychological and spiritual identification with the cultural and religious bonds of their African past.

Despite such significant resistance to Christian conversion, it was inevitable over time that many enslaved Africans, deprived of their tribal connections, would hunger for a religious belief system to fill in the gaps left by the slowly waning knowledge of specific tribal practices and rituals. During "The Great Awakening" of the 1740s, the conversion of enslaved Africans to Christianity began to occur for the first time in any significant way, although the total number of converts was still relatively small. As Albert Raboteau has pointed out in his landmark study of slave religion, there were several features of Christianity *when practiced true to its intent* that were compatible with basic features of African cosmology and which facilitated the slowly emerging positive (even if still reticent) response of African captives to Christian evangelistic exhortations. The presence of these compatible features made it possible for African American believers to "convert" to Christianity without compromising their core African religious sensibilities:

It is important to observe that on a very general level African religions and Christianity . . . shared some important beliefs. A

basic Christian doctrine which would not have seemed foreign to most Africans was belief in God, the Father, Supreme Creator of the world and all within it. The divine sonship of Jesus and the divinity of the third person of the Trinity, the Holy Spirit, would have also seemed intelligible to many Africans accustomed to a plurality of divinities. ... That adoration and prayer were owed by man to a god would have seemed obvious to Africans, for whom the essence of piety consisted in propitiating gods and ancestors. ... The differences between Protestant Christianity and African religious belief, were, of course, much more numerous and much more important than the similarities, but there were enough similarities to make it possible for slaves to find some common ground between the beliefs of their ancestors and those of the white Christians. *The theory that African acceptance of Christianity required the adoption of a totally alien world view needs therefore to be modified* (emphasis added).[12]

Those entering into the process of conversion to Christianity "distinguished the hypocritical religion of their masters from true Christianity and rejected the slave holder's gospel of obedience to master and mistress."[13] In one of the songs they sang as part of their new "Christian" consciousness, African converts contrasted their spiritual aspirations with those of their hypocritical oppressors:

> *Lord, I want to be a Christian* in my heart, in my heart,
> *Lord, I want to be a Christian,* in my heart![14]

Emphasizing the importance of being a Christian in the depths of one's heart, the African convert subtly mocked the superficial, hypocritical religion of the slave master. John Lovell has argued even further that this song was likely to have been employed as well by individuals who had not yet taken the step of converting to Christianity. In their case, argues Lovell, the song simply served as a mask for feelings of contempt for phony Christians:

> What has probably happened is that the group, as individuals, have seen a lot of people who profess Christianity and did not behave as Christians are supposed to behave. As though it has held a discussion of the matter, it has concluded that it wants to make known its disgust with phony, insincere Christians. It is tired, for example, of Christians who practice selfishness and

brutality. It is tired of so-called Christians who go to church on
Sunday morning and come home and beat their slaves on Sunday afternoon. So, using the mask of a song which seems to be
praying for the Christian experience, it makes a commentary on
the need for true religion, and the honest practice of the fine
set of doctrines encompassed in Christianity.[15]

Clearly, as enslaved Africans gradually converted to Christianity, they
were careful to be sure that the religion they were embracing was
radically different from the one practiced by their captors:

> *I got a robe,*
> *You got a robe,*
> *All God's children got a robe,*
> Everybody talkin' 'bout Heaven ain't goin' there. . . .

Although there were some beginning signs of the spread of Christianity in the slave quarters during the late eighteenth century, it was
not until the early nineteenth century and the emergence of significant numbers of black preachers that large masses of enslaved Africans took the formal step of conversion. The arrival of the black
preacher in the enslaved community was a significant development,
facilitating a creative transformation of Christianity into a form compatible with African experience, consistent with the actual needs of
the worshipers rather than the needs supposed or imposed by their
captors. Without the presence of black preachers, it is doubtful that
Christianity would have had so strong an influence among Africans
in America. Raboteau has underscored the critical role played by
these early African American religious leaders:

> The importance of these early black preachers in the conversion
> of slaves to Christianity has not been sufficiently appreciated.
> Emerging in the latter half of the eighteenth and the early dec-
> ades of the nineteenth centuries, they acted as crucial mediators
> between Christian belief and the experiential world of the slaves.
> In effect they were helping to shape the development of a bicul-
> tural synthesis, an Afro-American culture, by nurturing the birth
> of Christian communities among blacks, slave and free.[16]

It is not surprising that at the heart of the emergent Africanized
Christianity, the singing of spirituals provided a channel of expres-

sion for revitalized religious convictions. As we have seen, the spirituals, through their powerful symbolism, served important functions even among those who did not embrace Christianity. Conversion to Christianity by large numbers of enslaved Africans served to deepen even further the transforming power of this music, both for individuals and for the community at large. Frequently the call to secret meetings led by African American preachers was announced by the singing of a spiritual. For example, Dorothy Scarborough, reporting in 1925 on her conversations with the head of an African American Baptist organization, noted that singing of the spiritual "Steal Away to Jesus" was often used as a signal for the time of gathering, at which point worshipers would "steal away" into the secret cover of the backwoods to avoid the feared response of the slave master:

> Dr. Boyd told me incidents of the history of various songs. For example, he said of the familiar old spiritual, *Steal Away*, that it was sung in slavery times when the Negroes on a few plantations were forbidden to hold religious services. That was because the masters were afraid of gatherings which might lead to insurrections like some that had occurred.[17]

Such reports have been confirmed by former slaves, as in the following testimony:

> When de niggers go round singin' "Steal Away to Jesus," dat mean dere gwine be a 'ligious meetin' dat night. De masters . . . didn't like dem 'ligious meetin's, so us natcherly slips off at night, down in de bottoms or somewhere. Sometimes us sing and pray all night.[18]

In their singing and praying, worshipers embraced selectively those aspects of Christianity that were in harmony with their intuitive African frame of reference; even when they lost knowledge of specific tribal practices and ceremonies, they maintained a basic African world view, which was difficult to eradicate.[19] One of the principal features of this world view was the necessity for direct communication with the divine spirit, often in the heightened frenzy of spirit possession. Singing and dancing in the ring shout, participants entered into an altered state, much like their West African ancestors. Historian Margaret Washington Creel has described this phenomenon as it was experienced among the Gullah slave communities of South Carolina:

The Gullah ring shout . . . involved an altered state of consciousness and had the attributes of "possession." It represented either an unusual behavior, inspired and controlled by an outside agent, in this case the Holy Spirit, or the outside agent displaced the individual's personality and acted in its stead. The background of the Gullah ring shout, a manifestation of possession trance, was West African in origin.[20]

The singing of spirituals in the sacred circle of the ring shout provided an ideal setting for the emergence of spirit possession. It offered to the individual and the witnessing community a personally meaningful religious experience in which the participants consistently felt the presence, support and direction of the divine spirit. For such worshipers, the existence of God was not something to be abstracted intellectually; it was experientially immediate and real. One of the most familiar of the spirituals captures and expresses this deeply personal experience of God and its effects on the affected individual:

> Ev'ry time I feel the Spirit,
> Moving in my heart,
> I will pray (repeated).

> Up-on the mountain my Lord spoke,
> Out His mouth came fire and smoke.
> All around me looks so shine,
> Ask my Lord if all was mine.

> Ev'ry time I feel the Spirit,
> Moving in my heart,
> I will pray![21]

Singers of this highly animated song have long felt the burning presence of the spirit to accompany their singing and praying. Anyone who has sung this song with any sense of comprehension of its meaning knows the experience of progressively increasing ecstasy with each verse.

As John Lovell has noted, the phenomenon of spirit possession is not confined to African religion and song; it has appeared in a variety of cultures around the world. In fact there are songs in the white American Protestant tradition that reflect this theme. However, the African version of spirit possession carries with it an enhanced force and depth that makes it uniquely effective:

Among Protestant hymns honoring the theme of spirit possession are Isaac Watts' "Come Holy Spirit, Heavenly Dove," Samuel Longfellow's "Holy Spirit, Truth Divine," and George
Croly's "Spirit of God, Descend Upon My Heart." *But the possession theme in the Negro spiritual of North America seems a good
deal closer to the vigorous, dramatic concepts of the Africans.* These
songs do not describe a pale exercise. When the spirit captures
an individual . . . it is a memorable event. The spirit endows the
individual with great powers; it transforms him physically and
mentally. Expanding his role in life and death, the spirit gives
the individual new strength, new direction, new motives and
occupations, new capacity for wrestling with life, and above all,
a new sense of grandeur (emphasis added).[22]

Such immediate presence of the spirit reflected so strongly in the
spirituals offered much more than solace or comfort; it also provided
the courage, inspiration and energy for escape from or revolt against
slavery. A vivid illustration of a possession experience resulting in
the direct impetus to escape is seen in a slave narrative called to our
attention by theologian George C.L. Cummings:

Dey singin' an' shoutin' till de break of day. Some goin' into
trances an' some speakin' in what dey called strange tongues,
dis wuz a good chance for de slaves to run away, for wen' dey
would rise up from dey trance some would run like de debbil
wuz after him, an jes keep runnin' until he run clear off. So de
w'it folks den puts de trusty niggers to guard de door or dey
say dey leaves hit in de arbor, but hit is hard to make de trusty
catch dem for dey think hit de Holy Ghost dat is makin' dem
run, so dey is afraid to stop dem, claimin' dey can't stop de Holy
Ghost.[23]

Obviously, this was a person whose very personal religious experience, in the context of a ceremony involving hours of "singin' and
shoutin'," resulted in a decision to act immediately on the impulse
to escape from bondage. Furthermore, the presence of the Holy Spirit
informed the actions of a supportive community of worshipers, who
were unwilling to risk the consequences ensuing from their attempts
to interfere with divine will. In the experience of enslaved Africans,
this direct link between spirituality and concrete action was commonplace and highly at variance with the lingering stereotype of the

slave who was content to sing spirituals throughout life while passively awaiting an appointed time to enter heaven.

Not only was there often a direct link between the experience of the spirit and the decision to escape from slavery, but the most devoutly religious individuals were frequently active leaders of slave insurrections. One very potent example is Nat Turner, whose leadership of a bloody insurrection in Southampton County, Virginia, in 1831 was motivated in large part by deep religious convictions, bolstered and encouraged by frequent experiences of direct communication with the divine spirit. Stephen Oates, in his narrative account of the life of Nat Turner, has described the spiritually nurturing environment that encouraged Nat's evolution as a religious leader:

> At Negro praise meetings, he listened transfixed as black exhorters preached a different version of Christianity from what the white man offered, an alternate version that condemned slavery and fueled resistance to it. This was black religion — an amalgam of African mythology and Christian doctrines as slaves interpreted them, a unique religion that embodied the essence of slaves' lives. . . . Nat was quick to discern the power of the black preacher, who delivered his Bible sermons with stabbing gestures, singing out in a rhythmic language that was charged with emotion and vivid imagery. . . . And the slaves, swept along by his magic, hummed and swayed in constant motion, punctuating his exhortation with "*Amen*" and "*Hallelujah,*" with "*Tell it to them, preacher.*" And then all joined in a moving spiritual, "O my Lord delivered Daniel," clapping, clapping, "O why not deliver me." Until the power of the music, the clapping and shouting, drove old and young alike into a "frenzy of religious fervor."[24]

Raised in such an environment, it is not difficult to understand how the thirty-year-old Rev. Turner, closely attuned for years to a series of signs from the heavens, would call his co-conspirators together through the signal of a spiritual, the singing of which also communicated specific directions from the spirit:

> *Steal away, steal away,*
> *Steal away to Jesus!*
> *Steal away, steal away home,*
> *I ain't got long to stay here!*

My Lord calls me,
He calls me by the thunder;
The trumpet sounds within-a my soul,
I ain't got long to stay here!

Aside from its use as coded communication, this song also expressed poignantly the powerful nature of the relationship between Nat Turner and his God. Beginning in childhood, Nat had devoted most of his life to developing and strengthening that relationship. When he sang *"my* Lord," there would have been no question about the intimacy of his connection with the divine spirit. As a highly respected religious leader, Rev. Turner also would have been instructing the members of his community to develop and nurture their own relationships with that divine spirit. In addition, he would have been helping them to understand clearly the way in which religious faith was directly linked to the need to take action against the evils of slavery.[25]

One can draw similar parallels to the lives of numerous other insurrectionary leaders, many of whom, like Nat Turner, were preachers of the Gospel. Some of these preacher-insurrectionists continued to rely strongly on the African features of their religious consciousness, modeling for their followers the ability to infuse strong elements of Africanity into an evolving New World identity. One example of such a leader was Denmark Vesey, whose status as a "free Negro" in Charleston, South Carolina, only served to strengthen both his religious convictions and his determination to destroy the institution of slavery. Having served as a slave in both the Caribbean and the United States, Vesey was astutely knowledgeable of the complex African sensibilities of the enslaved community. He used this knowledge in his choice of comrades in the planning of an insurrection that was to take place in 1822. As Sterling Stuckey has pointed out, the story of Vesey's leadership illustrates the way in which ethnically divergent people in both enslaved and "free" African circles came together in the evolution of a new identity as African Americans and a correspondingly new, Africanized form of Christianity:

> In the Vesey conspiracy the very process by which Africans were being transformed into a single people is revealed. Vesey surrounded himself with lieutenants from several African ethnic groups: Monday Gell, an Ibo; Mingo Harth, a Mandingo; and Gullah Jack, an Angolan. His choice of leaders from different

African peoples was designed to maximize cooperation among elements further down. . . .

As study of the conspiracy indicates, the cultural outlook of the slave with the greatest exposure to whites was not always, perhaps not usually, unidimensional or even primarily American. . . . To find, for example, some aspects of Christianity extremely useful and satisfying did not mean — certainly not for most slaves or for most slave preachers — that they ceased to be African anymore than those blacks who embraced aspects of Christianity in Africa ceased to be African.[26]

Stuckey's analysis also serves to debunk another stereotype, the idea that "house niggers," the slaves with the closest contacts with whites, were necessarily less African in their orientation or less committed to the elimination of slavery. It is certainly true that there were some slaves (and also some "free Negroes") who attempted to set themselves apart from their less fortunate sisters and brothers. One such person, in fact, was responsible for the ultimate foiling of the Vesey conspiracy.[27] However, it is also true that a great many African Americans in the most privileged roles were not only closely identified with their comrades but also energetically involved in the ongoing struggle against slavery. Two of the most striking examples of such privileged servants who were nonetheless also involved along with less privileged comrades in the Vesey conspiracy were Ned and Rolla Bennett, who worked as trusted servants of the governor of South Carolina and who were also enlisted as two of Vesey's most enthusiastic deputies.[28] While not every enslaved African was so actively involved in plans for the overthrow of slavery — it is always a minority of the people who are involved actively as leaders in any revolutionary scheme — it is clear that few Africans in bondage harbored any delusions about the nature of the situation in which they found themselves or the kind of personal identification necessary to cope with their oppressive circumstances. Although religion served a variety of functions in the lives of different individuals, people who differed from each other in important ways also shared a common bond in using religion as an expressive outlet for their desires to be free. For example, theologian Will Coleman, based on his examination of a large volume of slave narratives, made the following observation:

Many slaves adopted the outward appearance of Christian conversion while they interpreted this religion very differently from their masters, and thus were inspired to rebellion. Others used this new religion to adjust themselves better to their condition of servitude. *However, they all discovered ways of describing religious experiences that were liberating within the conditions they lived under* (emphasis added).[29]

Like Nat Turner, Denmark Vesey and his co-conspirators were nurtured in the waters of an alive, highly Africanized Christianity. In a Charleston newspaper, one writer expressed his disgust in reaction to the obvious religious fervor evident among African worshipers in the years preceding the Vesey conspiracy. Obviously underlying his complaints was a thinly veiled fear of the inevitable consequences of such religious activity. His comments illustrate a commonplace and valid apprehension harbored by whites at that time:

> Almost every night there is a meeting of these noisy, frantic worshippers ... Midnight! Is that the season for religious convocation? Even allowing that these meetings were conducted with propriety, is that the accepted time? That the meeting of numerous black people to hear the scripture expounded by an ignorant and (too frequently) vicious person of their own color can be of no benefit either to themselves or the community is certain; that it may be attended with many evils is, I presume, obvious to every reflecting mind.[30]

Vesey was one of the leaders of such "noisy, frantic" meetings. An active member of an independent African church in Charleston, he was conscious of the importance of religious faith in the lives of his followers. The biblical texts that held much of his attention served to forge an identification with the liberation struggles recounted in the Old Testament. Historian Robert Starobin notes:

> At the church and in his home, Vesey preached on the Bible, likening the Negroes to the children of Israel, and quoting passages which authorized slaves to massacre their masters. Joshua, Chapter 4, verse 21, was a favorite citation: "And they utterly destroyed all that was in the city, both man and woman, young and old, and ox, and sheep, and ass, with the edge of the sword."[31]

In this context, it is not hard to imagine the singing that would have emanated from these unauthorized religious gatherings:

Joshua fit the Battle of Jericho, Jericho, Jericho,
Joshua fit the Battle of Jericho,
And the walls came tumbling down!

As it was, the insurrection Vesey and his comrades planned never came to pass; the walls of slavery were not yet ready to come down. The conspiracy was foiled by revelations to authorities by an African American informer who got wind of the secret plans in a conversation with one of the conspirators.[32] Nonetheless, the widely reported details of the planned conspiracy served as inspiration to many others who were in the process of forging a vital connection between their religious experiences and their aspirations of freedom. Nat Turner, for one, was certainly an indirect heir of the Vesey conspiracy, stepping into the same river in which the freedom aspirations of countless African American Christians and non-Christians alike were increasingly bathed.[33]

Along with their dreams of freedom, the nurturing of a direct, intimate relationship with the divine spirit was a serious matter for Africans in slavery. As the more devoutly religious members of the community strengthened their religious faith through daily worship and singing, they felt their spiritual legs grow, providing essential grounding as they climbed closer to God, experiencing deeper levels of faith with each advancing step:

We are climbing Jacob's ladder,
We are climbing Jacob's ladder,
We are climbing Jacob's ladder,
Soldier of the cross.

Every round goes higher'n higher,
Every round goes higher'n higher,
Every round goes higher'n higher,
Soldier of the cross.[34]

In the continual singing of their songs, both in formal worship and in conjunction with the everyday rhythms of work and social discourse, they continued the long-established legacy of a spirituality that was intricately connected to the routines of daily life. For such individuals, the idea of a separation between the religious and the secular was inconceivable; the very fact of life presumed the constant presence of spiritual forces.

As was true of their foreparents on the African continent, enslaved African Americans expressed their evolving religious faith in the context of a *multidimensional* experience of the spirit. In the religions of most West African societies, there was a belief in a hierarchy of divinities. At the top of the hierarchy was a High God or Supreme Creator, serving as the ultimate director of all other divinities. In many instances this High God was experienced as somewhat removed and distant from people in the tribe, whose personal experience of the divine was engaged through more intimate relationships with lesser gods. As Albert Raboteau has suggested, this complex hierarchy of divinities, along with the importance attributed to communication with the ancestors, was one factor that may have made the Catholic version of Christianity and its intercessory saints appealing to newly arrived Africans in the Caribbean and South America, where Catholicism was frequently the dominant religion.[35] Examination of the texts and themes of the spirituals suggests that this multidimensional aspect of the spirit in African religions may also have found its way into the Africanized version of Protestant Christianity that developed among Africans enslaved in the United States. In particular, the religious figures of God, the Lord and Jesus referred to in the spirituals may well have reflected different dimensions of the divine spirit.

As part of his comprehensive research on the spirituals, John Lovell took the time to catalog the references to God, the Lord and Jesus in a representative sample of songs. He made the following comments about the results of his investigation:

> If one makes a close examination of 260 spirituals, carefully selected for their representativeness, one will find about fifty developmental references (not simple mentions) of Jesus, the Lord, and God. Of these fifty, a little over half talk of Jesus, a little more than one-third of the Lord, and less than one-tenth of God. Rarely does the spiritual poet mix up the three except in by-words like "O my good Lord" or "Yes, my Lord" mingled with a reference to Jesus or God.
>
> On the basis of this examination one might, very cautiously, say that the spiritual poet thought of God as the ultimate and final source of power, more or less removed like an unbelievably massive and inexhaustible dynamo; of the Lord as a more available series of power stations; and of Jesus as readily available, always at hand. Angels are the messengers of any of the three.[36]

In his instructive exploration, Lovell's characterization of the roles of God, the Lord and Jesus is strikingly suggestive of the divisions between the High God and lesser divinities of traditional West African religions. Lovell's caution in drawing any definitive conclusions is certainly warranted. Such caution needs to be applied as well to any extrapolation to African cosmology. However, the link is highly suggestive; further exploration of these themes may well lead us to an even deeper understanding of the complex conceptual and experiential religious framework of our African American ancestors.

When they sang about God, enslaved Africans expressed their deference to a supreme divinity whom they viewed as the ultimate creator and ruler. As noted by Lovell, the specific reference to God is found in a minority of the spirituals, suggesting a somewhat distant relationship with this supreme divinity, much like the relationship seen in West African religions between tribal worshipers and their High God. Spirituals referring specifically to God reflect both a reverential deference and an appreciation of the gifts given by this powerful but somewhat remote spiritual force:

> God is a God!
> God don't never change!
> God is a God,
> An' he always will be God!

> He made the sun to shine by day,
> He made the sun to show the way,
> He made the stars to show their light,
> He made the moon to shine by night, sayin'

> God is a God!
> God don't never change!
> God is a God,
> An' he always will be God![37]

Such a God was also rock solid in providing rest and shelter for weary souls:

> My God is a rock in a weary land, weary land,
> In a weary land.
> My God is a rock in a weary land,
> And a shelter in the time of storm!

Moreover, this God's place in the universe was "so high, so low, and so wide" that it was difficult to gain access to him directly; communication had to flow through "the Lamb" (Jesus). Although this conception of Jesus as the channel through which believers must enter the Kingdom reflected a central feature of Christian theology, singers of the spirituals added another twist: Part of the reason why believers had to enter into communion with God through Jesus was because this (High) God was so powerful and all encompassing that he was inaccessible; a more immediate and intimate deity was required as an intercessor:

> *My God is so high, you can't get over Him,*
> *He's so low, you can't get under Him,*
> *He's so wide, you can't get around Him,*
> *You must come in, by and through the Lamb.*[38]

Clearly this high and mighty God was the supreme ruler, holding "the whole world in his hands." However, despite his omnipotence and his consistent and dependable love, it was difficult if not impossible to sing about him in any truly intimate way. In contrast, the Jesus of the spirituals was frequently much like an intimate friend, the kind of person one enthusiastically invites into one's home and welcomes by one's side throughout a long and difficult life journey:

> *I want Jesus to walk with me;*
> *I want Jesus to walk with me;*
> *All along my pilgrim journey,*
> *Lord, I want Jesus to walk with me.*[39]

In fact, the nature of the intimate relationship between the believer and Jesus was so close that it was often expressed in the metaphor of marriage:

> *I told Jesus it would be all right,*
> *If he changed my name,*
> *I told Jesus it would be all right,*
> *If he changed my name,*
> *I told Jesus it would be all right,*
> *If he changed my name.*[40]

As noted previously (see Chapter 3), Jesus, often referred to in the spirituals as King Jesus, was also actively involved in guiding the

ongoing struggle for the liberation of his people. With Jesus as a close
ally, each worker for freedom felt assured that "no man can hinder
me." In this role the benevolent but confidently righteous King Jesus
provided welcome leadership to members of his kingdom in their
attempts to utilize their spiritual strength as an empowering force in
their efforts to free themselves from their oppressive conditions. This
is not at all at conflict with the role Jesus played in providing solace
and nurturance for his people. Unfortunately, the idea of a comforting Jesus who walks and talks with folks and tends to their inner
spiritual needs is often misconstrued as simply a palliative agent, a
kind of "opium of the people," encouraging them to be passive and
to "adjust" to their oppression. As Lovell has pointed out, this reading of the inner spiritual experience of the enslaved African and the
outward expression of that experience in song fail to take into
account the preparations necessary for effective battle:

> If the reader is beginning to wonder how these private services
> relate to radical change, let us remind him that the slave felt
> that he had to be sustained from day to day before he could
> accomplish his transformation. American slavery with its isola-
> tion, its backbreaking toil under hot sun or in inclement
> weather, its lack of family life, its poor food and housing, its
> persistent threat of being sold "down the river," and its other
> disabilities was very hard to take. . . . These concepts of Jesus,
> were, in this regard, effective and necessary.[41]

It was only through such an *intimate* form of relationship with the
spirit that one could sustain the necessary balance between inner
solace and outer, effective action in the world.

As Lovell suggests, the Lord of the spirituals frequently appeared
to function as a kind of intermediate "series of power stations," possibly serving a connecting link between the intimate Jesus and the
omnipotent, overseeing force of God. The Lord, suggests Lovell, was
more available personally than God, but not as consistently available
as Jesus:

> The Lord in the spiritual is somewhat more comprehensive than
> Jesus and definitely farther away. But he is power beyond all
> the needs of the slave. The Lord readily cuts through laws, con-
> ventions, power structures, and all other sociopolitical forms to
> make things right for those he favors, for those who return his

trust. Thus, the slave creator appeals directly to the Lord when the need is great. The implied answers to his appeals often connote radical departures from natural as well as social law.[42]

Some songs expressed this idea of an intermediate spiritual force, which could come near and be very personal, but at times be experienced as far away:

> *Oh, my Good Lord's done been here!*
> *Blessed my soul and gone away,*
> *My Good Lord's done been here,*
> *Blessed my soul and gone.*[43]

At the same time, the Lord was certainly to be depended on in the struggle for freedom: "Didn't my Lord deliver Daniel? Then why not a every man?"

This complex of divine images (God, Jesus, the Lord) may well have reflected the continuation of a traditional, core African cosmology, preserved within the internal structure of the new Africanized Christianity that slowly evolved within the community of African American worshipers. However, even if there was no direct link between the African past and the appearance of these multidimensional images of the divine in the spirituals, it is clear that the religious experience of the creators of the spirituals was full and creatively comprehensive. It offered African American believers a varied repertoire of spiritual resources for their everyday confrontations with the forces of oppression, while at the same time providing an internal framework of sanity and justice in an insane and unjust environment. Among the creators and singers of the spirituals the experience of the divine was powerful and highly personal, and certainly not confined to weekly (or even daily) worship services; it was interwoven into the fabric of their daily life.

When early African Americans found themselves in the grip of the divine spirit, the influence of the spirit *required* that they express their experience publicly in songs, shouts, testimonies and prayers, often within the rhythmic dancing of the ring shout. In such outward expression they honored the African legacy of worship through music and dance, and they continued to nurture the kind of community solidarity that had been characteristic of generations of ancestors. At the height of their ecstatic experience of the presence of the spirit and their communion with each other, they sang,

I'm gonna sing (shout, preach, pray) when the Spirit says a-Sing,
I'm gonna sing when the Spirit says a-Sing,
I'm gonna sing when the Spirit says a-Sing,
And obey the Spirit of the Lord.[44]

This was a continuation of the best of the African oral tradition, nurtured and developed through the power of rhythm. Rhythm, embodied in the drum, had been a central feature of West African music. In fact, the drum had been regarded as a sacred instrument, the construction of which had followed the guidelines prescribed by the spirits. An example of such specific spiritual prescriptions for the construction of drums is seen in a passage from the writing of Chief Fela Sowande, called to our attention by religious music scholar Jon Michael Spencer:

> African musical materials and styles ... have mythological origins. ... Among the Yorubas of Nigeria (and presumably in other areas of Africa also), the very first step in the making of a drum is the ceremony which placates the spirit inhabiting the tree that is to be cut down for the wood from which the drum-frame will be subsequently carved. Furthermore, the Yorubas say that the tree must be one that has grown near the village, and is accustomed to hearing human voices. Only then will its wood "speak well" as a drum-frame. A tree in the forest, on the other hand, that has not been accustomed to hearing human voices will be unsatisfactory, or its wood will be "dumb" as a drum-frame. Moreover, every drum has its "altar" carved on the drum-frame. Here is the actual spot at which the drummer communes with the patron deity of drumming. The drummer who neglects his regular communion with this patron deity of drumming will find either that his drum goes to pieces or he will be constantly out of employment.[45]

The drum, providing the rhythms empowering the daily activities of West African peoples, was imbued with myriad sacred meanings and functions. However, because it was viewed with suspicion by uncomprehending Westerners, the drum was outlawed among Africans in America. Consequently, it quickly vanished from the enslaved community. However, the sacred functions of rhythm originally supplied by the drum survived within the souls of the people and were infused potently into the structures of their songs, which they sang to the accompaniment of the improvised rhythmic clapping of their hands and movements of their bodies and feet. These rhythmic accoutrements were supplemented by such improvised instruments as sticks, kitchen spoons, pans, cans and tin buckets.[46]

As Spencer has noted, rhythmic dance was an important catalytic agent in summoning the spirit within the circle of the ring shout. And as he has humorously observed, members of the ruling class would have faced quite a predicament if they had been able to understand the robust nature of the African tradition of rhythm:

> To the African the drum was a sacred instrument possessing supernatural power that enabled it to summon the gods into communion with people. However, to outside observers it was the drum alone that symbolized the "heathenism" of the "danced religion" practiced by these so-called "cursed sons of Ham." ... However, what they failed to realize was that the drum was not the cause of this so-called "paganism." It was actually rhythm that was largely responsible, for percussiveness produced the power that helped move Africans to dance and into trance possessions. Had missionaries, slave traders, and slave masters calculated this, they would have attempted to remove rhythm from the blood and bones of the African.[47]

As Spencer's observations also illustrate, the spirituality of early African American worshipers was made active and real not only by their singing, but also by their rhythmic dancing; their religion was literally one that encompassed both body and soul, a creative continuation of the best of African sacred tradition. The inner transformation that occurred as a result was one that permitted an experience of joy, even in the midst of horridly oppressive circumstances. Those fortunate enough to have such an experience could not help but share it with others:

> *This little light of mine,*
> *I'm gonna let it shine,*
> *This little light of mine,*
> *I'm gonna let it shine,*
> *This little light of mine,*
> *I'm gonna let it shine,*
> *Let it shine, let it shine, let it shine.*[48]

Singers of this song communicated their understanding that although each person is but a small part of the Kingdom, the collective shining of many "little" lights provides a powerful resource in the ongoing struggle for personal and social transformation.

In the context of such a rich religious experience, many spirituals, which to outsiders seemed to reflect an exclusively otherworldly orientation, were understood by those who sang them to be much more complex spiritually and psychologically. For example, songs referring to heaven, in addition to serving as code communication for plans to escape from slavery (see Chapter 3), also served to facilitate what theologian James Cone has called the experience of the "transcendent present":

> Even where there is no overt or hidden reference to specific historical events, the spirituals employ eschatological language to express transcendence in the slaves' present existence. . . . To be a child of God had present implications. It meant that God's future had broken in the slave's historical present. . . . The black slave could experience *now* a foretaste of that freedom which is to be fully revealed in the future.[49]

In one of the most important spirituals, they expressed this inner heaven of the present, one that has begun to feel like home. In a haunting melody, sung slowly to an emotionally powerful 6/8 rhythm, they sang,

> *I am a poor pilgrim of sorrow,*
> *I'm tossed in this wide world alone,*
> *No hope have I for tomorrow,*
> I've started to make Heaven my home.
>
> *Sometimes I am tossed and driven, Lord,*
> *Sometimes I don't know where to roam,*
> *I've heard of a city called "Heaven,"*
> I've started to make it my home.
>
> *My mother has reached that pure glory,*
> *My father's still walkin' in sin,*
> *My brothers and sisters won't own me,*
> *Because I am tryin' to get in.*

Sometimes I am tossed and driven, Lord,
Sometimes I don't know where to roam,
I've heard of a city called "Heaven,"
I've started to make it my home (emphasis added).[50]

In singing about their experience of having "started" to make heaven home, singers communicated that the task of integrating into one's life an effective, consistent sense of the spirit is a serious one, requiring conscious attention and effort and not accomplished in a single worship experience. Some, like "mother," have already reached an evolved spiritual plane. (Depending on the circumstances of the individual singer, this may have been in the form of mature spiritual development on earth or the "pure glory" of the hereafter.) Others, like "father," and "brothers and sisters," are still "walkin' in sin," not yet ready to take the step toward higher spiritual development.

The fact that the creators of the spirituals focused primarily on life in the present does not mean that they were never concerned with death. Tragically, death (especially the premature death of family or community members as a result of physical abuse) was a regular part of their existence, and there is no question that some of their songs communicated that reality. For example, there is no way to read any other meaning into the following song:

Death ain't nothin' but a robber, don't you see . . .

Death came to my house, he didn't stay long,
I looked in the bed an' my mother was gone, . . .

I looked in the bed an' my father was gone, . . .

I looked in the bed an' my sister was gone, . . .

I looked in the bed an' my brother was gone,
Death ain't nothin' but a robber, don't you see?[51]

At the same time, there is no evidence that they were preoccupied with concerns about death to the exclusion of embracing active aspirations for a meaningful life in the present. Rather, their songs reflected their ability to deal directly with the myriad of emotions that accompanied the loss of loved ones as well as their understanding of the need to prepare for spiritually meaningful life in the hereafter. To comprehend this fully, we have to recognize that in their still active African religious cosmology, the creators of the spirituals did not construct the kind of rigid boundaries between the worlds of life and death that are so characteristic of Western thinking. Communication with the ancestors and a holistic conception of the cycle of life and death served to remove from death the dreaded connotations awarded it by those outside of this traditionally African religious framework. John Lovell has provided one of the best explanations of this delicate balance seen in the spirituals between concerns about life on earth (particularly aspirations of freedom) and feelings about death:

> No one can begin to read spirituals for true meaning unless he accepts the slave's desire for freedom as his prime cause. It should be reiterated that the slave could discuss this prime cause only through symbols. Thus Death and Canaan are most often symbols of release from slavery without meaning release from life. . . .
>
> Where Death does mean release from life, the African concepts are likely to be present or pronounced. . . . In the dozens of songs which speak of reunion with mothers, fathers, sisters, brothers and other beloved dead, these African beliefs are assuredly being perpetuated.[52]

Because of this delicate balance between concerns of the here and the hereafter, songs could serve multiple functions. For example, when a singer declared, "I got a crown up in-a the Kingdom, ain't-a that good news?" the "Kingdom" could be the internal heaven of the present, earthly freedom symbolized as "Kingdom," or the world of the hereafter. None of these meanings would contradict the idea of active involvement in the realities of the present, whether in the form of the development of a mature religious faith or the involvement in preparations for escape from slavery. In fact, all of these concerns were quite complementary. For example, the almost unbearable suffering of the present was at times made more bearable by the ability to imagine a better life beyond death, which in turn helped provide the necessary energy to engage in the struggle to hasten the time of earthly freedom. Just as enslaved Africans transformed the time of the Old Testament into their time in the present (see Chapter 3), they also utilized their anticipation of the future within the frame of their present existence. James Cone has described this fluid sense of time in his description of what he calls "the transcendent future," seen in many of the spirituals:

> These songs emphasized the inability of the present to contain the reality of the divine future. In this sense the spirituals were "otherworldly." They stressed the utter distinction between the present and the future. The hope of black slaves was not of this world, not in the "hell of a completely understood humanity." . . .
>
> It was this transcendent element of hope (as expressed in black music) which elevated black people above the limitations of the slave experience, and enabled them to view black humanity independently of their oppressors.[53]

Continuing, Cone has also addressed the issue of the way in which this kind of "otherworldly" aspect of the spirituals (and black religion in general) has been misperceived by critics as an exclusively destructive element, cleverly employed by the oppressors to substitute "pie in the sky" for true freedom on earth:

> True, white oppressors did preach "pie in the sky" as a means to get black people to accept their exploitation. But white oppressors have also used, over the years, distorted versions of Democracy, Marxism, and even Black Power as their means to confuse and control the oppressed, and they will distort any world-view to camouflage their own interests. . . . The task, however, of black theologians is to move beyond the distortions of black religion to the authentic substance of black religious experience so that it can continue to serve as a positive force in liberating black people.[54]

I would add that this task is not limited to black theologians; it is appropriate for anyone interested in an accurate understanding of African American history and culture and in finding a way to extrapolate from the lessons of the past in order to guide meaningful and effective actions in the present. With specific regard to the issue of the meaning of the hereafter in the spirituals, it is clear that the "otherworldly" aspect of these songs was one that interacted actively with religious faith and hopes for freedom as well as with actions in the service of earthly liberation in the present. In our own time, we can certainly benefit from understanding and continuing this powerful part of the African American spirituals legacy as we search for effective approaches to the perplexing issues confronting us currently, both within and without the African American community.

The effective, everyday religion of early African Americans, passed on to us through the lyrics, rhythms and melodies of the spirituals, was a unique accomplishment. It would be difficult to find in history a more advanced example of a religious system able to integrate so effectively the seemingly contradictory tasks of inner solace and meaningful action in the world. It is clear that some of the best features of African religious traditions, interacting with the severely oppressive circumstances of slavery in America, resulted in a new, unique religious system of incomparable vision and power, expressed actively in an archetypally potent body of songs. If we are willing to draw on them, the lessons of this unique legacy can be highly instructive.

When official slavery ended, the spirituals' legacy was carried into later forms of African American spiritual music, including the blues, black hymnody and gospel music.[55] In many African American churches today, one can experience features of musical and religious expression that are strikingly similar to the ring shout and the spirituals as they were experienced in slavery. Writer James Baldwin, in *The Fire Next Time*, offered a vivid personal description of such experience when it is functioning at its best in the contemporary African American church:

> There is no music like that music, no drama like the drama of the saints rejoicing, the sinners moaning, the tambourines racing, and all those voices coming together and crying holy unto the Lord. . . . I have never seen anything to equal the fire and excitement that sometimes, without warning, fill a church, causing the church, as Leadbelly and so many others have testified, to "rock." Nothing that has happened to me since equals the power and the glory that I sometimes felt when, in the middle of a sermon, I knew that I was somehow, by some miracle, really carrying, as they said, "the Word" — when the church and I were one. Their pain and their joy were mine, and mine was theirs — they surrendered their pain and their joy to me, I surrendered mine to them — and their cries of "Amen!" and "Hallelujah!" and "Yes, Lord!" and "Praise His Name!" and "Preach it, brother!" sustained and whipped on my solos until we all became equal, wringing wet, singing and dancing in anguish and rejoicing, at the foot of the altar.[56]

In such experiences, the core elements of direct experience of the divine spirit in the context of music and dance reflect a continuation of the legacy of early African American religion and music.

On Sunday mornings in any number of traditionally African American churches in our time we can find devoted communities of "saints" who continue to immerse themselves in a kind of worship that provides immediate and powerful access to the divine spirit. This worship offers a reservoir of spiritual and emotional resources for people who must continue to cope with emotionally and physically crippling forms of unofficial slavery. In the church, people who are otherwise regarded as insignificant find themselves powerfully transformed in the nurturing environment of a caring and emotionally connected community. Often this environment is active in salvaging the lives of children who would otherwise be destined to failure. Child psychiatrist James Comer is one of those who has called this phenomenon to our attention. He has described an impressionable childhood experience in which he had taken time away from his family's own Baptist church to visit a storefront service with one of his classmates:

> Several of the choir members and ushers were people I knew from school. It seemed to me odd that some of these people were quite withdrawn in school and were hardly known to the teachers and staff, but in their church they were lively, active participants. At the storefront church that day, I found at least part of the answer. The choir gave a rousing rendition of a spiritual. The soloist responded to the audience's enthusiasm with these words, "One thing I like about this church is that if you have a speck of talent you can use it, and the people will love you and respect you for it."[57]

As Comer's observations illustrate, a central feature of the ongoing effectiveness of the traditional African American church is found in the role of music. In many settings the spirituals continue to live, both in their traditional form and in hymns and gospel songs that have been built on traditional melodies, rhythms and religious themes.

Despite the continuation of the spirituals in many church settings, it is also true that gospel songs have in large part supplanted the spirituals as the music of choice of the contemporary African American church.[58] There is no doubt that the same kinds of religious conviction and effective emotional transformation characteristic of the spirituals have found their way into the singing of gospel music. However, close examination of the themes dominant in the modern gospel repertoire reveals a subtle but significant difference. In contrast to the spirituals, gospel songs are in fact largely otherworldly in their focus, sometimes in a way that supports the development of inner faith to the exclusion of support for direct action in confronting the structures of oppression in the world outside of the church. As we have seen, one important strength of the spirituals has been their ability to promote *balance* between inner faith and social action. Gospel songs are less effective in promoting that balance. Lawrence Levine is among those who have commented on this important difference between the spirituals and their gospel song progeny:

> Changes in religious consciousness and world view are ... clearly delineated in the gospel songs, which from the 1930's on displaced the spirituals as the most important single body of black religious music. There were, to be sure, a number of important points of continuity in the consciousness of the gospel songs and the spirituals. In both, God was an immediate, intimate, living presence. ... Like the spirituals the gospel songs were songs of hope and affirmation. ...
>
> As important as these similarities are, they are overshadowed by the differences. The overriding thrust of the gospel songs was otherworldly. Emphasis was almost wholly upon God with whom Man's relationship was one of total dependence.[59]

Jon Michael Spencer has provided one of the most illuminating explorations of this strongly otherworldly theme in gospel music. In describing it as a music that reflects the idea of "Christ against culture," Spencer leads us into an understanding of how a people, thoroughly discouraged in their dealings with a persistently abusive and sinful world, would take refuge in the comforting support and spiritual nurturance found in an exclusive relationship with Jesus Christ. In his analysis Spencer gives examples of songs written by composers who have inspired the development of the gospel tradition:

> The single stream of thought that issues through the history of the gospel music movement is the notion that Jesus Christ is "Everything." For instance, Jones says, "Christ is all," or further, "all in all." Tindley also claims Jesus as his "all," adding that his

allness is such that "there's nothing between." Morris sings, "Christ is all, all and all this world to me." The Lord is "all and all" to Brewster because he is friend to the friendless, mother to the motherless, and father to the fatherless. Dorsey lyricizes, "He's ev'rything, dear Lord, You are the source that I draw from; My joy, my strength, Oh Lord, is in You."

In gospel music Jesus Christ is Everything—Friend, Protector, and Liberator—because he is portrayed as the Ultimate Alternative to a world that is essentially nothing, that is, no friend, offering no protection, and conditioned by captivity.[60]

Spencer has opted not to compare the gospel and spirituals traditions, preferring instead to "take gospel as it is and determine just were it stands theologically."[61] However, I do not think that comparing the two is necessarily critical of the gospel movement. Rather, I believe that we benefit greatly from our understanding of history; some of our most "radical" advancements have come from our ability to learn from the best features of past traditions.

The gospel tradition represents a significant development in the religious music of African Americans; there are countless gospel songs that are highly moving and effective. I, for one, have often found myself visiting particular churches simply because of their reputation for having strong gospel choirs and effective music ministries. I experience a great deal of emotional and spiritual renewal when I immerse myself in such an environment. However, the strengths of this important contemporary music movement will be even further enhanced if it can continue to be infused periodically with the memory and transformative vision of the spirituals. Without that kind of periodic renewal, gospel music, with its largely escapist leanings, may be in danger of fostering the kind of passivity and withdrawal from social action which many have always feared to be a necessary by-product of black religion.

In fact, a kind of periodic reemergence of the spirituals has occurred, and it is important for us to recognize that the idea of a simple, linear, and chronological evolution of African American religious music, beginning with the spirituals and ending with gospel music, is a simplification of the historical facts. As music historian John Storm Roberts has reminded us in his comments about black religious music, "Its many styles may perhaps be arranged chronologically according to which began first, but all are still sung today and are widely popular."[62] In support of Roberts's view, Wyatt Tee

Walker has called our attention to four distinctive periods since "emancipation" when spirituals have reemerged to assume a prominent position in the African American sacred music environment. These include the period following the tours of the Jubilee Singers, the period between 1914 and 1930 (aided by the contributions of John W. Work), the period of World War II (a national crisis time during which the Wings Over Jordan radio choir brought spirituals to Americans over the air waves), and the period of the freedom movement of the 1960s (another crisis period, during which many old spirituals were reworked to aid in the struggle; see Chapter 3). Clearly, the evolution of African American religious music has not followed a straight line. Rather, the influence of the root music, the spirituals, continues to reassert itself (especially during crisis periods), evidencing its continuing power alongside other musical forms derived from it. In turn, other African American sacred music forms are highlighted and strengthened, offering a whole spectrum of music serving multiple purposes in the adaptation and resistance struggles of African peoples in America.[63]

Hopefully, we will again find ourselves open to the possibilities for an infusion of the best features of the spirituals legacy. In a time in recent years that has seen the expansion of the so-called black underclass and the increasing abandonment of government programs serving the poor and oppressed, we are in need more than ever of a renewed vision of ourselves as potent and able agents of social change. Although it is tempting to withdraw into the world of the spirit to the exclusion of social action, the legacy of the spirituals reminds us that even in the most desperate of times African Americans have transcended their conditions to serve as leaders in the building of a just world. If we can hear and experience the socially empowering messages of the spirituals alongside the potently nourishing voices of the gospel movement, we will indeed have something to sing about!

Outside of the African American community, America at large also appears to be searching desperately for a meaningful spiritual vision. The reappearance of interest in the occult and the rise of various forms of fundamentalist and New Age religions are just a few examples of that search. Unfortunately, some attempts at spiritual renewal have been forged in the service of the status quo or even regression in social progress rather than forward-looking change. Still, in the spirited singing frequently evident in the rapidly growing fundamentalist Christian movement, one can recognize the strong influence of the African American spirituals tradition. Members of fundamentalist communities who are open to a deeper understanding of the spirituals might find to their surprise that transcending the individualistic (and sometimes materialistic) focus of their new movement to join in the legacy of a spirituality active in the confrontation of oppressive circumstances would not only uplift those who are members of "officially" oppressed groups, but would free members of their own fundamentalist groups as well from the oppressive circumstances with which they themselves are frequently familiar. Too often, critics of contemporary Christian movements have failed to look beyond the surface to recognize the underlying experience of oppression among some of their most enthusiastic adherents.[64] Such victims of oppression have more in common with the creators of the spirituals than they imagine. If they are open to the lessons of this tradition they may find themselves strengthened rather than, as they appear to fear, weakened.

Many Americans and others in the Western world, feeling that institutionalized religion in *any* form has lost any sense of personal meaning for them, have turned to other, creatively alternative channels in order to develop a sense of connection with the realm of the spirit. The Swiss psychiatrist Carl Jung was one of those who was disenchanted with institutionalized religion. Raised in the latter part of the nineteenth century in what he experienced as a religiously sterile environment, his nevertheless intimate involvement with the church (his father and several uncles were Christian clergymen) motivated him to engage in a lifelong attempt to transform Christianity into a form that would once again have the chance to carry power and meaning in the personal lives of Christian believers. In both his theoretical writings and in the psychological method of deep unconscious exploration that he developed, his determination to revive the power of Christianity is evident.[65]

Jung's ideas have had a profoundly widespread impact, especially in the last two decades; those who have discovered his work or who have (sometimes unknowingly) been influenced by it indirectly have embraced the idea of an "inner" spirituality in which they can experience a deeply personal sense of the numinous, finding clearer personal definition and direction as they discover a personal "myth" or life purpose. In some respects this approach to spirituality has much in common with the core features of traditional African and African American religion, which also, as we have seen, relies heavily on the development of an intimately personal experience of the spirit, one which guides and directs life purposes. For example, much of what the insurrectionist leader Nat Turner experienced in his attention to visions and signs from God could easily be explained and construed within a Jungian framework. Like many Jungians, Nat was confident about his life purpose, which for him emerged clearly in his experience of the spirit and his attention to what Jungians might call synchronous signs in nature. A more recent example of the close link between Jungian thinking and some of the best of the African American religious tradition is found in the work of the great African American mystic Howard Thurman, which also focuses strongly on the voice of the spirit as it is experienced within.[66] In addition, the work and underlying spiritual framework of traditional African healers have much in common with the work of analysts and psychotherapists trained in the Jungian school.[67]

In my own encounter with Jung's ideas over the last several years I have come to believe that Jung's greatest contribution is found not in his original theoretical ideas (although it is difficult to overestimate the importance of some of those ideas), but rather in his unique standing as one of the few European thinkers with the vision and courage to align himself with the wisdom of centuries of geographically diverse cultural traditions, including many non-Western traditions. In their narrowly myopic conceptualizations, most other Western theoreticians operate as if the world of sophisticated thought began on the European continent. In contrast, Jung, who was able to demonstrate the presence of myriad archetypal commonalities among cultures in such geographically ranging areas as China, Africa, India and Europe, was successful in calling our attention to concepts that, in the astoundingly similar way in which they appear in such varied contexts, can confidently be considered universal in their ability to instruct us about the nature of core features of human functioning that transcend the particulars of any specific cultural framework.

One of the important areas that Jung focused on was the *necessity* to consider the realm of spiritual functioning if one is to have any valid understanding of human nature or work effectively with anyone in the process of developing a meaningful life plan. In this area Jung again stands apart from many other European thinkers, particularly those in the mainstream of Western mental health disciplines, who have somehow managed to construct elaborate theories of human psychology without any attention at all to the clearly universal dimension of spirituality, which is present in every culture in history.[68] It is therefore easy to understand why Jungian ideas have become popular in many religious communities. However, it is curious that even American Jungians have virtually ignored the limitless wealth of spiritually significant material found in traditional African American folksongs and folktales. Many American Jungians, familiar with esoteric myths and folklore from such places as Greece and India, have virtually no knowledge of the rich body of material contained in the spirituals, representing one of the most important pieces of their own country's history. When they have focused on American folk material, much of the attention has been on Native American traditions. And sadly, some of this interest in the culture of Native Americans seems motivated by the perceived "exotic" nature of these traditions. In my opinion, the Jungian community must come to terms with the fact that even in its professed commitment to being fully "conscious," it has been infected by some of the same negative racial influences that have invaded most other aspects of American society. Part of the effect of this process has been the pervasive assumption that there is very little of value to be found in African American culture aside from its importance as a symbol of pride for African Americans. The idea that there might be material that has application to the lives of people of non-African descent has somehow escaped any serious consideration.[69]

One example of a song that has the ability to capture the imagination of anyone seriously interested in exploring its far-ranging archetypally symbolic meaning is the spiritual "Wade in the Water," whose underlying significance in encouraging deep immersion in the spiritual waters of the soul is readily evident when one takes the time to think about it in that way:

> Wade in the water,
> Wade in the water, children,
> Wade in the water,
> God's-a gonna trouble the water!

On this level the lyrics communicate that if one follows the song's advice about engaging in a process of deep exploration of the waters of the spirit (or "the unconscious"), a transformation will occur; "God's-a gonna trouble" these spiritual waters, and the affected person will never be the same. And when one listens to or sings this song, the lively rhythm and infectious melody provide further confirmation; one is indeed a new person! Countless other spirituals, examined from a similar perspective, communicate equally rich meanings concerning the nature of and possibilities for human transformation.

In addition to providing an expansion in the body of archetypal material that is available to them, Jungians and others interested in inner dimensions of the human spirit will find that the spirituals also encourage their ability to understand the ways in which a *collective* or community-encouraged experience of the spirit enhances the effectiveness of that experience for each community member. Most adherents of inner spiritual approaches to religion have been individualistic in their orientation and have failed to understand the unlimited potential of communal sharing as a facilitator of individual growth. In addition, although Jung and others of his persuasion did not intend it, the emphasis on deep spiritual exploration central to this tradition sometimes encourages a kind of preoccupation with the self to the exclusion of developing any meaningful strategies for concrete action in the world. Exposure to the strong social action messages of the spirituals would serve to correct this imbalance. Additionally, the emphasis on oral expression and body movement found in the spirituals tradition would serve to enrich the body-oriented expansions of Jungian work that are becoming increasingly popular.[70]

Even among those in Europe and America who have continued to find meaning in traditional, institutional religion, the concept of spirituality appears to encourage a primarily individualistic, private form of spiritual practice, one that is lacking both in its social dimension and in the idea of responsibility for confronting the structures of social oppression. This development is part of the increasingly popular concept of spirituality which has emerged in response to modern secular society's search for meaning. The insightful British Anglican priest Kenneth Leech has commented on this situation:

> Today "spirituality" is marketed as a product, in competition with others, on the book stalls. It belongs to the area of "private life." . . . Within Western societies religion itself has come to be seen as an option, one of the wide range of choices that consumerism offers. Spirituality is widely seen not as a way of living in every sphere but as a sphere in its own right: "the spiritual dimension." The action of God is thus confined within extremely narrow limits. It is not surprising that in much of the popular literature that has emerged from the spiritual revival of recent

years, prayer and meditation are offered as ways of coping with existing reality, not as ways to change it.[71]

The legacy of the spirituals and the African American religious tradition with which it is associated has much to offer those who are currently bombarded with such a compartmentalized conception of spirituality. In fact, much of America in particular, largely in search of a soul, would find itself enriched immensely in its sense of purpose if it could be open to the challenges found in the tradition of African American song, with its integrated attention to the multiple dimensions of faith, "inner" centeredness and meaningful action in the world.

Fortunately, there are many, both in and outside of America, who are beginning to understand the important example provided by the African American tradition of spirituality and particularly the critical importance of the songs that both nurtured that tradition and were produced by it. Increasingly, those committed to spiritually informed social action are recognizing that music is not only helpful but frequently necessary in the mobilizing of people to action. Continuing his discussion, Kenneth Leech argues that

> the Christian in politics must be joyful, celebrating the victory over injustice and oppression in the midst of failure and trial. Politics needs songs and dances, wildness and jubilee, and the dimension of celebration should be something that Christians can bring to political struggles. Today we need to learn afresh from Latin America, South Africa, and the countries of the East about the power of liberatory music and the importance of celebration in the midst of strife. For no vigorous political movement has ever existed or can exist without resistance music.[72]

I would add that Leech's analysis is also pertinent to those outside of the Christian tradition, encompassing myriad worldwide religious movements. There can be no question about the influence of the African American spirituals tradition in contributing to the growing recognition worldwide of the importance of song in movements for justice and freedom in the context of such widely varied settings. Early African Americans set an invaluable example in both the practice of an effective, everyday spirituality and in the creation and singing of songs that encouraged and promoted the connection between their religious faith and their active engagement in the struggle for revolutionary change. Any group of people willing to learn from this historical example will find themselves engaged in the same kind of two-sided spiritual connection. In fact, like the community of Africans enslaved in America for nearly two hundred and fifty years, they will come to understand that freedom is meaningless unless the life of each free person is informed by a meaningful spirituality, one that promotes a sense of accountability to self, to God, and to one's fellow human beings.

∽

It is Sunday morning early in 1965 in one of the large African American Baptist churches in Chicago. Mahalia Jackson, one of the most important pioneers of the gospel movement, is preparing to sing. As members of the congregation, we find ourselves excitedly anticipating Mahalia's ministry of song. We all know that whenever she sings we are not only deeply touched by her singing but we are also drawn into a wonderfully intimate connection with the divine spirit; when Mahalia sings, the *whole church* is filled with the presence of the spirit. This morning, Mahalia has chosen the spiritual "City Called Heaven" as her anthem. As she begins her song, accompanied effectively by the resonant, enveloping sound of the organ, our expectations are indeed confirmed; we find ourselves entering into the realm of that inner heaven that was so familiar to our foreparents. Mahalia *caresses* the words and melody of this powerful song, sensitively drawing us deeper into heaven with each new phrase. We can also feel the depth of her own faith as she sings, in her magnificent contralto voice,

> *Sometimes I am tossed and driven, Lord,*
> *Sometimes I don't know where to roam.*
> *I've heard of a city called "Heaven,"*
> *I've started to make it my home.*

We find ourselves undergoing a slow but steady inner transformation as our weary bodies and spirits experience a welcome renewal, bolstering our determination to go on with our lives. As she completes her song, we find that Mahalia's singing has also helped us to renew our connections with one another, guided by a fresh awareness that our God demands not only faith, but also consistent accountability in our actions with each other and with our sisters and brothers in the world outside of our cherished Sunday haven.[73]

∼ Chapter 5 ∼

"Scandalize' My Name"

Accountability

O, Lord, teach us who love Liberty and long for it, to realize its costs and purpose. There can be no freedom in a just and good world, if freedom means to do as we please, and where all about us in this life, as in this school, lie bars and bonds and limits. The free are those who know the rules which God Himself has set and go their way within these metes and bounds full freely. Truth is the knowledge of these strait and narrow ways. It is the Truth that makes us free and this it is we linger here to learn, O Lord. Amen.

—W.E.B. Du Bois[1]

I met my brother (sister, preacher) the other day,
Gave him (her) my right hand.
But just as soon as ever my back was turned,
He (she) took an' scandalize' my name!

You call that a brother (sister, preacher)?
No, no!
You call that a brother (sister, preacher)?
No, no!
You call that a brother (sister, preacher)?
No, no!
Scandalize' my name!

—Traditional African American Spiritual[2]

Often ignored in discussions of the spirituals is the rich commentary they provide on issues of values, particularly with respect to human relationships. Consistent with their experience of the Holy

101

Spirit, the creators of the spirituals felt the necessity to honor that spirit through the channel of humane and loving dealings with family and community members. These values are reflected clearly in many of the songs they have passed on to us. In revealing their deepest thoughts and feelings concerning such issues, the creators of the spirituals have provided us important information regarding exactly what they were striving for in their fight for freedom and justice. They made it clear that in their minds the struggle to end slavery (and all other forms of external oppression) would be fruitless without an adequate answer to the question, Freedom to do what? or When we obtain our freedom, what will be our highest priorities as a people?

When singers exhorted their oppressors to "Let my people go!," they were directing attention to passages from the Old Testament that gave clear direction concerning the purpose of liberation for the Israelites, and by extension, for Africans and all others in the history of the world who have been victims of oppression. As Kenneth Leech has indicated,

> The cry "Let my people go" has as its purpose "that they may serve me." The deliverance is therefore both from slavery to the economic and political bondage of Egypt and from captivity to idols and false gods. The liberating God of the Exodus calls this oppressed and fragile people to serve that ultimate Freedom that is Godself (emphasis added).[3]

For the creators of the spirituals, "that they may serve me" included not only prayer and worship, but most important, the enactment of God's Kingdom on earth in the form of caring relationships with sisters and brothers in the community, avoiding the idolatrous worship of possessions or of self-interest. They encouraged anyone confused on such matters to

> Give me yo' hand,
> Give me yo' hand,
> All I want is the love of God,
> Give me yo' hand,
> Give me yo' hand,
> You must be loving at God's command.

For those who had actually succeeded in obtaining their freedom (either in the flesh or in the freedom of the spirit) the exhortation from the singers was even more direct and repetitiously clear; the song leader provided the questions and the responding community provided the simple and consistent answer:

Call: You say you're aimin' for the skies,
Response: You must be lovin' at God's command.
Call: Why don't you quit your tellin' lies?
Response: *You must be lovin' at God's command.*

Call: You say the Lord has set you free,
Response: You must be lovin' at God's command.
Call: Why don't you let your neighbor be?
Response: *You must be lovin' at God's command.*

Call: You seek God's grace but don't seek right,
Response: You must be lovin' at God's command.
Call: They pray in the day, but none at night.
Response: *You must be lovin' at God's command!*[4]

The message was crystal clear: One's purpose in life, beyond obtaining freedom, is to deal honestly and lovingly with members of one's community. There is no place for mistreatment of others; there is certainly no place for hypocrites, who profess one set of beliefs verbally and exhibit an entirely different set of beliefs in their behavior. There is only one way to put it: "You must be lovin' at God's command!"

Those who doubted the necessity to follow these directives from their sisters and brothers would be reminded that there is no avoiding the watchful eye of God, whose light is reflected through both his human servants and the elements of nature. To underscore the seriousness of these admonitions, potential transgressors were reminded about the horrors of hell, into which they would inevitably descend if they persisted in their behavior. In the process they would discover that "there's no hidin' place down there!" These admonitions were offered through the powerful voice of personal experience:

There's no hidin' place down there,
There's no hidin' place down there,
Oh, I went to the rock to hide my face,
The rock cried out, "No hidin' place,"
There's no hidin' place down there![5]

The issue of the final judgment of God, either on Judgment Day or in the Promised Land on earth, was always lurking beneath the surface meanings of such songs. In this regard, singers were certain that God's command required that they follow only God's directions, not those of any earthly master. In thus preparing for their freedom (whether on earth or in heaven), members of the community were confident that God would reward their obedience. Nowhere is the judgment (and final rewards) theme more evident than in one of the most majestic of the spirituals, "In That Great Gittin' Up Morning." In a rousing call-and-response celebration, excitement built steadily as they sang verse after verse of this inspirational song:

Call: I'm-a gonna tell you 'bout the comin' of the Saviour,
Response: Fare you well, fare you well.
Call: I'm-a gonna tell you 'bout the comin' of the Saviour,
Response: Fare you well, fare you well!

Call: There's a better day a-comin',
Response: Fare you well, fare you well,
Call: Oh, preacher, fold your Bible,
Response: Fare you well, fare you well!

Call: Gabriel, blow your trumpet,
Response: Fare you well, fare you well.
Call: Lord, how loud shall I blow it?,
Response: Fare you well, fare you well.
Call: Loud as seven peals of thunder,
Response: Fare you well, fare you well.
Call: Wake the livin' nations,
Response: Fare you well, fare you well! . . .[6]

In frenzied ecstasy they sang on and on, affirming among themselves their joyful confidence in the abundance of God's rewards for the righteous. This was surely cause for celebration, even if the tragic circumstances of the present made it clear that there was still a long way to go before the day of reckoning; they were still "a long ways from home." As they sang, the future became now, and the motivation to persist was strengthened. Beneath the surface of jubilant celebration, the agenda for the life of the future as well as the life of the present remained consistently present: "You must be lovin' at God's command!"

"Follow the drinking gourd ... " Harriet Tubman (extreme left), with a group of ex-slaves whose escape she assisted.

"Joshua fit the Battle of Jericho ... " The discovery of Nat Turner (1800-1831), leader of a slave insurrection in Virginia.

"There is a balm in Gilead to make the wounded whole." The first touring choir of the Fisk Jubilee Singers. All but one were born in slavery. On tour in 1871 they made history by introducing the spirituals to a wider American public. This portrait by Edmund Havel, Artist to Queen Victoria, was painted in 1872.

"Steal away, steal away home." Frederick Douglass (1817-1895), ex-slave and abolitionist. In writing about the spirituals he described the double meaning of such lines as, "I don't expect to stay much longer here."

"Scandalize my name!" Roland Hayes, singer, son of ex-slaves, and a member of the early Fisk University touring choirs, photographed in 1937.

"Go down Moses ... " Paul Robeson, son of a slave, singer and actor of renown, gave many concerts devoted to the spirituals.

"My God is a rock in a weary land." In 1939, Marian Anderson, the noted Black contralto, was barred from singing in the concert hall of the Daughters of the American Revolution. Instead, at the invitation of Secretary of the Interior Harold Ickes, she performed a program of spirituals and other songs in an open-air concert at the Lincoln Memorial.

"I want to be a Christian *in my heart*." Dr. J. Lesley Jones directs the Metropolitan Community Church Choir in Chicago in a performance of spirituals in 1948.

"Oh, freedom over me!" Students in Birmingham march in protest of segregation. Singing freedom songs and spirituals, they face high-pressure fire hoses and police dogs.

In 1963 Dr. Martin Luther King, Jr., delivers his famous "I Have a Dream" speech at the Washington Monument, concluding with the "words of the old Negro Spiritual, 'Free at last, free at last, thank God Almighty, we are free at last!'"

"Go tell it on the mountain, to let my people go!" In 1964 Fannie Lou Hamer, a former sharecropper and leader of the Mississippi Freedom Democratic Party, sought to challenge the segregationist Democratic Party delegation at the Party's National Convention in Atlantic City. The MFDP was refused credentials.

"Sometimes I am tossed and driven, Lord." Mahalia Jackson, one of the most important pioneers of the gospel movement, sings at a rally for Civil Rights in Chicago in 1964.

"Everybody talkin' 'bout Heaven ain't goin' there." The Rev. Martin Luther King, Sr., listens as a choral group sings at the Canaan Baptist Church in Harlem.

"Marching up the heavenly road, I'm bound to fight until I die." Martin Luther King, Jr., leads civil rights marchers during the Selma-to-Montgomery march for freedom in 1965.

"Sinner, please don't let this harvest pass." Opera diva Jessye Norman. Her 1990 concert with Kathleen Battle at Carnegie Hall was devoted entirely to spirituals.

UPI/Bettmann

"Go Down, Moses ... " The Harlem Spiritual Ensemble, the only professional group in the world dedicated exclusively to performing spirituals.

Elaine Beery

Although singers understood the importance of calling others on their transgressions, they also knew that the ultimate responsibility for transforming their lives rested entirely on their own shoulders. They could not depend on others to change them; they had to do it themselves. However, in such an enormous undertaking, they needed everything they could get in the way of help from the Almighty:

> *It's me, it's me, it's me, O Lord,*
> *Standin' in the need of prayer.*
> *It's me, it's me, it's me, O Lord,*
> *Standin' in the need of prayer.*
>
> *Not the preacher, not the deacon, but it's me, O Lord,*
> *Standin' in the need of prayer.*
> *Not the preacher, not the deacon, but it's me, O Lord,*
> *Standin' in the need of prayer.*
>
> *Not my father (mother, sister, brother, stranger, neighbor), but*
> *   me, O Lord,*
> *Standin' in the need of prayer!*[7]

Singers were clear in their understanding that responsibility for change rested with *nobody but themselves*. Although help from God would certainly be welcome, each singer stood alone in the task of obeying God's commands concerning the treatment of others in the community. Prayers would be unheard without the full assumption of personal responsibility. And lest one who has in fact acted responsibly be tempted to feel self-righteous, there was another song on hand to put things in proper perspective: If one truly feels the "bell" of the Spirit in one's heart, then humility and not self-righteousness will be the result:

> *Live a-humble, humble, humble yourselves,*
> *The bell done rung.*
>
> *Glory and honor!*
> *Praise the Lord!*
> *Live a-humble, humble, humble yourselves,*
> *The bell done rung!*[8]

The theme of ultimate personal accountability is pervasive in the spirituals. However, it would be a mistake to assume that this reflected an individualistic orientation. Rather, the idea was that a large community of fully responsible individuals was necessary in order to produce an effective and accountable collective force. In other words, the transformation of the group resulted from the forging of changes within each individual group member, as pointed out by John Lovell:

> The theory of the spiritual poet is that, if one person can be transformed ... why cannot the same thing work for a whole crowd or nation of people? This theory is very little different, in the poetic sense, from a doctrine of implied revolution; only the method needs working out. ... The spiritual poet often initiates the revolution in himself. *The "I" of the spiritual, however, is not a single person. It is every person who sings, everyone who has been oppressed and, therefore, every slave anywhere* (emphasis added).[9]

During the freedom movement of the 1960s, many of the original "I" spirituals and gospel songs were changed into "we." For example, "I shall not be moved" became "We shall not be moved," and "I shall overcome someday" became "We shall overcome."[10] While these changes were helpful in encouraging solidarity among freedom workers, many of the singers of these transformed songs may not have been aware of the implied "we" in the original versions. This subtle underlying meaning in the traditional spirituals (and their gospel song progeny) is highly instructive as a manifesto for social change. Often, significant changes begin with the actions of one individual or with a small community of dedicated workers; this provides the impetus for larger waves of change. And clearly, freedom is not the final object of personal changes. Even after freedom has been attained, one has a responsibility to "serve God" through the fair treatment of others in the community.

In the various songs that commented on basic human values, song writers rarely addressed the issue of the behavior of slave holders. This lack of attention to the ruling class was probably the result of several factors. On one level, it was simply dangerous to make one's sentiments on such issues too obvious. However, in some respects the slave holder's outrageous behavior was so extreme as to be beyond the limits of ethical comment. Subtly, singers smirked, "Everybody talkin' 'bout heaven ain't goin' there!" But occasionally, the underlying sentiments leaked out from behind the mask, emerging in more direct form:

> *You may be a white man,*
> *White as drifting snow,*
> *If your soul ain't been converted,*
> *To Hell you're sure to go.*[11]

In the day of final reckoning the tables will be turned; the oppressed will be in heaven and the oppressors will be in hell. In Southampton, Virginia, in May of 1828, one singer was certain that the tables would be turned *soon*; he had just been informed about it:

> I heard a loud noise in the heavens, and the Spirit instantly appeared to me and said the Serpent was loosened, and Christ had laid down the yoke he had borne for the sins of men, and that I should take it on and fight against the Serpent, *for the time was fast approaching when the first should be last and the last should be first* (emphasis added).[12]

Nat Turner and countless others took on the task of *ensuring* that the tables would be upset once and for all. However, all of these warriors in the freedom struggle also knew that even though the behavior of those who ran or supported the slave system was despicable, scandalous behavior within the enslaved community was equally revolting. The slave holder was *expected* to be immoral; one's friend or neighbor was *not*. Uncaring actions perpetrated by members of one's own community were therefore seen as particularly destructive. The response from the unexpecting victim of such actions often revealed a combination of outrage and sadness, and the supporting community frequently joined in commiseration:

The offended one:	You call that a brother?
Community:	No, no.
Offended one:	You call that a brother?
Community:	No, no.
Offended one:	You call that a brother?
Community:	No, no!
Offended one:	Scandalize' my name!

In such songs, singers highlighted a truth that we as heirs of the songs have sometimes attempted to avoid: *Race by itself does not determine morality.* Immoral and offensive actions, regardless of the color of the offender, are simply wrong. In other words, when freedom finally arrives, the spirit of the hard-fought freedom struggle is scandalously violated if the beneficiaries of that new freedom forget their purpose as liberated people. If those who were previously oppressed construe freedom to mean that they are now "free" to mimic the behavior of their former oppressors, then all of the struggles, all of the songs, have been for nought.

As we stand on the threshold of the twenty-first century, those of us in the African American community, we who are the direct descendants of the creators of the spirituals, are faced with perhaps the most demanding moral challenge of any community in America. We have to ask ourselves how we can best be accountable to those nameless and faceless song writers and to the hundreds of songs that filled the air for countless years of toil and struggle. If we can somehow manage to continue to hear the songs and their messages, perhaps we will learn some helpful lessons and also be in place to continue to stand as moral leaders in a society much in need of our leadership. We might ponder, for example, what it would mean to absorb into our senses the full meaning of:

> *It's me, it's me, it's me, O Lord,*
> *Standin' in the need of prayer.*

Perhaps it would help us to see more clearly some of the ways in which we ourselves, as individuals and as a community, have failed to be accountable to our ancestors' demand that we bring our *best* selves to every situation, no matter how apparently hopeless.

In our individual and collective prayers we might learn that one of our most formidable enemies, much more foreboding than anything confronting us from the outside, is the internal slavery of the mind, which has welcomed itself into our communities, enthusiastically ready, willing and able to stand in the place previously occupied by the tangible chains of our previous, physical enslavement. Psychologist Na'im Akbar is among those who have been pleading desperately for us to come to terms with the painful reality of this new psychologically and spiritually destructive form of slavery:

> As cruel and painful as chattel slavery was, it could be exceeded only by a worse form of slavery. . . . The slavery that captures

the mind and incarcerates the motivation, perception, aspiration, and identity in a web of anti-self images, generating a personal and collective self-destruction, is more cruel than the shackles on the wrists and ankles. The slavery that feeds on the psychology, invading the soul of man, destroying his loyalties to himself and establishing allegiance to forces which destroy him, is an even worse form of capture. The influences that permit an illusion of freedom, liberation, and self-determination, while tenaciously holding one's mind in subjugation, [are] the folly of only the sadistic.[13]

While we might be tempted to become obsessed with the ways in which even this psychological form of slavery is the product of our continuing external oppression, at some point we have to hear the message of the ancestors: It is *we* who are in need of prayer, and only *we* can remove the shackles of our increasingly destructive internal, psychological slavery. Beyond such easily identified symptoms as self-hatred and black-on-black violence, our psychological slavery has also produced more subtle but equally destructive effects. For example, as some opportunities previously denied us have begun to open up (primarily as a result of the efforts of centuries of struggle by our people), we have to confront the reality of how easy it has become for us to abandon our legacy of service to each other in exchange for a copy-cat version of the individualistic, competitive value system that formed the very basis of our original enslavement as a people. Shortsightedly, many of us have rushed to climb the ladder of "success," anxious to claim our long-overdue pieces of the American economic pie. In rushing so quickly to mimic the dominant behavior pattern of the majority culture, we have failed to notice that such "success" has not brought happiness to mainstream white America.[14] It is not likely to produce any enduring sense of happiness for us either. Increasingly, in my work as a practicing psychologist, I have encountered members of a new community of psychological casualties: "successful" African American couples whose rapid rise into the upper middle class and rush to live in "comfortable" suburban communities, with their children attending "superior" (that is, predominantly white) schools, has left those children clinically depressed, socially isolated and unconnected to any emotionally satisfactory sense of themselves.[15] The lack of a coherent, thoughtful way of understanding themselves and their "success" has resulted in a new psychopathological syndrome among such couples and their families, a syndrome which psychologist Beverly Daniel Tatum has aptly termed "the assimilation blues."[16] (And why is it so difficult to see that even the behavior exhibited by drug-dealing members of youth gangs is in some respects part of the same mimicry of the dominant culture pattern of obsession with power and material acquisition?)

I am certainly not arguing that we should shy away from opportunities for professional and personal advancement; that would contradict everything we have worked for in nearly four centuries of life in America. Rather, I am suggesting that our "psychological slavery" has sometimes interfered with our ability to be thoughtful in envisioning such opportunities in terms that are consistent with the legacy of our foreparents' teachings about accountability, so clearly reflected in the spirituals: "You must be lovin' at God's command." If those of us who are fortunate to have opportunities to enter into new positions of professional and occupational achievement would think consistently first in terms of how our new skills and accomplishments could benefit others in the community who have been less fortunate, not only would we be contributing to the collective well-being of our community, but we would also be involving ourselves in actions that have the potential to give us an *enduring* psychological and spiritual satisfaction, considerably more substantive than the superficial and insatiable rewards that result from our too frequent preoccupation with power and material acquisition.

Marian Wright Edelman, president of the Children's Defense Fund, always has understood the importance of honoring the legacy of the ancestors' vision of service. Her own genuinely "successful" life as an attorney who works untiringly for the just and compassionate treatment of children is a living testimony to her clarity. Reflecting on the lessons of her youth, she recalls:

> We were told that the world had a lot of problems; that Black people had an extra lot of problems, but that we were able and obligated to struggle and change them; that being poor was no excuse for not achieving; and that extra intellectual and material gifts brought with them the privilege and responsibility of sharing with others less fortunate. In sum, we learned that service is the rent we pay for living. It is the very purpose of life and not something you do in your spare time.[17]

Edelman's life work stands as an inspirational example of someone who has been accountable to the central teachings of her (our) elders.

In her writing these central teachings seem so simple and so clear. Yet, for most of us, these lessons are easy to forget. One resource we frequently neglect is the motivating and energizing power of the spirituals. Continuing, Edelman writes about one of the ways she regains her clarity when she is tired and confused:

> When I don't know what to do, which way to go, or feel profoundly inadequate to the task at hand, an echo of my father's frequent off-key humming of the spiritual "There is a Balm in Gilead" wells in my heart, reminding me that I don't have to preach like the Apostle Paul or Martin King or Jesse Jackson or meet Harvard or Yale or congressional or White House or society's decreed standards of anything to be a useful messenger or servant in the world.[18]

As Edelman's reflections illustrate, the lessons of the spirituals are simple yet profound and are uncluttered with the tangential distractions and "shoulds" that come from other voices and other places. When we are able to be clear that "it's *me*, O Lord, standing in the need of prayer," then paradoxically we are not alone; there is always assistance from the spirit to lend clarity and direction to any confused and weary soul. The voice of that spirit rings loudly and clearly through the words, melodies and rhythms of our traditional music.

All of us have a responsibility to make ourselves aware of the numerous ways in which our tendencies toward psychological slavery are manifested, in our individual lives as well as in our relationships with each other. We also have to examine the extent to which we sometimes automatically assume that someone who is biologically black will be true automatically to the legacy of accountability associated with the best of African and African American cultural traditions. Electing an African American person to an important public office, for example, is meaningful only if that person lives and practices the lessons of accountability. As an old African American proverb wisely comments, A white snake and a black snake are exactly alike; they both bite. And as writer Alice Walker has courageously brought to our attention, such behaviors as the sexual mutilation of women in Africa cannot continue to hide behind the cloak of cultural relativism easily invoked by those of us who do not want the bubble of our romantic idealization of everything African to be burst; mistreatment of human beings is simply wrong, no matter what the context.[19] Moreover, we do not have to go to Africa to find significant exploitation of women and other African peoples; these patterns are prevalent in our communities in America. And although it is tempting for us to blame the continued influence of colonialism and racism for our troubling patterns of exploitation of each other, those of us interested seriously in addressing these issues must take responsibility for our own psychological slavery; it is *we* who need prayer in our efforts to change our own behavior, not historical or contemporary colonizers or racists: "It's me, it's me, it's me, O Lord."

Increasingly, those within our communities who are serious about genuine accountability are beginning to step up to the challenge of uncovering and confronting patterns of personal and interpersonal slavery among ourselves as a necessary preparation for meaningful action in facing continuing external forms of oppression. For example, I have had the experience of participating in two groups recently that have taken on the painfully difficult challenge of addressing the issue of exploitation of women in the African American community. As the spotlight has focused on the ways in which *we ourselves* are willing participants in these patterns of exploitation, the process of necessary self-examination, for all of us (women and men) has been *very* painful; sometimes there has seemed to be no satisfactory resolution in sight. However, our knowledge that ultimately such struggles will strengthen us has provided the motivation to persist. On the horizon, equally difficult challenges, such as the issue of the too frequent hateful treatment of African American lesbians and gay males, await similar, painful but necessary confrontation.[20]

Although not at all apparent from the distorted media accounts of happenings in our communities, there are countless sisters and brothers around the country who, amid the continuing struggle of confronting our own issues as a community, are working humbly and daily within a framework of strong personal and social accountability to engage external structures of oppression and to establish compassionate and caring community environments for our families and neighbors. Consistent with their humility, most of these workers for justice and compassion do their jobs quietly, rarely if ever taking any time to bask in the spotlight of public recognition. For example, there are the scores of people who are involved daily in a committed effort to provide compassionate care for women and men afflicted with AIDS and to help African American churches step up to the challenge of this critical but tragically neglected need. There are numerous women and men involved in the training of physicians who, in their hierarchy of values, place service and integrity above materialism and financial success. There are also women and men who are daily risking their lives to make the small areas served by their religious or community groups places in which the best of the African American tradition of accountability not only lives but thrives. In addition, there are dozens of researchers and practitioners who are utilizing their skills and positions of power to develop research programs and thoughtful clinical interventions that have the potential to forge substantial progress in diminishing the effect of significant medical and psychological ills, such as hypertension, sickle cell anemia, gang violence and problems of self-esteem and self-doubt among African American children and adolescents. And always present to address a multitude of spiritual and ethical concerns, whenever and wherever needed, are countless sisters and brothers who have been working steadily and consistently for decades as front-line workers for justice and freedom.

Most encouragingly, there are countless *young* people, women and men in their teens and twenties, whose highly effective actions in a variety of spheres serve to put many of us in older generations to shame with respect to levels of commitment and creative vision. In the ongoing "Spirit and Struggle" group organized by Vincent Harding as a forum for the empowerment and renewal of African American sisters and brothers from around the country, one unplanned development has been the emergence of many of these young people as leaders and visionaries with respect to critical areas of concern. As with their older counterparts, most of these young women and men do their work quietly, in areas including such diverse arenas as education, literature and community organization and service. With such people at the front lines in the coming century we have a lot to be encouraged about. We simply have to ensure that at moments of despair we focus on the "good news" brought by such visionary leaders rather than on the negative images favored by those who would have us believe that the legacy of accountability forged by the ancestors is no longer alive. The unheralded actions of these young sisters and brothers serve as examples of the best of the African American tradition of accountability.

Outside the boundaries of the African American community, in the society at large, the spirituals and their messages of accountability have the potential to serve as a catalyst for the appearance of any number of opportunities for growth and redirection. Perhaps more critical than any other issue of accountability is the task of coming to terms with the reality of the pathological foundation of racism and human exploitation on which this country was built and which continues to be a significant factor operating beneath the surface of cliched proclamations of family values and the American way. Without confronting the fundamental processes of greed and exploitation that continue to constitute a significant part of its collective shadow, America is certain, in my opinion, to suffer an even further expansion in the psychopathological symptoms of emptiness and lack of purpose which are so prevalent currently. This is an inevitable consequence of a nation that stubbornly and consistently has been unwilling to look itself in the mirror. Moreover, such continuing blindness will ultimately destroy all of us unless it is interrupted and corrected by those with the courage to open their eyes and steer others into a clear-sighted confrontation with reality.

Historian Nathan Huggins has provided one of the most effective descriptions of America's consistent unwillingness to confront the full meaning of slavery in its history. In a discussion of what he calls "the deforming mirror of truth," Huggins describes the way in which historians and other scholars have been primary contributors to the creation of a fictional history:

> Slavery has been seen as a pathological condition, studied as a disorder which had consequences leading to the Civil War. At most, it was the Old South's particular pathology to be ultimately excised for the health of the nation. Racism and racial caste—which issue from racial slavery—have been, in their turn, studied as the "tangle of pathology" of blacks and the so-called underclass. Very little thought has been given to the general health of the society that created and sustains them. Society and its historians have treated all these phenomena as aberrations, marginal to the main story, to be quarantined if we extend the metaphor. Thus, our national history has continued to amplify the myths of automatic progress, universal freedom, and the American Dream without the ugly reality of racism seriously challenging the faith.[21]

Huggins's comments on America's longstanding penchant for ignoring its ugly, shadow sides very easily could be expanded to include persistent distortions concerning its treatment of Native Americans and numerous other communities of people, whose exploitation has been viewed as minor "aberrations," rare examples of a departure from the central American perception of itself as a champion of freedom and justice. But no matter how it is rationalized, it is impossible to avoid the truth forever:

> *I went to the rock to hide my face,*
> *The rock cried out, "no hidin' place."*

As with all ugly realities, any change in the large picture must begin with the efforts of individuals and small groups of people working to transform their own small worlds: "It's me, O Lord, standing in the need of prayer." In America-at-large, groups of clear visioned, "conscious" sisters and brothers will have to provide leadership within their own cultural circles to help their compatriots come to terms with the fact that racism is not a minority problem, but rather a manifestation of a deep-seated illness in the majority culture. They will have to assist others in seeing that efforts to create change in this area cannot be focused on the underclass or solved by token gestures of opportunity to members of communities of color. Rather, the people who are suffering from the illness, members of the dominant culture, will have to come face to face with their own ugly shadows.

Joseph Barndt, a white Christian minister working in the Bronx, New York, is among those who have had the courage to assume leadership in the important area of assisting members of the majority culture in confronting directly their own complicity in the creation and perpetuation of racism:

> The racial problem of the United States is not a minority problem. It is a majority problem. The cause is in the white society. The effects are felt in the communities of color. The problems of African Americans, Native Americans, Hispanics and Asians are only the symptoms of European America's sickness. ... All the programs in the world aimed at changing the victims of racism will ultimately be useless if those institutions and structures that create and control the conditions in the first place are not changed. This is very hard to accept for those of us who are white because our own happiness and lifestyle depend on these institutions and structures in their present form.[22]

Barndt has argued effectively that although the process of self-examination and change concerning racist attitudes and actions is painful, the end result of such a process will not only be beneficial to the victims of racism, but, equally important, to the victimizers, whose significant personal transformation will contribute to the emergence of a more substantive experience of "happiness," free of the demand to exert endless energy in the sole service of continuing the exploitation and disenfranchisement of others for self-gain. Barndt has also had the courage to point out that even those who do not harbor strong internal prejudices are nonetheless active participants in the process of institutional racism when they fail to challenge the continuation of structures (in virtually every educational, governmental and private enterprise institution in America) that perpetuate the exploitation of significant portions of the American population.

Fortunately, there are also numerous other women and men in various spheres of American life who are attempting to confront directly issues which have for some time been either ignored or distorted by mainstream America and its governmental representatives. One of those areas is the area of child abuse and neglect. The crisis in America is minimized by those (particularly in government) who acknowledge it as a problem but who refuse to come to terms with how this national emergency reflects some of the fundamental problems of an American culture which has failed to provide adequate care and protection to its children, a reflection in turn of a larger neglect of primary human issues. In an extensive review and careful study of the problem, the U.S. Advisory Board on Child Abuse and Neglect concluded in 1991 that

> the costs of child abuse and neglect are so grave that the emergency represents a threat to national survival: such negligence threatens the integrity of a nation that shares a sense of community, that regards individuals as worthy of respect, that reveres family life, and that is competent in economic competition. ... In such a context ... all Americans share an ethical duty to ensure the safety of children.[23]

Within this framework the Board recommended that an effective policy in addressing this major issue would need to include a focus on demonstrated programs, which have shown that by providing assistance to families-at-risk in the form of home visits and by strengthening naturally occurring networks of family and community caring, the scope of the national emergency in this area could be significantly reduced. Moreover, by referring to documented research indicating that such systems of community caring networks are effective, the Board was challenging the American government to be consistent with all its popular proclamations of interest in families and family values. Those who are interested in taking on the difficult issues of accountability facing the nation at large will have to be ready to demand that the courageous work of groups like the Advisory Board on Child Abuse is not swept aside and discounted, like the work of so many boards and commissions which have identified and made recommendations concerning the confrontation of serious failures of accountability at deep levels of American consciousness.

Ironically, despite the clear history of Africans in America who resisted for a significantly long time the process of assimilation into the dominant society, their cultural legacy has ultimately become one of the most significant components of what most outsiders now think of as distinctly American. The spirituals, in particular, reflect a core of hopeful possibilities for the transformation of America, a transformation in the direction of eliminating the dramatic contrasts between its written and spoken creeds and its substantially hypocritical actions. In effect, the legacy of African American culture that is reflected so clearly and strongly in the spirituals represents one of the best hopes for the development of any significant sense of accountability for all of us who now share the common destiny dictated by our existence as American citizens. African American scholar and social critic Cornel West has pointed out that, for better or worse, diverse American peoples must learn to talk productively about their differences (racial and otherwise), and also about their unquestionably common future:

> To establish a new framework, we need to begin with a frank acknowledgment of the basic humanness and Americanness in each of us. And we must acknowledge that as a people — *E Pluribus Unum* — we are on a slippery slope toward economic strife, social turmoil and cultural chaos. If we go down, we go down together. The Los Angeles upheaval forced us to see not only that we are not connected in ways we would like to be but also, in a more profound sense, that this failure to connect binds us even more tightly together. The paradox of race in America is that our common destiny is more pronounced and imperiled precisely when our divisions are deeper. The Civil War and its legacy speak loudly here. Eighty-six percent of white suburban Americans live in neighborhoods that are less than 1 percent black, meaning prospects for the country depend largely on how

its cities fare in the hands of a suburban electorate. There is no escape from our interracial interdependence, yet enforced racial hierarchy dooms us as a nation to collective paranoia and hysteria — the unmaking of any democratic order.[24]

In a sense, West has provided us a set of considerations for what it might mean for Americans of all colors to embrace genuinely the idea of a truly multicultural society. In such a society each ethnic group would be acknowledged and recognized for its important contributions. As West suggests, our failure to find a way to forge that kind of respectful unity will be tragic for us all: *If we go down, we go down together.* In a genuinely multicultural America one of the most significant contributions of its African American contingent would be the spirituals, with their effectively transformative messages of accountability, and of hope.

∾

It is December 29, 1947. The great African American tenor Roland Hayes and his accompanist, Reginald Boardman, are preparing to record a group of spirituals at Hayes's farm in North Georgia, the place of his birth. In many of his recitals, Hayes, who has performed in front of enthusiastic audiences around the world for more than thirty years, has highlighted the spirituals. As the son of ex-slaves and a member of one of the early Fisk University touring choirs, Hayes is intimately acquainted with the depth of meaning contained in the melodies, rhythms and lyrics of the spirituals. In fact, as the current recording session is getting under way, it is very possible that Hayes is reviewing in his mind some thoughts concerning the completion of his book, entitled *My Songs*, which will include his interpretations and original musical arrangements, for voice and piano, of thirty-five songs.[25]

In the early part of his career, outraged by racial discrimination against African American singers of classical music, Hayes, intent on proving himself as a singer, had not performed spirituals at all. Later, recalling those early days, he commented,

I am embarrassed to recall that in my preoccupation with the European composers, and with learning French and German, I had become neglectful of Afro-American music. . . . I was unconsciously putting myself into competition with white singers, whose spotlight I wanted to share. I had not yet received the revelation which was presently to give my ambition its native direction. . . . It remained for me to learn, humbly at first, and then with mounting confidence, that my way to artistry was a Negro way.[26]

But this temporary blindspot in Hayes's perception of himself was never to recur. He went on to become one of the greatest interpreters of the spirituals, one of those most responsible for the expansion of the spirituals within the consciousness of America and the world at large.

This December day in 1947 Hayes and Boardman are recording one of their arrangements of a spiritual entitled "Scandalize My Name." In his uniquely sensitive way, Hayes begins:

> *I met my brother the other day,*
> *Gave him my right hand . . .*

Hayes's trademark lyric tenor voice fills the room, conveying the complex emotions of sadness, hurt and anger, all at the same time. He continues:

> *You call that a brother?*
> *No, no,*
> *You call that a brother?*
> *No, no,*
> *You call that a brother?*
> *No, no,*
> *He done scandalize my name!*

As he sings, we have the feeling that Hayes understands intimately the intense hurt some of our foreparents experienced as they absorbed into their consciousness the emotional impact of hateful actions directed at them by sisters and brothers whom they had loved and trusted. Hayes, also regarding this song as symbolic of Judas's betrayal of Jesus, feels at a very deep level the song's multiple meanings. He goes on:

> *You call that a sister?*
> *No, no . . .*

We now experience another emotion entering into Hayes's exquisitely sensitive interpretation of this important song: love. We can sense Hayes's understanding that one of the most significant pieces of the legacy of all of the early African American ancestors' singing is the fact that even in the face of direct emotional assaults they could not bring themselves to stop loving. In the process, they retained a faith that their relationships with those whom they loved could be repaired. In fact, regardless of the circumstances, nothing in the human realm could remove the feelings of faith and hope from their stubbornly persistent place in the center of their emotional and spiritual consciousness.[27]

Chapter 6

"There Is a Balm in Gilead"

Hope and Healing

There is a balm in Gilead,
To make the wounded whole,
There is a balm in Gilead,
To heal the sin-sick soul.

Sometimes I feel discouraged,
And think my work's in vain,
But then the Holy Spirit,
Revives my soul again.

There is a balm in Gilead,
To make the wounded whole,
There is a balm in Gilead,
To heal the sin-sick soul.
                —Traditional African American Spiritual[1]

~

It is the middle of the summer—July 1978. Jessye Norman, grand
diva of the Western opera world, is recording a program consisting
exclusively of African American spirituals. The site for this recording
is London, the capital of the British Empire, the same empire responsible in large part for the proliferation of the African slave trade. In
an interesting kind of irony, African American conductor Willis Patterson is directing the Ambrosian Singers to sing the background
choral accompaniments for Norman. In the process Patterson has
shown that indeed this music can be performed effectively by singers

outside of the African diaspora. In his unique demonstration Patterson has also affirmed the accessible, archetypal core of the spirituals, which have the ability to speak to broad human issues far afield from the specific context of African American slavery.

Patterson's achievement represents a continuation of a legacy begun over a hundred years previously, when the Fisk Jubilee Singers introduced to the world a repertoire of music that diverse audiences would find extraordinarily effective in its communication of the most important message of the spirituals, the message of hope. Almost as if in conscious honor of that legacy, and the continuation of that legacy forged by such concert singers as Roland Hayes, Paul Robeson and Marian Anderson, Norman takes the time midway through the program to offer a solo rendition of "Balm in Gilead":

> *There is a balm in Gilead,*
> *To make the wounded whole,*
> *There is a balm in Gilead,*
> *To heal the sin-sick soul.*

Norman has never communicated more effectively. Successfully forging a marriage between her deeply spiritual instincts and the technical skills she has gained in her Western vocal training, the voices and energies of generations of African American sojourners seem to be flowing through her body as she sings. As a result, we have immediate access to the soothing, confident message of hope contained in this significant song. Indeed, the Fisk Jubilee Singers would be honored if they could be present to witness the continuation of the worldwide celebration of African American music that they began. As Norman sensitively embraces every phrase, offering a seemingly endless variety of dynamic contrasts with each new verse, she provides us the knowledge that, even in this wretched land, which stands as a symbol of the deep-seated evils of racism and colonialism, "There is a balm"; a strong sense of hope and the promise of healing are present.[2]

⁓

Following the end of official slavery, one of the most important historical events was the establishment of the Fisk School, which opened its doors in Nashville, Tennessee, in 1866. Begun as a high school, Fisk eventually developed into a college and normal school, providing one of the first sites of training for African American elementary school teachers. The beginning years at Fisk were difficult; the school operated precariously, consistently on the edge of financial collapse. It was in this climate that George L. White, a musician and treasurer of the school, came up with the idea of forming a small touring choir of Fisk students who could raise money on concert tours to help with Fisk's serious financial problems. White received very little encouragement from his administrative and faculty colleagues at Fisk. Nevertheless, he was confident that his fund-raising plan would succeed.

White, impressed by the spontaneous singing of spirituals among Fisk students, many of whom had been slaves, believed that spirituals would provide unique concert material, giving his group an edge over the offerings of competing choirs. However, the nine young women and men who comprised the first Fisk touring choir in 1871 resisted strongly the idea of singing their songs in public. One important reason was their belief, based on experiences with whites, that their music would be ridiculed and perceived as simpleminded or "primitive." Some of the students also wanted to forget the songs reminding them of the horrors of slavery; all except one member of the group (Minnie Tate) had been born in slavery. Accordingly, Isaac Dickerson, Green Evans, Benjamin Holmes, Jennie Jackson, Maggie Porter, Thomas Rutling, Ella Sheppard, Minnie Tate and Eliza Walker began their tour in October of 1871 with a concert program consisting of classical choral works and popular folk tunes; no spirituals were included. Although they sang beautifully, the entrenched racism of white audiences made it difficult for the singers to receive much support for their concerts. In the first few concerts they were lucky if they raised as much as fifty dollars; audiences frequently consisted of twenty or fewer people. Understandably, the young singers quickly became discouraged and disillusioned.

Eventually, an event occurred in Oberlin, Ohio, that would have a profound impact on the survival and influence of African American spirituals in the twentieth century. At a religious conference in Oberlin, the Fisk singers waited in the back of the church, hoping that an opening in the program would give them a chance to perform. Finally, when there was a brief lapse in the program, the Fisk singers, under direction from White, began singing. The historical record indicates that this was a major turning point in the tour. From this point on, the touring students began to earn significant money from their concerts. Writer Arna Bontemps, in an attempt to sketch a picture of what it was actually like in Oberlin, described it in this way:

A whisper of strange harmony rose in the back of the auditorium. Members of the council in the front seats looked around in puzzlement. What was it? Where was it coming from? The tone increased in volume as the ministers listened, and their eyes showed that it was wonderful to hear. By the time it reached full voice, there was no longer any secret about its source ... The weary and perplexed members of the council turned their heads in pleasant surprise.

As they did so, Jennie Jackson raised her eyes to the ceiling and cried in an agony of deep melody:

> "My Lord he calls me,
> He calls me by the thunder,
> The trumpet sounds within-a my soul,
> I ain't got long to stay here. . . ."

It was a slow song with many lines repeated, and it faded as hauntingly as it had begun. But it left the audience in a bewildered attitude. Some mouths that had been opened to say "Ah!" couldn't seem to close. Heads that had turned to see the group of young people on the back seat remained turned after the song ended.[3]

History had now been made. The singers, encouraged by the positive audience response, sang on and on, one spiritual after another. Contrary to their apprehensions, there was no sign of ridicule. The extraordinary power of the music, much of which had not been heard before in a public arena, appeared to counteract the prevailing negative racial atmosphere. Momentarily forgetting that these were African American singers, many of the listeners cried, obviously touched by the music. Although created by African Americans in slavery for exclusive use within the African community, these songs nonetheless touched something deep in the psyches of this predominantly non-African audience, providing one of the first affirmations of the archetypal and transforming power of the spirituals outside of the context of slavery.

The experience at Oberlin marked a historic turning point for the students from Fisk. Eventually known as the Jubilee Singers (a name chosen by George White in honor of the spiritual "The Day of Jubilee"), the students went on to complete their tour, no longer hesitant about performing spirituals in public. They toured the northeastern seaboard and eventually were invited to sing for President Grant at the White House. When they returned to Nashville at the end of their first tour, they had earned twenty thousand dollars! In 1873, after adding additional singers, the group embarked on a European tour. Their tour itinerary included performances for royalty in several European countries. By the end of their European tour the Jubilee Singers had earned one hundred fifty thousand dollars, ensuring a future for Fisk as one of the most important of the universities providing first-rate education for African American students.[4]

The tours of the Fisk Jubilee Singers contributed significantly to the emerging worldwide appeal and influence of the spirituals. The Jubilee Singers set a precedent that led to the establishment of similar groups at other schools, most notably Hampton Institute, Tuskeegee Institute and Howard University.[5] We might wonder what would have happened without the serendipitous occurrences of the Fisk Singers' first tour. It is possible, for example, that we would not have the knowledge of spirituals available to us today. However, it is also very possible that some other equally compelling circumstances would eventually have led to the same results, for the Fisk singers or for some other group.

In historical accounts of the Fisk experience it is clear that people hearing spirituals for the first time, performed by singers who understood and felt their deep meanings, invariably found themselves touched deeply by the melodies, rhythms and lyrics of these songs. The same power that formed the basis of their effectiveness as songs of resistance, personal transformation and religious conviction appeared to contribute to the ability of the spirituals to communicate effectively in widely divergent places and circumstances.[6] It did not take long for it to become apparent that this was a body of music with unique powers of transformative emotional and spiritual healing. Recognition of this fact motivated numerous observers to attempt to preserve spirituals in voluminous published collections, beginning during the Civil War and continuing through most of the first half of the twentieth century.[7] These collections, in turn, contributed further to the proliferation and influence of spirituals.

One additional development was the emergence of arrangements of spirituals for solo and choral performers, spearheaded by several gifted composer-arrangers trained in the European classical music tradition. These composers were very much in touch with the rich heritage of the spirituals, as is evident in the powerfully emotional arrangements they created, highlighting the beauty and transformative potency of a number of traditional songs. Following the lead of such pioneers as Harry T. Burleigh, a large number of these gifted composers contributed to the influence of the spirituals by providing creative arrangements for use by artists in concert performance.[8] Along with others who have performed spirituals in their more traditional, a cappella forms, these artists have expanded dramatically the numbers of people around the world who are familiar with spirituals.[9]

While concert singers have contributed significantly to the preservation of the spirituals, the most important continuing expression of their legacy is found in churches, community gatherings and worldwide movements for freedom and justice, within and without the African diaspora. In these widely diverse settings people continue to draw on the power of the spirituals as functional music, expressing deep religious convictions as well as facilitating personal and social transformation. At its best, this music is as effective in our time as in slavery, assisting human beings in maximizing their potential as free people leading full lives. At the center of the ability of spirituals to serve such vital life functions is the fact that the most significant outcome of the transformation process assisted by these songs is the emergence of *hope* and the promise of healing.

Out of personal and communal suffering, out of tired and long-fought struggles for freedom, out of the actively spiritual core of traditional African American religious folk songs, hope consistently emerges as the most salient experience of both singers and listeners. In the process, emotional and spiritual wounds are healed. Above all else, it was the experience of hope that was conveyed in the concerts of the Fisk singers, leaving unsuspecting and unprepared audience members suddenly vulnerable and open to their own needs for emotional and spiritual healing. The message of hope and healing has also rendered spirituals consistently in demand in concert halls around the world.[10] Hope was present strongly among singers in the U.S. freedom movement of the 1960s. The activism guided by their music brought significant healing for them and for the nation at large. Hope was strongly present as well in China and other movements for freedom and justice around the world in the 1980s, as freedom workers in countless places adopted African American spirituals as an expression of their aspirations and as a channel for personal and social change. In impossible situations of suffering and oppression everywhere, the spirituals have brought the message of hope, the comfort of healing, and the motivation to persist in ongoing struggle and resistance.[11]

The important spiritual "Balm in Gilead" expresses the predominant experience of hope and healing that has been at the center of the African American experience since the beginning of slavery and has always received direct expression in the spirituals. This song, with its gently soothing melody and lyrics, offers the final word on matters of suffering, struggle and resistance. Howard Thurman, one of the most knowledgeable interpreters of the spirituals, has highlighted this point in his analysis of "Balm in Gilead":

> The peculiar genius of the Negro is revealed here in much of its structural splendor. . . . The prophet has come to a "Dead Sea" place in his life. Not only is he discouraged over the external events in the life of Israel, but he is also spiritually depressed and tortured. As a wounded animal he cried out, "Is there no balm in Gilead? Is no physician there?" It is not a question of fact that he is raising—it is not a question directed to any particular person for an answer. . . . He is searching his own soul. . . . He straightened the question mark in Jeremiah's sentence into an exclamation point: "There is a balm in Gilead!" Here is a note of creative triumph.[12]

As Thurman indicates, "Balm in Gilead" is an especially important song in the spirituals tradition, expressing the ability of enslaved Africans to transform sorrow into joy, to make a way where no way seemed possible. That ultimate message of hope and healing is found as well in the archetypally powerful music and lyrics of hundreds of other spirituals; it is the product of a creative tension between awareness of painful oppressive circumstances and the simultaneous envisioning of a hopeful future. This is not a naive optimism, but rather a genuine inner transformation following from a process which consistently leads singers and listeners onto an emotionally and spiritually triumphant high plain. In this sense "Balm in Gilead" simply provides summary punctuation, the final confirmation of a transformation process constantly at work wherever singers of spirituals are found.

The Roman Catholic Sister Thea Bowman, who had an especially rich understanding of African American religious music, was one of those who understood the long-established African American tradition of fashioning positive spiritual and emotional material out of a field of apparent contradictions:

African people are a diunital people, seeking richness of meaning in *apparent* contradiction. They are comfortable bringing
together realities which may appear contradictory or in oppo-
sition. . . . They reach toward unification or synthesis of oppo-
sites. . . . African Americans for 400 years have used symbol and
song to express a faith too high, too low, too wide, too deep for
words, too passionate to be confined by concepts.[13]

The hope and emotional healing, which were the products of one of
those "apparent contradictions" (despair *vs.* the wish for a better life),
were described by W.E.B. Du Bois, who made it clear that his use of
the term "sorrow songs" was never intended to convey the impression that sorrow was the salient emotional experience of the enslaved
Africans who created and sang spirituals:

Through all of the Sorrow Songs there breathes a hope — a faith
in the ultimate justice of things. The minor cadences of despair
change often to triumph and calm confidence. Sometimes it is
faith in life, sometimes a faith in death, sometimes assurance of
boundless justice in some fair world beyond. But whichever it
is, the meaning is always clear: that sometime, somewhere, men
will judge men by their souls and not by their skins.[14]

In his analysis Du Bois simply enriched the observations of scores of
witnesses who have found in the spirituals an extraordinary ability
to forge deep transformations out of apparent contradictions, with
hope and emotional healing emerging as the final and most important end results.

Despite a clear record of effectiveness in the lives of individuals
and communities, spirituals have still been misinterpreted and misunderstood by many Americans. Although it might be expected that
those outside of the African American experience would misunder-
stand this music, it is particularly distressing that such misunder-
standings are common as well among African Americans. A product
of complex historical and social factors, the growing ignorance of the
meanings and historical impact of the spirituals threatens the functional preservation and continuation of this important body of music.
John Lovell has offered a helpful commentary on this puzzling predicament:

Many members of the present Afro-American community have
dismissed the spiritual as a religious cry of slavish people. They

feel the present community needs neither religion nor slavishness. Quite obviously, they have read the songs on the surface. They associate them with some of the people who still sing them, people of a fundamentalist religious cast. They also are not well acquainted with the slaves who produced them, men and women of considerable self-respect and courage.

Many of the people who still sing the spirituals in churches and in other congregations think and feel likewise. For them the songs are precious because of a surface sentimentality, or because they are associated with ancients in their families, or because they are beautiful and touching. Quite often these "lovers" of the spiritual are not well acquainted with the deep underlying meanings of individual songs, and certainly not with the powerful meanings of a number of songs on the same subject, taken together.[15]

Written more than twenty years ago, Lovell's comments seem to have gone largely unheard, as there remains today a widespread ignorance of the depth of meaning and emotional power contained in the spirituals.[16] Bernice Johnson Reagon is among those who have lamented this situation. In reflecting on her upbringing, she contrasts her personal experience with that of many children being reared today:

I felt like there was no air I breathed that these songs didn't exist in. . . . They are not being passed today in the same way. I'm not sure if black people can get through the next century without this repertoire.[17]

I agree completely with Reagon about the necessity to do something to correct the current circumstance, which finds so many African American children without the transformative resource of our important ancestral music.

As Lovell has intimated (see passage above), there are myriad reasons for the lessening awareness and understanding of spirituals. Certainly the long history of co-optation of African American music, beginning with the pejorative portrayals of African music in the early minstrel tradition, has to be considered one factor.[18] Additionally, as Lovell further suggests, the singing of spirituals in some fundamentalist settings, where the important balance between religious faith and social action has often been lost, has to be considered another contributing factor. However, in my opinion the most important contribution to poor understanding and knowledge of the spirituals is the "mis-education" that still prevails in much of the educational process to which contemporary African Americans continue to be subjected. In this process not only are the spirituals misunderstood but numerous pieces of our history as a people, both in America and on the African continent, are distorted as well. The mis-education process exerts constant pressure on African Americans to see cultural contributions outside of the African tradition as always more valuable than those from within that tradition.[19]

When spirituals are experienced within a context of accurate understanding, the messages of hope and healing emerge consistently as the salient themes, along with an understanding of the history of suffering and transformation, struggle and resistance, spiritual excellence and accountability that has been associated with this music. These lessons have been carried into the ongoing evolution of music in the African American religious tradition, including meter music, hymns and gospel singing.[20] With the spirituals as the ancestral foundation, the transformative product of hope and healing has been a necessary ingredient in the survival and progress of African peoples in America. The songs in this tradition have provided not only personal comfort but, most important, the motivation for continued participation in the struggle for change. As Wyatt Tee Walker reminds us, this balance between inner sustenance and ongoing activism is one of the great gifts of the African religious music tradition in America:

> The music of the Black religious tradition operates on two levels: first psychologically and emotionally—it locates the people's sense of heritage, their roots, where they are and where they want to go; and secondly, it mobilizes and strengthens the resolve for struggle. ... Black sacred music is the primary reservoir of the Black people's historical context and an important factor in the process of social change.[21]

It is not only desirable, but absolutely essential that this tradition be preserved. The warnings of African American sage Bernice Johnson Reagon are critical for us to understand; African people may in fact have great difficulty dealing with current and future challenges without our traditional song repertoire. Not only is this a tradition that is important to the continued struggle of Africans in America, but it is also one that provides much of the basis for the role of African Americans as moral leaders and agents of transformation of the larger society. Wyatt Tee Walker continues:

> Through their music, Black people have made a singular contribution to Americana. It is very likely that if the integrity of Black music is maintained, they may, as well, make a singular contribution religiously by restoring America to its humanity.[22]

Although Walker focuses his discussion on the music of the African American church, his comments can be extended to include the important leadership channelled through the African American spirituals tradition outside the specific arena of the church. In fact, Walker himself has made such an extension in commenting that the use of spirituals in the freedom movement of the 1960s contributed to "minimizing the distinction between sacred and secular within the Black music tradition."[23]

As we have seen, melding of the sacred and secular stands squarely in the center of an African tradition that has never made such rigid distinctions (see Chapters 1 and 4). In fact, the ability to infuse spiritual and moral considerations into daily life outside of the church is one of the important reasons why the African American legacy of struggle may well represent the best hope for the necessary transformation of American society. Many will see such visions as naive. As Harding has pointed out, this perception is not new. In fact, that perception provided a challenge to the integrity of the freedom movement of the 1960s in its early days:

> When Martin King first came among us speaking of the need to carry on a struggle for justice and truth that would "redeem the soul of America," many of us tended to smile patronizingly or to turn away in annoyed disbelief at such naivete. It appears to me now that we rather than he may well have been the innocents.[24]

As in the 1960s, we have to believe in the potential of the African American community, armed with its songs, to push pass misplaced perceptions of naivete and mis-education to reassert its rightful position in the vanguard of ethical leadership in America. However, that opportunity may be lost if we fail to remind ourselves periodically about the critical role of our music in the ongoing struggle.

As I reflect on these issues I am taken back in time to my experiences in the early 1960s as a member of a group comprised of singers from the more than one hundred public high schools in New York City. Each Saturday morning during my junior and senior years, I joined more than two hundred other young women and men from throughout the city who came together for rehearsals in a high school auditorium in downtown Manhattan. Singers came by bus and by subway from Bensonhurst and Harlem, from Chinatown and Little Italy, from Eastside and Westside, from Staten Island and Manhattan Island, from Brooklyn, Queens and the Bronx—from every conceivable corner of the embattled city. The young singers were black, Puerto Rican, white, Jewish, Chinese, Japanese, poor, middle class, wealthy, "A" students and "D" students, basketball players and bookworms, heterosexuals, gays and lesbians. Most of us had no musical training to speak of; a few were fortunate to have had some training in voice or in one or more musical instruments. The only thing we all had in common was the love of singing and our common bond as survivors of the audition process that led to membership in the New York All-City High School Chorus.

The hard work and the discipline of preparing for each annual concert were frustrating but highly fulfilling in the end, when we found ourselves performing before a television audience at Carnegie Hall or Lincoln Center. We were proud of our accomplishments. Our director, Peter Wilhousky, was successful in introducing us to the world of professional music; many in our group who planned careers in the performing arts had an excellent head start on the fulfillment of their ambitions. However, these were not the most significant aspects of the experience for me or for many of my singing comrades. For many of us, the important piece, the piece that has left a lasting impression, was the effect of the music on our lives as emerging adults and on our ability to come together as diverse young people in a unique kind of communal experience.

Our sense of ourselves as a community gelled most successfully in the informal times before and after the rehearsals. Bands of us, often as many as forty or fifty, would get together informally to sing. We sang repertoire from the current and past years of work in the chorus, but we also sang music we decided, spontaneously, to sing that day. Each week after rehearsal, groups of us sang together on subway platforms, often letting several trains go by as our enthusiasm mounted and our cohesiveness grew. Frequently, some of us gathered to sing in Central Park.

Most salient in my memory of these informal moments is the times when we sang spirituals. Walking down the street or singing in the park, we were free from the written harmonies and rhythms that constrained us in rehearsals. We could improvise, make up harmonies, do anything we liked. Those were the times when we truly came together as a group; the music and the communal experience are still fresh in my memory and in my body. I can still hear and feel the sounds: "I'm gonna ride in the chariot in the morning, Lord, I'm gonna ride in the chariot in the morning, Lord. I'm gettin' ready for the judgment day, my Lord, my Lord!" The sopranos, floating their sound above us: "Are you ready, my brother?" Our reply: "Yes, Lord!" "Are you ready for the journey?" "Yes, Lord!" "Well, I'm goin' to see my Jesus!" "Yes, Lord!" All together now: "I'm ready for the chariot 'cause I'm ready to go!"

I doubt that there were many in our group who knew the full history of these songs. There were probably not many who knew about the ring shout, who understood the African background of the music, or who knew very much at all about the transformed Christianity practiced by Africans enslaved in America one hundred years before. Still, the music was felt deeply by these largely uninformed singers. Curiously, our diverse religious roots—Jewish, Christian, Muslim, Buddhist, atheist, agnostic—had little influence on the level of enthusiasm individual singers brought to the songs. The music, the words, the rhythms were infectious. Our singing of spirituals was our most joyous experience; we found ourselves literally dancing as we broke out into various call-and-response songs, with different groups and different individuals taking turns with the lead. It was as if the message of the early African American ancestors had somehow gotten through: "This is music that will change the way you experience yourselves and each other!"

None of us had death in mind when we sang about our impending "ride in the chariot" or when we boarded, in the words of another song, "the little black train." We had *joy* in mind, and our singing brought (and still brings, as I think about it now) that joy. In our lives outside the chorus, many of us continued to experience the racism, the hatred, the tensions, the deeply chronic problems passed on to us as part of our rite of passage into the burdensome responsibilities of adulthood. But in the chorus those tensions and divisions were transformed into something much more meaningful, and certainly more memorable.

So it was that Peter Wilhousky, after observing a number of us singing spirituals before rehearsal one Saturday morning, remarked at the beginning of our formal work session, in front of all of our teachers and coaches, "I'm sorry, but when people tell me about how terrible and criminal our youth are today, I simply don't buy it. Any group of kids who dedicate their Saturdays every week to come together around the discipline of music, and who sing so beautifully, cannot be anything like the stereotypes we are sold!"

The depth of emotion Wilhousky felt was quite evident; he had to take a few moments to gather himself before beginning the rehearsal. This was the same stern man who rarely smiled in rehearsals and who would, at the drop of a hat, toss someone from the auditorium for singing even slightly off pitch! It is clear to me now that the decision of this world-famous composer and conductor to devote a substantial amount of his time to working with high school students was based largely on his knowledge of the transforming power of music and his commitment to passing the knowledge and experience of that power on to members of younger generations. He took that task very seriously. At no time was that transforming power more evident than when we sang spirituals.

After our final concert in the spring of 1963, my choral comrades and I stepped into a world that was attempting to grapple, somehow, with one of the most violent and racially divided periods in human history. Less than twenty years previously the world had seen the massacre of millions of innocent women, men and children in the concentration camps of Germany and in the thriving Japanese cities of Hiroshima and Nagasaki. For decades in our own country the "strange fruit" of African bodies hanging from trees had been the most salient sight on the Southern landscape. In the urban North the bodies of African men and women had experienced daily the abuses of police brutality, often succumbing through death. (Later, in 1991, many of us would wonder how America could be "shocked" by a videotape simply documenting on camera one of scores of such incidents occurring daily in African communities across the country for decades.)

A few short months after our final concert, four young children attending Sunday school would be murdered inside the protective walls of a church in Birmingham, Alabama. The same year, the life of the president of the United States would be taken in Dallas, Texas. Before the decade was over, thousands of our sisters and brothers, many of them citizens of color from America and Vietnam, would slaughter each other in Southeast Asia. Over the next several years scores of freedom workers would risk the threat of vicious dogs and white citizens in forging their determined struggle to secure just a few of the "rights" supposedly guaranteed by a constitutional document signed nearly two hundred years before. A number of those freedom workers would in fact give their lives in the struggle.

In just two short years after our final concert, our "shining prince," Malcolm X, would be assassinated in New York. Three years later, Martin Luther King, Jr., would experience the same fate. Martin's assassination would be followed by African American uprisings in the great urban centers of our country, calling the attention of the world, at least momentarily, to the rapidly spreading cancer comprised of American racism, greed and neglect.

In striking emotional contrast to the ugly historical events that were to follow, Martin Luther King, Jr., five years before his death, delivered his now-famous "I Have a Dream" speech in the nation's capital. This was less than four months after our final All-City concert. Is it possible that Martin had our group in mind, as our community of singers had actually embodied the contours of his dream? Not likely. Martin's dream was much broader than that. It echoed centuries of hope, encapsulated most effectively in the spirituals. In the final section of his speech Martin gave explicit credit to that legacy:

> . . . when we allow freedom to ring, and when we let it ring from every village and every hamlet, from every state and every city, we will be able to speed up that day when all of God's children, black men and white men, Jews and Gentiles, Protestants and Catholics, will be able to join hands and sing in the words of the old Negro spiritual: "Free at last. Free at last. Thank God Almighty, we're free at last."[25]

Martin was in fact calling up the ancestors. It was they who had created and sung one of the most important songs of the spirituals tradition:

> *Free at last, free at last,*
> *Thank God a'mighty I'm free at last.*
>
> *Surely been 'buked,*
> *And surely been scorned,*
> *Thank God a'mighty, I'm free at last.*

But still my soul is-a heaven born,
Thank God a'mighty, I'm free at last.

If you don't know that I been redeemed,
Thank God a'mighty, I'm free at last.

Just follow me down to Jordan's stream,
Oh, thank God a'mighty, I'm free at last![26]

Those allowing themselves to experience the power of this song had been able to comprehend, at a deeply personal level, the meaning of hope in the midst of tragedy. Proclaiming "I'm free at last," they had put the world on notice that however hopeless their external circumstances, they were experiencing directly the presence of a fiercely stubborn internal liberty, spurring them on in their continuing fight for external freedom, secure in the confident knowledge that "my God is a rock in a weary land!" The heaven they sang about referred at critical times to the potent simultaneous presence of internal peace in the present and imminent change in the future.[27] Martin Luther King, Jr., commander of an entire movement based on the creative tension between these seemingly contradictory forces, understood this paradoxical message at its deepest level. This message was carried into the air on the wings of hundreds of African American spirituals, continually transforming the lives of all of those who heard or sang them.

Unknowingly, dozens of young people opening themselves to the powers of song in New York City on Saturday mornings in the 1960s found themselves involved in a similar kind of transformation. In an urban environment full of hatred and torment, realistic possibilities for any personally meaningful multicultural experience were virtually unheard of. Yet, these young singers had put into action that very impossibility. Intuitively, they had grasped the fact that effective attempts at social change begin within one's own small social sphere. ("It's me, O Lord, standing in the need of prayer!") Metaphorically, this basic principle was reiterated in a comment made recently by one of my colleagues in a meeting I attended in which the topic of discussion was how one stays motivated to remain on the front lines in the increasingly frustrating struggle for social change. My colleague pointed out to the group that frequently the necessary catalyst for the emergence of health in a sick body is the healing of one small part of that body. This sets off a chain reaction resulting in the final outcome of total health:

There is a balm in Gilead,
To make the wounded whole,
There is a balm in Gilead,
To heal the sin-sick soul.

In the long sojourn of Africans in America, there has always been an abundantly rich knowledge of the unlimited possibilities for healing, even in a hopelessly sick society. Most often the rehabilitation process was begun in one small segment of the oppressed community, where bands of visionaries worked within their small social sphere to create changes that carried the seeds of hope for change within the larger environment. So it was with Gabriel Prosser and his band of conspirators in Richmond, Virginia, in 1800. A similar vision captured Denmark Vesey in Charleston, South Carolina, in 1822. In 1831 Nat Turner, taking his orders directly from the spirits, led his band of determined insurrectionists into acts whose effects were felt for decades, possibly serving as one of the critical factors in the gradual unraveling of the entire institution of slavery. Similarly, workers for freedom in such lonely and dangerous places as Selma, Alabama, in the mid 1960s drew their motivation to persist from their knowledge that healing is contagious. They succeeded in dismantling one of the most elaborate structures of oppression in modern history, the laws of the Jim Crow South. In all of these sites throughout the history of African America, the spirituals have been present to renew the spirits of people when they have lost hope:

Sometimes I feel discouraged,
And think my work's in vain,
But then the holy spirit,
Revives my soul again.

There is a balm in Gilead!

When Africans in America have functioned at their best levels, they have brought the lessons of the spirituals to bear on ever more distressing and destructive patterns of oppression. This is an example that can well serve *all* Americans as we recognize that in our current world our destinies are inextricably interlinked.

Those of us who are knowledgeable about the rich legacy of the spirituals must continue to pass the torch to new generations. With the challenges facing us more ambiguous, more disturbing and more complex than ever, we and our children need desperately to hear our music in the air, signalling the presence of an omnipresent spiritual force larger than ourselves, offering support, reassurance and new direction as we step up to the overwhelming challenge of accountability in our ongoing struggle for justice, freedom and meaningful life. This struggle, begun by our foreparents, must be continued by us, their twentieth- and twenty-first-century daughters and sons. But not without the transforming power of music. In order for us to succeed, we will have to carry that empowering force with us into the final battles.

But just as we might be tempted to believe that the voices of the creators of the spirituals might actually recede from our collective consciousness, sisters and brothers in new generations call to our attention fresh, creative ways to keep those voices alive. So it is currently, as the distinctively African sounds and rhythms of the rap movement make their way through a maze of racially and sexually exploitive messages to reach new transformative heights, strengthening again our spiritual connection with our ancestral teachers. Refreshingly, new sounds rise up into the air, again providing us music which signals the arrival of new hopes and new visions:

> Let it rain, let God's water feed me,
> The water of life, mentally rinsing me,
> Physically drenching me.
> Most are frowning upon your arrival,
> But I need you for survival,
> And when you fall on my community,
> I run to properly greet you.
> Let it rain, take my pain, I'm glad to meet you.
> Fill my eyes with a colorful rainbow,
> Every drop that hits me,
> Fills me with an unmeasurable amount of security.
> Knowing my God acknowledges me,
> My Lord thanks for life, thanks for my rain.
> My Lord thanks for life, thanks for my rain,
> It's raining revolution,
> It's raining solution.

The ancestors, I am sure, are quite pleased. They must certainly feel a significant bond with these wise young workers for freedom, who understand that wading in the internal spiritual rain waters of revolutionary change is a prerequisite for any substantive outer revolution:

> *I feel the rain enhances the revolution,*
> *Of a spiritual solution,*
> *And reminds us of a natural,*
> *Yet unnatural solution,*
> *It's raining revolution.*[28]

Of course, we have no way to know exactly what lies ahead in our ongoing struggle for justice, peace and meaningful human life. But whatever form our struggle takes, we can be confident that renewed hopes, continued healing and new victories will be part of the picture. We can also be certain that the powerful sounds and teachings of the spirituals will remain with us, in the air above our heads and in the secure, nurturing wombs of our deepest selves.[29]

Postscript

When *Wade in the Water* first appeared in 1993, I had no idea that I was joining a wave of renewed interest in the spirituals. Perhaps this is how the *zeitgeist* works; one becomes part of an idea whose time has come, even without conscious awareness of one's place in the larger fabric. Regardless, it has been a joy and a privilege to experience myself as a part of this phenomenon, and to receive many positive reactions from others who share my interest in honoring and preserving the spirituals for future generations.

The new wave of interest in spirituals has been multifaceted. For example, new performance groups, ranging from the classically influenced New England Spiritual Ensemble, to the folk-oriented sounds of Linda Tillery's Oakland, California, Cultural Heritage Choir, have emerged. There have also been several new jazz musicians joining the stream, including such varied artists as Hank Jones, Charlie Haden, Cyrus Chestnut, and Jubilant Sykes. And all along, the McIntosh County Shouters of coastal Georgia have continued to perform spirituals in the traditional ring shout, in the manner prescribed by their ancestors nearly two centuries ago.

There are important applications of the spirituals in community work, by people like the Rev. Yvette Flunder, whose Bay Area ministry utilizes the spirituals in its work with disenfranchised women and men living with AIDS and other crippling conditions. Organizations like The Spirituals Project in Denver and the Spiritual Renaissance Singers of Tampa, Florida, have provided exposure to the spirituals in programs across the country. Finally, a growing cadre of church musicians have re-integrated the spirituals into weekly worship services, supplementing a number of Black churches in the rural South, where people have never *stopped* singing the spirituals.

It is my hope that the re-release of *Wade* will provide yet another contribution to this new wave of interest in the spirituals. To aid in this effort, I am pleased to include an expanded discography of recommended recordings. I remain hopeful that folks will not only read about the spirituals, but that they will also listen, and *sing*! This is the most effective way to learn about the power and the magic of these amazing songs.

Arthur C. Jones
Denver, Colorado
March, 1999

Notes

1. "Over My Head I Hear Music in the Air"

1. Throughout the text the words of traditional songs are presented in standard English in order to avoid confusion, except where the use of dialect is necessary to convey the essential meanings or rhythms of a song. However, knowledgeable use of dialect when performing these songs can increase their power and effectiveness. The problem comes with exactly how to indicate the dialect in writing, since there is no standard convention. For a useful discussion of the issue of dialect, including an excellent guide for pronunciation during performance, see the historic discussion of this issue by James Weldon Johnson. (James Weldon Johnson and J. Rosamond Johnson, *The Books of American Negro Spirituals*, N.Y.: Da Capo Press, 1969, Preface to Book One, pp. 43-46, originally published as two separate volumes by Viking Press in 1925 and 1926. For the complete words and melodies of this song, see *Songs of Zion* (Nashville, Tennessee: Abingdon Press, 1981), selection 167. This book, used in many African American churches of various denominations, is easily available and familiar to many. Because it is so well-known, and contains a good collection of familiar spirituals, I have referred the reader to it whenever it contains the words and melodies of songs I have discussed. Of course, many of these songs appear in an infinite variety of other collections and publications, often in many different versions.

2. Sterling Stuckey, *Slave Culture* (New York: Oxford Press, 1987). Stuckey discusses the cultural characteristics of the various tribes from central and western Africa, from which most Africans enslaved in America were drawn. The main areas involved, according to Stuckey, were Congo-Angola, Nigeria, Dahomey, Togo, the Gold Coast, and Sierra Leone. There were undoubtedly countless tribal groups involved. Stuckey mentions the Yorubas, Akans, Ibos, Ibibios, Efiks, Angolans, Ekoi, Bakongo, Mende and Temme, but emphasizes the cultural commonalities among all of these groups, especially with regard to singing and dance rituals. Vincent Harding adds to his list the Bambara, Malinka, Fon, Dinka and Ewe, and adds "hundreds more." Harding, too, stresses the commonality among these groups, and ease with which they were able to join with each other in common cultural expressions of the urge for freedom, often through singing (Vincent Harding, *There is a River* [New York: Vintage Books, 1983; originally published New York: Random House, 1981]). Lerone Bennett includes in his list the Mandingos, Krus, Fantins Dahomeans, Binis and Sengalese (Lerone Bennett, Jr., *Before the Mayflower*

[4th ed.] [Chicago: Johnson Publishing Co., 1969]). John Hope Franklin, in his discussion, focuses primarily on the nation-states of Ghana, Mali and Songhay, with less attention to specific tribal groups. He too, however, stresses cultural commonalities between Africans from varied regional backgrounds, especially with respect to the role of music (John Hope Franklin, *From Slavery to Freedom* [4th ed.] [New York: Knopf, 1974]).

3. John Lovell, Jr., *Black Song: The Forge and the Flame: The Story of How the Afro-American Spiritual Was Hammered Out* (New York: Paragon House Publishers, 1986; originally published New York: Macmillan, 1972). In conducting his research, Lovell not only did exhaustive archival work, but also extensive interviews with numerous people around the world with special insights concerning African and African American music. This included interviews with tribal leaders and musicians in nine African countries. This comprehensive empirical framework gave him some particularly important insights and perspectives concerning important qualitative aspects of African music and particularly the retention of Africanisms in music created by enslaved Africans.

4. Eileen Southern, *The Music of Black Americans* (2nd ed.) (New York: W.W. Norton, 1983).

5. Southern describes the unfortunate experience of a European visitor in an African village who, to his chagrin, found himself the subject of a song of ridicule, improvised with elaborate poetry (ibid. pp. 18-19).

6. LeRoi Jones (now Amiri Baraka), *Blues People* (New York: William Morrow and Company, 1963), pp. 28-29.

7. For a succinct but illuminating description of how different facets of African life are interrelated, see Wade Nobles, "African Philosophy: Foundations of Black Psychology," in Reginald L. Jones (ed.), *Black Psychology* (3rd ed.), Berkeley, CA: Cobb & Henry, 1991, pp. 47-63. One of the most effective explanations of the key role played by oral expression and body movement in this holistic philosophy of life is provided by Molefi Kete Asante in *The Afrocentric Idea*, Philadelphia: Temple University Press, 1987.

8. This is not to suggest that people who unite in the face of a threat by a common enemy instantly lose the memory of their specific traditions and heritages. Attendance at any one of numerous pow wows held annually in the United States by Indian peoples is a powerful illustration of the way in which common bonds and separate heritages can be celebrated simultaneously. A parallel example in the African American community is the widespread use of "brother" and "sister" to refer to members of the community from geographically diverse areas, retaining such designations as "homeboy" to identify persons with roots in one's specific childhood community.

In another context the Ghanaian scholar Kwame Anthony Appiah has criticized the idea of any kind of significant link between diverse African cultures, and particularly between African American culture and the cultures of African peoples on the continent (*In My Father's House: Africa in the Philosophy of Culture* [New York: Oxford Press, 1992]). Appiah's argument is provocative and is helpful in tempering our tendencies to go too far in our concepts of Pan-Africanism. It is clear to me that one of the major issues is that of perspective. From the perspective of blacks in America who have been taught for decades that they are entirely unrelated culturally to their African ancestors, the links with the continent, when we become aware of them, appear *very* significant. For one raised in a specific African culture (such as Ghana), the cultural links with other Africans may appear much less compelling.

9. Stuckey, *Slave Culture*, p. 13. The quotations are from Melville J. Herskovits, *Dahomey* (New York: Augustin, 1938).

10. Nobles, "African Philosophy," p. 54.

11. John Mbiti, quoted in Nobles, p. 55.

12. For a lyrical, scholarly and historically detailed account of the spirit of resistance in America during the slave period, see Harding, *There Is a River*.

13. One of the strongest proponents of the view that slavery all but obliterated any remnants of African culture was E. Franklin Frazier. See especially Frazier's *The Negro in the United States*, rev. ed. (New York: Macmillan, 1957). Frazier's most vociferous opponent, Melville J. Herskovits, argued strongly for the survival of African cultural traits among enslaved Africans. See especially Herskovits's *The Myth of the Negro Past* (Boston: Beacon Press, 1958). It is now clear that Herskovits's position was closer to the actual reality. Over time researchers have uncovered increasingly more evidence of African survivals, extending to current African American culture. An excellent sampling of writings on this subject is provided in Joseph E. Holloway, ed., *Africanisms in American Culture* (Bloomington: Indiana University Press, 1990). With respect to music, John Lovell establishes conclusively that African cultural traditions figured strongly in the development of African American folk music, including songs now referred to as spirituals (see Lovell, *Black Song*). Stuckey, *Slave Culture*, provides corroboration for Lovell's view.

14. Sterling Stuckey has provided a fascinating explanation of the importance of the ring shout as a unifying force among Africans in America. Stuckey argues convincingly that the ring shout was the most important channel for the preservation of African cultural traditions during the transition to slavery. See Stuckey, *Slave Culture*, chap. 1.

15. Lydia Parrish, *Slave Songs of the Georgia Sea Islands* (New York: Creative Age Press, 1942), p. 54. See Wyatt Tee Walker's *Somebody's Calling My Name* (Valley Forge, Pennyslvania: Judson Press, 1979) for a more extended discussion of the evolution of African American religious songs from shouts and moans to spirituals and eventually to modern gospel music.

16. The terms *gospel song* and *spiritual* are often used interchangeably, but the style and form of the two types of music are very different. Spirituals are folk songs that were created in slavery and not credited to any known composer. In the early twentieth century, the spirituals tradition, along with the blues, provided the foundation for the emergence in African American churches of composed songs with lively rhythms and significant improvisation. These songs came to be known as gospel songs. Thomas A. Dorsey is generally recognized as the father of gospel music. A readable and inform-

ative historical sketch of African American religious music is found in Walker. A wonderful sampling of songs from both the spirituals and gospel traditions, with informative commentary concerning both traditions, as well as the tradition of African American hymns, is found in *Songs of Zion*.

17. Some attempted, with painstaking effort, to wage an argument for the view that the spirituals of the slaves were actually impoverished imitations of white hymns. John Lovell, among others, has conclusively dismissed this view (Lovell, chaps. 8-13). Clearly, slaves borrowed material (such as material from the Bible) from their captors, just as any creative poet or song writer draws material from the cultural environment in which she or he is immersed. The use of this environmental material does not make the poet's or song writer's creation an imitation. In the case of African American spirituals, the final result was unmistakably African and original, both with respect to the song melodies and rhythms and the poetic content and flavor of the lyrics. One of the first to demonstrate the largely African influence in the spirituals was New York music critic Henry Edward Krehbiel (*Afro-American Folk-Songs* [New York: Frederick Ungar Publishing Co., 1962; originally published 1913]). For one of the most interesting examples of an attempt to force the white hymn to Negro spiritual evolution interpretation, see George Pullen Jackson, *Spiritual Folk-Songs of Early America* (Gloucester, Massachusetts: Peter Smith, 1975; originally published New York: Augustin, 1937).

18. See Stuckey, *Slave Culture*, chaps. 1-4, for a discussion of the important core African elements of the new religion which emerged among Africans in slavery. See also Albert J. Raboteau, *Slave Religion* (New York: Oxford University Press, 1978), for a detailed account of the gradual process of conversion, with African American religious leaders at the center of the conversion of captives who were weary of the religion of a people who equated religion with obedience to masters. This issue is discussed in detail in Chapter 4 of the current book.

19. See *Songs of Zion*, selection 82.

20. Lovell, *Black Song*, pp. 150-51.

21. Numerous authors have catalogued the variety of folk songs created during the slave period, including but not limited to songs typically referred to as spirituals. A classic work of this variety is *Slave Songs of the United States* by William Francis Allen, Charles Pickard Ware and Lucy McKim Garrison (New York: Peter Smith, 1951; originally published in 1867). Part 4 of Alan Lomax's *The Folk Songs of North America* (Garden City, New York: Doubleday, 1960), is a more recent example. Other important examples are John W. Work, *American Negro Songs* (New York: Bonanza Books, 1940); Walker, *Somebody's Calling My Name*; Harold Courlander, *Negro Folk Music, U.S.A.* (New York: Columbia Press, 1963); and Parrish, *Slave Songs*. Stuckey, *Slave Culture*, and Lovell, *Black Song*, discuss at some length the issue of spirituality and its pervasive operation throughout both "secular" and "spiritual" songs among enslaved Africans in America.

22. Of course, religious in the African sense is much broader than the way that concept reveals itself in European and American cultural contexts. The

distinguishing spiritual content of the songs is more a function of the fact that they comment on large issues of philosophical or ethical concern, in contrast to work songs, for example, which are more rhythmical accompaniments to a physical task and not particularly philosophical or religious in content. See Johnson and Johnson (preface to Book 2, pp. 12-13) for a helpful discussion of the broad-ranging philosophical character of spirituals as contrasted to work and sex songs.

23. Lovell, *Black Song*, pp. 223-24.

24. The misunderstanding and co-optation of African American music have formed a recurring theme in American history. For an extensive discussion of this issue, and especially its reflection in American music, see Sam Dennison, *Scandalize My Name: Black Imagery in American Popular Music* (New York: Garland Publishing, Inc., 1982).

25. In *Hope and History* (Maryknoll, New York: Orbis Books, 1990), Vincent Harding, in his effective lyrical style, discusses the critical importance of preserving the memory of that movement, including the memory of the singing that derived directly from the spiritual commitments of its participants. Harding is providing here an important link with the enslaved past, which he discussed thoroughly in *There Is a River*. He helps to remind us that the powerfully effective spirit of the freedom movement of the 1960s was a continuation of the long-existing struggle for freedom forged by Africans in America since the beginning of the slave trade. The powerful spirit of celebration and life affirmed in the '60s freedom movement is documented effectively in the P.B.S. Television series *Eyes on the Prize*. The constant accompaniment of songs derived from the spirituals is vividly evident throughout the series.

26. Paul Robeson, *Here I Stand* (Boston: Beacon Press, 1958), p. 100.

27. Lovell, *Black Song*, p. 384.

28. Walker, *Somebody's Calling My Name*, pp. 43-44. Walker uses the metaphor of the holocaust, deliberately drawing our attention to the similarities with Nazi Germany. As Walker notes, the slavery experience has never been dealt with adequately in the collective consciousness of Americans.

29. Frank Cooper, from a U.S. Library of Congress slave narrative, quoted in Julius Lester, *To Be a Slave* (New York: Scholastic, Inc., 1968), pp. 33-34.

30. For one of the most effective descriptions of the daily experiences of enslaved Africans, and the music that experience generated, see Lovell, *Black Song*, pp. 142-47.

31. Stuckey, *Slave Culture*, has shown that some of the most effective moments of social change in the African American community have been associated with recognition and use of the powerful cultural weapons found in the ring shout and the spirituals. African American activists who have understood the critical importance of these African-derived cultural forms have been particularly effective in their ability to motivate their people. Prominent examples cited by Stuckey are W.E.B. Du Bois and Paul Robeson. An obvious more recent example is Martin Luther King, Jr., whose powerfully effective leadership was bolstered substantially by the constant singing

of songs derived directly from spirituals. For the story of the 1960s freedom movement through the perspective of African American song, see *Sing for Freedom*, compiled by Guy and Candie Carawan (Bethlehem, Pennsylvania: Sing Out Corporation, 1990).

32. The Swiss psychiatrist C.G. Jung used the term *archetype* to refer to potentialities deep in the human psyche that have universal significance, beyond the life of the individual experiencing them. Jung noted in his clinical observations that archetypal material would frequently emerge during times of extreme crisis or trauma. It is my belief that the unusual worldwide appeal of African American religious folk songs derives in part from the fact that they are archetypal in nature, created during the most extreme crisis of the spirit imaginable, the interminably long experience of American slavery. The second half of Lovell's *Black Song* is devoted to an extensive documentation of the unprecedented enthusiasm and interest around the world that the spirituals have received. Lovell provides a helpful, comprehensive discussion of the typical evolution of folk music and he demonstrates convincingly that the spirituals have been extraordinarily unusual in their ability to engender such intense, worldwide attention. Even if one does not accept the Jungian theoretical notion of the archetype, it is unquestionably clear that spirituals are inspired folk music, unusual in their ability to communicate deep emotional meanings to people of widely diverse ethnic and cultural backgrounds.

33. Carter G. Woodson, *The Mis-education of the Negro* (Trenton, New Jersey: Africa World Press, 1990). Woodson details the pervasive nature of the cultural ignorance that results from the way African Americans are educated. His book, first published in 1933, is sadly still relevant today and has enjoyed intensely renewed attention as a result of the Afrocentric movement.

34. A delightful discussion of the way in which these basic African American sensibilities appear in various spheres of life is found in Joseph L. White and Thomas A. Parham, *Psychology of Blacks* (Englewood Cliffs, New Jersey: Prentice-Hall, 1990).

35. Although somewhat dated, Joel Kovel's *White Racism: A Psychohistory* (New York: Vintage Books, 1971), still provides, in my opinion, one of the most revealing and incisive explorations of the deep roots of the disease of racism. Although I disagree with some of his psychoanalytic formulations, I am in complete agreement with Kovel with respect to the pervasive nature of this disease and the idea that it serves important psychological functions for its victims (members of the dominant culture). One result is the inability to assign proper value to the cultural contributions of African peoples. It therefore becomes difficult to entertain the notion that anything of value beyond curious "folklore" could have been contributed by unschooled enslaved Africans to the European American cultural environment.

Internalization by African Americans of negative racial attitudes remains a significant problem but is potentially counteracted by bolstering the influence of traditional cultural values. I have discussed some of the complexities of these psychological dynamics in two clinically oriented articles (Arthur Jones, "Psychological Functioning in Black Americans: A Conceptual Guide for Use in Psychotherapy," *Psychotherapy* 22 (2S), 1985, pp. 363-69; reprinted in Reginald L. Jones, ed., *Black Psychology*, 3rd ed. (Berkeley, California.: Cobb and Henry, 1991), pp. 577-89; and idem, "Psychological Functioning in African American Adults: Some Elaborations on a Model, with Clinical Applications," in Reginald L. Jones, ed., *Black Adult Development and Aging* (Berkeley, California: Cobb & Henry, 1989), pp. 297-307.

36. Johnson and Johnson, *American Negro Spirituals*, preface to Book 2, pp. 12-13.

37. Asante, in *The Afrocentric Idea*, has provided an informed, comprehensive discussion of the nuances of African and African American oral communication. For an instructive understanding of how attention to oral expression and body movement expands one's ability to understand the messages of African American folk music, see the videotape recording of the P.B.S. Bill Moyers program, *The Songs Are Free*, featuring one of the statespersons of the 1960s freedom movement, Bernice Johnson Reagon (Cooper Station, New York: Mystic Fire Videos, #76204, 1991). In this magnificent program, historian-singer-activist Reagon (Smithsonian Institution curator and founder of the singing group "Sweet Honey in the Rock") is interviewed by Moyers on the subject of the African American folksong tradition. In addition, there are clips of Reagon leading congregational singing workshops, where she exhibits her encyclopedic knowledge of the songs and some of the lessons they provide about the African American experience. Most helpfully, she demonstrates the power, experience and knowledge one gains from singing the songs, far beyond what would be possible from simply studying the words or even listening to the music passively.

38. C. G. Jung's notion of the four functions of thinking, sensation, intuition and feeling is a helpful framework for understanding such differences. In Jung's conception, people (and cultures) vary with respect to the dominant manner in which information is processed and in which decisions, based on that information, are made. Jung asserted that no specific approach is better than any other, but that understanding the approach used in a specific personal or cultural context facilitates understanding of the person or culture involved. (C. G. Jung, *Psychological Types*, Collected Works, vol. 6. Princeton, N.J.: Princeton University Press, 1971.) In this framework, it is clear that Western cultures favor thinking (logic) as a dominant channel, while African (and many other non-Western) cultures favor feeling. Unfortunately, the dominance of the Western framework results in a misinterpretation of feeling-based approaches to knowledge as inferior, when the main problem is that they are unfamiliar to people of a Western mind set.

39. Paul Robeson, quoted in Stuckey, *Slave Culture*, p. 336.

40. Robeson, *Here I Stand*, p. 15

41. W.E.B. Du Bois, *The Souls of Black Folk* (New York: Bantam Books, 1989; originally published in 1903), p. 178. The Bantam Books edition is a reprint of the revised 1953 edition. These words by Du Bois, a visionary in so many respects, are as relevant today as when they were written in 1903. Although some would argue that jazz has supplanted spirituals as "the greatest con-

tribution of the Negro people," that argument becomes specious when we recognize the early African American folksong as the cultural foundation for the blues, jazz and gospel music, which are all developments that have occurred since Du Bois's classic statement. See LeRoi Jones, *Blues People*.

42. Kathleen Battle and Jessye Norman, *Spirituals in Concert* (Hamburg, Germany: Deutsche Grammophon, Compact Disc Number 429790-2, 1991). Also available on cassette tape and VHS videotape.

2. "Sometimes I Feel Like a Motherless Child"

1. Linda Brent (Harriet Jacobs), *Incidents in the Life of a Slave Girl*. In Henry Louis Gates, Jr., ed., *The Classic Slave Narratives*, N.Y.: Penguin Books, 1987), pp. 350-51.

2. See *Songs of Zion*, selection 83.

3. Crista Dixon has noted that in some African patriarchal societies it was the father who was responsible for providing food and protection to his family. Accordingly, the phrase "My father is dead" was frequently used symbolically to communicate the experience of a desperate situation in which ordinary human needs have gone unmet. Dixon suggests that this metaphorical reference to the father was shifted to the mother during slavery because the father in slavery was not allowed to assume his traditional role as provider and in fact, more often than the mother, was sold away from his family. She suggests that "the shift from the African idiom, 'my father is dead,' to the Afro-American expression 'I feel like a motherless chile' reflects the fact that after the physical father had been sold the mother was the only lasting provider of care, support and love." When the mother too was then auctioned off, Dixon suggests, " 'Sometimes I feel like a motherless chile, / A long, long ways from home' therefore expresses utmost desperation." While it is impossible to determine the validity of Dixon's speculation about the African roots of this type of metaphorical expression, her ideas are intriguing. See Crista Dixon, *Negro Spirituals: From Bible to Folksong* (Philadelphia: Fortress Press, 1976), pp. 35-36.

4. At lecture-recital programs on spirituals, I hand out questionnaires, asking audience members to complete them anonymously, providing information about their ethnic and religious backgrounds, and reactions to the program. Next to a listing of each song performed during the program respondents are asked to indicate the extent of their familiarity with that song prior to attending the program. The choices are "not familiar," "somewhat familiar," and "very familiar." Invariably, "Sometimes I Feel Like a Motherless Child" is at or near the top of the list of the songs most frequently endorsed as "very familiar," more often endorsed this way than such other familiar songs as "Joshua Fit the Battle of Jericho" and "Go Down, Moses." Frequently, respondents who endorse all other songs as "not familiar" will indicate that "Sometimes I Feel Like a Motherless Child" is "very familiar." This is true for African Americans as well as for audience participants from disparate ethnic and religious backgrounds. While there are a number of

possible explanations for the special familiarity this song enjoys (such as its history of performance by well-known concert artists, for example), we certainly have to consider strongly the possibility that song themes and melodies with particularly enduring power have managed to make their way frequently into the repertoire of concert singers, worshipers, and the general folk community.

An example outside of the spirituals tradition that many people would agree has such enduring power is "Amazing Grace," which seems to connect emotionally with Americans from widely varied cultural backgrounds. That song, actually written by a reformed slave trader, is embraced intensely and enthusiastically by many people, most of whom are unaware of its origins. See the excellent Bill Moyers documentary on "Amazing Grace," recorded on videotape (Los Angeles: PBS Home Video #102, 1990). I believe that "Sometimes I Feel Like a Motherless Child" has a similarly archetypally powerful ability to connect with people from varied ethnic backgrounds. Similar to "Amazing Grace," both the melody and the words of "Motherless Child" appear to communicate an important message about matters of concern to the universal human spirit.

5. Brent, *Incidents in the Life of a Slave Girl*, p. 383.

6. Ex-slave and abolitionist Frederick Douglass also commented on this phenomenon of the reciprocal suffering and moral deterioration of the slave holder. See "Narrative of the Life of Frederick Douglass," in Gates, *The Classic Slave Narratives*. See especially pp. 274-77.

7. Although there is some disagreement on this issue, some scholars have felt that much of the symbolism in the spirituals referred to the motherland, Africa, and longing for "home" in that sense. See especially Fisher, *Negro Slave Songs* (Ithaca, New York: Cornell University Press, 1953). Lovell, in *Black Song*, argues strongly that most slaves, especially after several generations, had no wish whatsoever to return to Africa, but rather to be free, in this country, to live outside of slavery, and that the "home" in their songs was simply symbolic of freedom. In either case, it is clear that the condition of slavery left people with a longing to be "home," somewhere different from their current condition, and that longing made its way into the poetic symbolism of their songs. See Nathan Irvin Huggins, *Black Odyssey: The African-American Ordeal in Slavery* (New York: Vintage Books, 1990; originally published 1977), for a particularly powerful and emotionally moving discussion of the traumatic impact on Africans who were taken from their homeland into slavery. See especially pages 25-27. Huggins's description leaves us feeling that the effect of separation from the homeland must have certainly lingered in the collective memories of enslaved Africans in slavery and may well have made its way into images of separation from "home" in spirituals.

8. See Johnson and Johnson, *American Negro Spirituals*, Book 1, p. 120.

9. Ibid., p. 108.

10. The term *post-traumatic stress* emerged in the official American psychiatric nomenclature during the 1980s. It was employed to describe the experiences and psychiatric symptoms of individuals exposed to extraordi-

narily traumatic experiences, such as active participation in combat, child-hood sexual abuse or ritualistic satanic abuse. *Post-traumatic stress* replaced older terms, like *battle fatigue* or *shell shock*, and expanded the understanding of trauma to include experiences outside of the exclusive arena of war. Util-izing current diagnostic criteria, many victims of slavery would undoubtedly qualify for a diagnosis of post-traumatic stress syndrome (see *The Diagnostic and Statistical Manual of Mental Disorders* [Washington, D.C.: American Psy-chiatric Association, 1987], pp. 247-50).

11. Howard Thurman, *Deep River and The Negro Spiritual Speaks of Life and Death* (Richmond, Indiana: Friends United Press, 1975, p. 42; originally pub-lished in 1945 and 1947 as two separate volumes.

12. Harding, *There Is a River*, p. xxv.

13. Reagon, *The Songs Are Free*.

14. See Lovell, *Black Song*, chaps. 1-3, for an extensive, general discussion of how folk music is created and what functions it serves in various cultural contexts (see chaps. 14-15 for a discussion of the specific origins and functions of African American religious folksongs, or spirituals).

15. James Miller McKim, "Negro Songs," in *The Social Implications of Early Negro Music in the United States*, ed. Bernard Katz (New York: Arno Press and the *New York Times*, 1969), p. 2.

16. The modern field of music therapy is built on an understanding of the healing power of music. See, for example, Robert F. Unfeker, ed., *Music Therapy in the Treatment of Adults with Mental Disorders* (New York: Schirmer Books/Macmillan, 1990). Unfortunately, the mainstream mental health dis-ciplines of social work, psychiatry and psychology have been very slow to incorporate these ideas into standard clinical practice.

17. One of the most moving and illuminating discussions of this issue is found in W.E.B. Du Bois's classic autobiographical text, *Dusk of Dawn* (New York: Harcourt, Brace and Co., 1940), in a chapter entitled "The Colored World Within" (chap. 7).

18. See Reagon, *The Songs Are Free*.

19. See Thurman, *Deep River*.

20. Frederick Douglass, *My Bondage and My Freedom*, reprinted in Eileen Southern, ed., *Readings in Black American Music* (New York: W.W. Norton, 1971), p. 84.

21. This issue is explored more fully in Chapter 4.

22. Jung first published his ideas about the healing power of symbols in *Symbols of Transformation*. See *Collected Works of C. G. Jung*, 2d ed., vol. 5 (Princeton, New Jersey: Bollingen Foundation, 1967; first edition published 1956). For a comparative study of the similarity between Jungian uses of symbols for healing and traditional African methods, see M. Vera Buhrmann, *Living in Two Worlds* (Wilmette, Illinois: Chiron Publications, 1986).

23. For an especially effective recording of both versions of "Mary Had a Baby" see *Black Christmas: Spirituals in the African-American Tradition* (Dobbs Ferry, New York: ESS.A.Y. Recordings, Compact Disc No. 90998-1011-2, 1990). See also Johnson and Johnson, *American Negro Spirituals*, Book 2, p. 124.

24. See Lovell, *Black Song*, p. 249, for a discussion of the significance of train symbolism in spirituals.

25. See Harding, *There Is a River*, and also Harding's *The Other American Revolution* (Los Angeles: Center for Afro-American Studies, 1980). The reflection of that struggle in the spirituals is discussed more extensively in Chapter 3.

26. See Roland Hayes, *My Songs* (Boston: Little, Brown and Co., 1948), pp. 98-102.

27. Testimony of Charity Bowery, interviewed by Lydia Maria Child in 1847 and 1848. Reprinted in John W. Blassingame, ed., *Slave Testimony* (Baton Rouge: Louisiana State University Press, 1977), p. 263.

28. Report of interviews in 1910 by Mary White Ovington of former slaves from Alabama. Reported in Blassingame, *Slave Testimony*, pp. 537-538.

29. See especially Roland Hayes's effective arrangement of this song for voice and piano, in which the piano accompaniment accentuates the rhythmic movements of the mother rocking the child (Hayes, *My Songs*, pp. 98-102). This song is also recorded in *Black Christmas* (see note 23).

30. See *Songs of Zion*, selection 126.

31. Blassingame, *Slave Testimony*, p. 163.

32. James Cone, *The Spirituals and the Blues* (Maryknoll, New York: Orbis Books, 1991, originally published 1972), p. 49.

33. See *Songs of Zion*, selection 101.

34. One of the most inspired interpretations of this song is found in a recording by the great contralto, Marian Anderson, one of the first professional singers to include spirituals as a regular part of her solo concert repertoire, following the lead of tenor Roland Hayes (*Marian Anderson*. New York: RCA Victor, Compact Disc. No. 0-7863-57911-2-9, 1989).

35. Matthew 27:46, Mark 15:34: "My God, my God, why have you forsaken me?"; Luke 23:34: "Father forgive them, for they do not know what they are doing"; John 19:11: "You would have no power over me if it were not given to you from above. Therefore the one who handed me over to you is guilty of greater sin" (*Holy Bible, New International Version* [Grand Rapids, Michigan: Zondervan Bible Publishers, 1984]).

36. This song is not included in the *Songs of Zion* collection, but see Dett, *Religious Folk-Songs of the Negro as Sung at Hampton Institute* (New York: AMS Press, 1972), p. 235.

37. See Edward Boatner, *The Story of the Spirituals* (Miami, Florida: Belwin Mills, 1973), pp. 67-71.

38. See Raboteau, *Slave Religion*, pp. 72-74, for a discussion of African-derived cultural forms and performance styles, including the role of the ring shout, in the singing of spirituals during slavery. See also Stuckey, *Slave Culture*, pp. 25-30, for a specific discussion of spirituals sung in the context of the ring shout. Current continuations of the combination of shout and song may be witnessed in such settings as worship services in traditional African American churches, such as the Church of God in Christ ("Holiness" Church), or some churches in the Baptist tradition. The essential difference

between those current parallels and the role of the shout and singing in slavery is that current church settings rarely provide an opportunity for participants to integrate these experiences of religious ecstasy into their daily struggles at home and in the world. In this respect they may sometimes reflect a kind of escapism that was rarely characteristic of the worship experience in slavery. See Chapter 4 for a further discussion of this issue.

39. A very effective rendition of this song is found in a recording by the wonderful folk singer Odetta, entitled *Odetta, Christmas Spirituals* (Waterbury, Vermont: Alcazar Productions, Compact Disc No. 2166-10104-2, 1988). In this recording one gets a sense of the soothing, emotionally deepening rhythms, and can almost feel oneself propelled into the circle of the ring shout. See Jung, *Collected Works*, Volume 12 (*Psychology and Alchemy*, London: Routledge and Kegan Paul, 1953), pp. 119-122, 134-136, 183-185 and 189-90, for a discussion of the symbolism of the left as a channel into the deep human unconscious, found in cultures around the world.

40. See *Songs of Zion*, selection 164.

41. See Johnson and Johnson, *American Negro Spirituals*, Book 1, p. 96.

42. There are growing numbers of Americans engaged in discussions about these crises and concerned about developing programs to address them. For example, the U.S. Advisory Board on Child Abuse and Neglect recently reported that "child abuse and neglect in the United States now represents a national emergency.... Each year hundreds of thousands of children are starved and abandoned, burned and severely beaten, raped and sodomized, berated and belittled; ... the United States spends **billions** of dollars on programs that deal with the **results** of the nation's failure to prevent and treat child abuse and neglect" (U.S. Department of Health and Human Services, Office of Human Development Services, Advisory Board on Child Abuse and Neglect, *Child Abuse and Neglect: Critical First Steps in Response to a National Emergency* Washington, D.C.: U.S. Government Printing Office Document No. 017-092-00104-5, August, 1990). The advisory board's report indicates that such abuse and neglect are by no means confined to the poor and dispossessed. This conclusion is illustrated by the recent public revelations of former Miss America Marilyn Van Derbur, who reported a period of severe and ongoing sexual abuse as a child; her father, a respected and wealthy businessman, was the perpetrator. The advisory board has outlined a series of strategies to deal with the serious problem of child maltreatment. In 1991 the U.S. Senate Judiciary Committee released a report whose findings indicated that the United States is now "the most violent society on earth," with incidents of rape, murder and other violent crimes at levels far above those of any other countries in the world, including countries where problems of extreme poverty prevail. The report seemed to provide an occasion for serious discussions around the country. Hopefully, these important government studies will not follow the precedent of previous "official" alarms, which have gone unheeded.

43. See Paul L. Wachtel, *The Poverty of Affluence: A Psychological Portrait of the American Way of Life* (New York: Free Press, 1984).

44. For a sampling of some of the important spiritual and meditative reflections of the great African American preacher, teacher, mystic and theologian Howard Thurman, see *Deep River and The Negro Spiritual Speaks of Life and Death* and *With Head and Heart: The Autobiography of Howard Thurman* (New York: Harcourt Brace Jovanovich, 1979); helpful reflections on Thurman's work by others include Mozella G. Mitchell, *Spiritual Dynamics of Howard Thurman's Theology* (Bristol, Indiana: Wyndham Hall Press, 1985) and Luther E. Smith, Jr., *Howard Thurman: The Mystic as Prophet* (Washington, D.C.: University Press of America, 1981). See Nobles, "African Philosophy," p. 53, for a discussion of the African concept of the living-dead. The quotation is from the character Bynum in playwright August Wilson's *Joe Turner's Come and Gone* (New York: NAL Penguin, Inc., 1988), p. 71. The story of the life of Harriet Tubman, fugitive slave and leader of the Underground Railroad, which provided escape for enslaved African Americans, is detailed in Sarah Elizabeth Bradford, *Harriet Tubman, the Moses of Her People* (New York: Corinth Books, 1961; originally published 1886). Another account, written for children but appealing to readers of all ages, is found in Jeri Ferris, *Go Free or Die: A Story About Harriet Tubman* (Minneapolis: Carolrhoda Books, 1988).

45. Anyone interested in spirituals should be aware of the recording of this concert, available commercially as *The Harlem Spiritual Ensemble, in Concert*, through Arcadia Records (New York: United Music Management. Compact Disc No. 26072-1991-2, 1991).

3. "Joshua Fit the Battle of Jericho"

1. David Walker, *Walker's Appeal in Four Articles* (Salem, New Hampshire: Ayer Co., 1989; originally published 1829), p. 80.

2. See *Songs of Zion*, selection 96.

3. Harding, *There Is a River*, p. 19.

4. See the Introduction to *There Is a River* for a description of the river metaphor, how it evolved, and what meanings Harding intended. See especially p. xix. In *The Other American Revolution* Harding continues the story of the river's course into the twentieth century. Clearly the story of the struggle has a past, a present and a future.

5. See Molefi Kete Asante, *Kemet, Afrocentricity and Knowledge* (Trenton, New Jersey: Africa World Press, 1990), pp. 80-96.

6. See Harding, *There Is a River*, chap. 3.

7. See *Songs of Zion*, selection 106.

8. See Raboteau, *Slave Religion*, chap. 6, "Religion, Rebellion and Docility."

9. Lawrence Levine, *Black Culture and Black Consciousness* (New York: Oxford University Press, 1977), p. 51.

10. See Nobles, *African Philosophy*, pp. 51-54.

11. Frederick Douglass, *My Bondage and Freedom*. The section from which this passage is drawn is reprinted in Southern, *Readings in Black Music*, pp. 82-87. The quotation is on page 87.

12. See *Songs of Zion*, selection 112.

13. See *Songs of Zion*, selection 134.

14. Aside from the already cited observations by Frederick Douglass, see Lovell, *Black Song*, pp. 195-97, for a discussion of the use of spirituals for a variety of purposes, including secret communication. Also see Southern, *The Music of Black Americans*, pp. 140-44, Levine, *Black Culture and Black Consciousness*, pp. 51-52, and John W. Blassingame, *The Slave Community*, rev. ed. (New York: Oxford University Press, 1979), pp. 120-22; 139-44. See Harding, *There Is a River*, p. 69, for an intriguing discussion of the Vesey situation and the possible "Go Down, Moses" connection. See Courlander, *Negro Folk Music, U.S.A.*, for a general discussion of secret meanings, including the connection of Harriet Tubman and "Go Down, Moses." That connection is touched on as well in Bernard Katz's Introduction to *The Social Implications of Early Negro Music in the United States* (New York: Arno Press, 1969) and Lovell's article, "The Social Implications of the Negro Spiritual," in the same book, pp. 128-37. See also Irwin Silber, *Songs of the Civil War* (New York: Columbia Press, 1960), p. 270, who identifies Harriet Tubman as the "Moses" of "Go Down, Moses." That connection is documented as well in a description of an interview with Tubman reported in Blassingame, *Slave Testimony*, p. 458. Harriet Tubman as "Moses" and Nat Turner's use of "Steal Away" are touched on as well by Russell Ames in *The Story of American Folk Song* (New York: Grosset & Dunlap, 1955), chap. 6. Fisher, in *Negro Slave Songs*, argues for Nat Turner as the composer of "Steal Away" and dates "Go Down, Moses" as appearing no later than the end of the eighteenth century. We may question in particular Fisher's ability to be so specific in his dates and connections. However, his general argument of spirituals as songs of secret communication is supported by many other sources, as illustrated in the above citations.

15. Ames, *The Story of American Folk Song*, p. 151.

16. Southern, *The Music of Black Americans*, p. 144. Additional verses are found in Silber, *Songs of the Civil War*, pp. 278-80. See also Ames, *The Story of American Folk Song*, p. 159.

17. See *Songs of Zion*, selection 88.

18. Fisher, *Negro Slave Songs*, p. 29.

19. See Raboteau, *Slave Religion*, pp. 305-12.

20. See Lovell, *Black Song*, pp. 397-585 for a detailed and extensive discussion of the worldwide interest and attention enjoyed by spirituals, particularly those engendering deep religious feelings.

21. Courlander, *Negro Folk Music, U.S.A.*, p. 43.

22. Levine has provided an illuminating discussion of the fact that even now many people do not recognize the complexities of religious experience found in the spirituals. See *Black Culture and Black Consciousness*, especially pp. 51-55.

23. Excerpt from the well-known spiritual "Wade in the Water." See *Songs of Zion*, selection 129.

24. One of the most insightful discussions of the nature and functions of improvisation in spirituals is found in Levine, *Black Culture and Black Con-*

sciousness, pp. 40-41. Other helpful discussions are found in Southern, *The Music of Black Americans,* pp. 172-177, and Johnson and Johnson, *American Negro Spirituals,* Preface to Book 1, pp. 21-23, and Lovell, *Black Song,* pp. 40-41. For an illuminating perspective on the continuing functional role of improvisation as it is expressed in jazz, see Ferdinand Jones, "Dancing to the Music in Our Heads," *Brown University Alumni Monthly* 90 (2) (October 1989), pp. 30-37. As Jones indicates, psychologist Adelbert Jenkins, in his important book, *The Psychology of the Afro-American: A Humanistic Approach* (N.Y.: Pergamon Press, 1982), has documented the many ways in which the lifestyle of Africans in America has always been creatively improvisational.

25. In *Black Song* Lovell interlaces a discussion of mask and symbol throughout his thorough, comprehensive analysis (see especially pp. 45-46, 132-33, 190-93 and 340-43, although a full appreciation of the complexities of mask and symbolization comes only from a full reading of this very important work).

26. Ames, *The Story of American Folk Song,* p. 160. See *Songs of Zion,* selection 129, for the more standard version of "Wade in the Water." See Parrish, *Slave Songs of the Georgia Sea Islands,* pp. 168-71, for a discussion of the original baptismal purpose of this song, and see Stuckey, *Slave Culture,* pp. 34-35, for an account of how traditional African religion often merged with the Christian rite of baptism, accompanied by the singing of "Wade in the Water." Some of the words in the improvised version of "Wade in the Water" used by Tubman were also used frequently by African Americans in other songs, such as "Swing Low, Sweet Chariot" (see *Songs of Zion,* selection 104), another song employed frequently for secret communication. See also Southern, *The Music of Black Americans,* p. 144.

27. See Harding, *Hope and History,* pp. 2-5, for reflections on the worldwide influence of the long-fought African American struggle for freedom, which began in slavery, and the songs expressive of that struggle.

28. See Harding, *There Is a River,* for an especially inspirational account of the work of these and numerous other African workers for freedom throughout the period of official slavery.

29. Stuckey, *Slave Culture,* pp. 48-49.

30. Lovell, *Black Song,* p. 229.

31. Levine, *Black Culture and Black Consciousness,* pp. 37-38.

32. Cone, *The Spirituals and the Blues,* pp. 43-44.

33. See *Songs of Zion,* selection 77.

34. One very effective recording of this song is by the mezzo-soprano Florence Quivar in an inspirational album which actually has *Ride On, King Jesus!* as its title (Hayes Middlesex, England: EMI Records, Compact Disc No. 7-49885-2, 1990). Quivar is joined by the Harlem Boys Choir and accompanied on piano by two brilliant musicians, Joseph Joubert and Larry Woodard. The album is a tribute to Quivar's upbringing in the African American community, where she heard and sang spirituals from an early age. In the liner notes of her album, Quivar comments, "I've grown up in a world of music all my life, and I've been truly blessed to have been able to sing on so many

great operatic and concert stages throughout the world. But nothing has given me as much joy as working on this recording of Negro spirituals. They are part of my own beginnings. Of my own roots. Of family. Of friends. Of an American dream. With love, Florence Quivar." An interesting Gullah variation on "Ride On, King Jesus" is found in Margaret Washington Creel, *A Peculiar People* (New York: New York University Press, 1988), p. 270. The lyrics are "Jesus make de blind see, Jesus make de cripple walk, Jesus make de deaf to hear. Walk in, kind Jesus! No man can hinder me." Creel discusses its dual use as both a religious and resistance song.

35. See *Songs of Zion*, selection 93.

36. The phrase "watch as well as pray" may possibly have been inspired by the biblical text "Watch and pray so that you will not fall into temptation" (Matthew 26:41, *New International Version*). It is interesting to note that this statement of Jesus comes shortly before the crucifixion story, providing an interesting parallel to people in the slave community, who frequently had to prepare themselves for similar imminent experiences of abuse. These, of course, are speculations, since it is impossible to know the intentions of the original composers or of all the singers who embraced this song. Still, it is interesting to see the many possibilities for symbolic and thematic improvisation in slave songs, appropriate to individual circumstances and singers. See a related but different analysis of the meaning of "Keep A-inchin' along" by Lovell in *Black Song*, pp. 231-32. Lovell emphasizes the issue of endurance rather than the active struggle for freedom. We are in agreement, however, with respect to the idea that this was probably not often used as a song about the anticipation of death.

37. Lovell, *Black Song*, p. 367.

38. Blassingame, *Slave Testimony*, p. 458.

39. As an example in support of his argument, Lovell reports the 1850 census figures, which revealed that 45 percent of the slaves in the South were under 15 years of age, 56 percent were under 20, and almost 74 percent were under 30. Lovell summarizes the available data as indicating that "the folk community of the American slave is predominantly that of tough, resilient, overworked young people, generally in their late teens and twenties." Yet, "the plantation tradition stereotype of the typical slave is a white-thatched, bald-on-top old man, or a correspondingly elderly old woman, who had grinningly given up on life and thought only of pleasing 'ol massa' and 'ol mistus' as he stepped gingerly toward the grave." See Lovell, *Black Song*, p. 140.

40. See *Songs of Zion*, selection 97. Miles Mark Fisher makes the allusion to "I yearde from heaven to-day" (*Negro Slave Songs*, p. 57), in his comprehensive study, linking that phrase to songs composed in response to the receipt of mail in the Port Royal Islands from newly arrived Liberian colonists in 1825. Again, we have to question Fisher's ability to be so confident in the dating of composition of songs and their association with specific events. Lovell, in particular, questions Fisher's specific conclusions, especially with regard to the idea of many spirituals having a back-to-Africa connection (see

Black Song, pp. 112-13). More important than the specific facts (which are impossible to determine) is that Fisher has sparked our imagination in understanding how songs previously interpreted as otherworldly were probably employed for numerous *present world* purposes. As plausible as the back-to-Africa connection is the jubilant announcement, "I heard from heaven today," in response to news from a fugitive in the North or in Canada.

41. Cone, *The Spirituals and the Blues*, p. 86.

42. Lovell, *Black Song*, p. 371.

43. See *Songs of Zion*, selection 102.

44. See Southern, *The Music of Black Americans*, pp. 215-16.

45. Reagon, *The Songs Are Free*.

46. Frederick Douglass, from Foner's *The Life and Times of Frederick Douglass*, quoted in Harding, *There Is a River*, p. 147.

47. See *Songs of Zion*, selection 138.

48. James Cone, *Martin and Malcolm and America: A Dream or a Nightmare* (Maryknoll, New York: Orbis Books, 1991).

49. See Harding, *The Other American Revolution*, for a sketch of the course of the African American freedom struggle after the end of official slavery. See the two volumes by Tony Martin (*Literary Garveyism* and *African Fundamentalism* [Dover, Massachusetts: Majority Press, 1983]) on the often misunderstood and underestimated role of Garvey and the Harlem Renaissance. See Stuckey, *Slave Culture*, chap. 6, for an important treatment of Paul Robeson, his knowledge of African cultural foundations, and his contribution to the Black Nationalist stream of the struggle. For an important discussion of the long-term psychological fallout from the extended oppression of Africans in America, see Na'im Akbar, *Chains and Images of Psychological Slavery* (Jersey City, New Jersey: New Mind Publications, 1983). Again, see Cone, *Martin and Malcolm and America*, for a sketch of the two main wings of the 1960s phase of the struggle.

50. Carawan and Carawan, *Sing for Freedom*, p. 77.

51. For an account of the story of all of these and numerous other song adaptations and compositions during the movement, see Carawan and Carawan, *Sing for Freedom*, which is indexed by song title. See Harding, *Hope and History*, for an inspirational reflection on the meanings of the movement, including its songs, and for a set of arguments concerning the crucial need to preserve the movement's history.

52. See Cone, *Martin and Malcolm and America*, especially chap. 4.

53. Paul Robeson, *The Power and the Glory* (New York: Columbia Records, Compact Disc No. 0-7464-47337-2, 1991).

4. "City Called Heaven"

1. Harding, *Hope and History*, p. 77.

2. See *Songs of Zion*, selection 135.

3. For a discussion of the role of the Colonization Society, see Harding, *There Is a River*, especially pp. 66; 87; 132; 184. Also see Franklin, *From Slavery*

to Freedom, pp. 184-87; Lerone Bennett, *The Shaping of Black America*, Chicago: Johnson Publishing Co., 1975, p. 133; and John Lofton, *Denmark Vesey's Revolt*, Kent, Ohio: Kent State University Press, 1983, pp. 94-95. In addition, Lofton's book throughout provides a helpful understanding of the status and mind set of "free" Negroes. See especially Chapter 7, entitled "The Half Free Community."

4. Raboteau's *Slave Religion* was the first major work sketching the details of the African American community's transition to Christianity. Raboteau was somewhat cautious in his conclusions, arguing that African influences were strong in the Caribbean and South America, but considerably less strong in the United States. Stuckey, in *Slave Culture*, has expanded our understanding of the African influences in the United States. This enriched understanding is continued in Margaret Washington Creel's *A Peculiar People*. Levine's *Black Culture and Black Consciousness* provides an exploration of the robust aspects of African consciousness that remained as Africans in America converted to Christianity. John Blassingame, in his 1979 revision of *The Slave Community*, also seemed to be incorporating some of the new knowledge concerning African influences. Recently, as the use of slave narratives as a source of historical information has gained more widespread acceptance, the kind of perspectives offered by such scholars as Stuckey and Creel have gained even more support. See, for example, Dwight N. Hopkins and George C.L. Cummings, eds., *Cut Loose Your Stammering Tongue: Black Theology in the Slave Narratives* (Maryknoll, New York: Orbis Books, 1991), which offers a helpful and precise understanding of religious beliefs during slavery, gleaned from the undistorted testimonies of ex-slaves. Clearly, the "Christianity" that emerged and evolved among enslaved Africans was very different from the religion of their oppressors. Of course, it is also important to note that the religion that emerged in slavery was a unique new development, different in many respects both from its original African root forms and the Christianity borrowed from the oppressor. An excellent exploration of the highly complex issue of similarities and differences between current African and African American theologies is found in Josiah U. Young, *Black and African Theologies: Siblings or Distant Cousins?* (Maryknoll, New York: Orbis Books, 1986).

5. Stuckey, *Slave Culture*, p. 27.

6. See *Songs of Zion*, selection 129.

7. See for example, Parrish, *Slave Songs of the Georgia Sea Islands*, pp. 168-72. Of course, this song was undoubtedly sung at times to convey a deeper, more symbolic meaning as well. See especially Thurman, *Deep River*, pp. 90-96.

8. Stuckey, *Slave Culture*, p. 35.

9. Ibid., pp. 35-36.

10. Testimony of Mrs. Joseph Smith, 1863, in Canada. Blassingame, *Slave Testimony*, p. 411.

11. Will Coleman, "Coming Through 'Ligion," in Hopkins and Cummings, *Cut Loose Your Stammering Tongue*, p. 71.

12. Raboteau, *Slave Religion*, p. 127.

13. Ibid., p. 294. Those slave holders who allowed their slaves to worship were always sure to highlight one passage: "Slaves, obey your earthly masters with respect and fear, and with sincerity of heart, just as you would obey Christ. Obey them not only to win their favor when their eye is on you, but like slaves of Christ, doing the will of God from your heart" (Eph 6:5-6 NIV).

14. See *Songs of Zion*, selection 76.

15. Lovell, *Black Song*, pp. 191-92.

16. Raboteau, *Slave Religion*, pp. 136-37.

17. Dorothy Scarborough, *On the Trail of Negro Folk-Songs* (Cambridge, Massachusetts: Harvard University Press, 1925), pp. 22-23.

18. Testimony of Wash Wilson, quoted in Raboteau, *Slave Religion*, p. 213.

19. Those who have focused concretely on the number of African "retentions" among Africans in America have failed to understand the robustness of cultural frames of reference, even when specific "retentions" are no longer obvious. Linda James Myers has provided a helpful overview of the basic elements of an African world view that have survived among Africans in America even into the twentieth century (*Understanding an Afrocentric World View: Introduction to an Optimal Psychology* [Dubuque, Iowa: Kendall/Hunt Publishing Co., 1988]). In an altogether different context, Monica McGoldrick and the various authors in her important book on ethnically oriented family psychotherapy have discussed the robust continuation of diverse cultural value systems from the traditional cultures of the various people who now call themselves American. McGoldrick and her colleagues demonstrate convincingly that various root culture value systems (Irish, Russian, Chinese, African, etc.) determine the behavior of "Americans" far more than they are aware, and that mental health practitioners unknowledgeable of these traditional cultural influences are practicing under considerable handicap (Monica McGoldrick, John K. Pearce, and Joseph Giordano, eds., *Ethnicity and Family Therapy* (New York: Guilford Press, 1982).

20. Creel, *A Peculiar People*, p. 299.

21. See *Songs of Zion*, selection 121.

22. Lovell, *Black Song*, p. 29.

23. Testimony of Joe Oliver, quoted in Hopkins and Cummings, *Cut Loose Your Stammering Tongue*, p. 53.

24. Stephen B. Oates, *The Fires of Jubilee: Nat Turner's Fierce Rebellion* (New York: Mentor Books, 1975), pp. 28-29.

25. As noted previously, Miles Mark Fisher, in *Negro Slave Songs*, argues that Nat Turner was actually the composer of "Steal Away." The fact that Nat was so highly attuned to signs in nature (an eclipse of the sun, blood on the leaves of corn, shifts in the coloring of the sun and the movements of the wind, etc.) makes it plausible that such lyrics as "My Lord he calls me, He calls me by the thunder" may well have been of Nat's creation. Regardless, numerous observers have linked the singing of "Steal Away" and the Turner rebellion (see chap. 3, note 14). The ability to imagine the

power of the song in that connection does not require the assumption that Nat was its composer. See Oates, *The Fires of Jubilee,* for an excellent attempt at a narrative reconstruction of Nat's attention to the signs in nature as communication from God. Also see Nat's own testimony as recorded in Thomas R. Gray, *The Confession, Trial and Execution of Nat Turner,* in F. Roy Johnson, *The Nat Turner Slave Insurrection* (Murfreesboro, North Carolina: Johnson Publishing Co., 1966), pp. 225-48.

26. Stuckey, *Slave Culture,* p. 47. For the complete story of the life of Denmark Vesey and the historical backdrop of his planned insurrection, see John Lofton, *Denmark Vesey's Revolt.*

27. See Lofton, *Denmark Vesey's Revolt,* pp. 146-47.

28. See Lofton, *Denmark Vesey's Revolt,* pp. 134-35. See also Chapter 7, "The Half Free Community," which provides an illuminating discussion of the various ways in which "privilege" was only relative, even among so-called "free Negroes." Clearly, a relatively privileged status did not prevent most Africans from being aware of the deep-seated racism that ultimately had pervasive effects on the lives of all people in America of African descent. See also Harding, *There Is a River,* which provides numerous sketches of the way in which this theme reasserted itself throughout the history of the freedom struggles of the slavery period.

29. Will Coleman, "Coming Through 'Ligion," in Hopkins and Cummings, *Cut Loose Your Stammering Tongue,* p. 94.

30. Quoted in Lofton, *Denmark Vesey's Revolt,* p. 92.

31. Quoted in Stuckey, *Slave Culture,* pp. 48-49. See Lofton, *Denmark Vesey's Revolt,* for an outline of the various African churches that emerged in Charleston and the membership of Vesey in the Hampstead branch of one of the African associations (p. 93).

32. See Lofton, *Denmark Vesey's Revolt,* pp. 146-47.

33. See Harding, *There Is a River,* especially chap. 4.

34. See *Songs of Zion,* selection 205.

35. See Raboteau, *Slave Religion,* chap. 1.

36. Lovell, *Black Song,* p. 230.

37. See *Songs of Zion,* selection 140.

38. An effective rendition of this popular spiritual is found on Battle and Norman, *Spirituals in Concert.*

39. See *Songs of Zion,* selection 95.

40. See *Songs of Zion,* selection 118.

41. Lovell, *Black Song,* p. 233.

42. Ibid., p. 234.

43. *Songs of Zion,* selection 163.

44. *Songs of Zion,* selection 81.

45. Quoted in Jon Michael Spencer, *Protest and Praise: Sacred Music of Black Religion* (Minneapolis: Augsburg Fortress Press, 1990), p. 136.

46. See Spencer, *Protest and Praise,* for a comprehensive discussion of the role of rhythm in African and African American sacred music (chap. 6). The issue of improvised instruments is discussed on p. 142.

47. Ibid., p. 135.

48. *Songs of Zion*, selection 132.

49. Cone, *The Spirituals and the Blues*, pp. 83-84.

50. *Songs of Zion*, selection 135.

51. Cited in Lovell, *Black Song*, p. 299.

52. Ibid., p. 307.

53. Cone, *The Spirituals and the Blues*, p. 90.

54. Ibid., p. 91.

55. For effective accounts of these later developments, see Walker, *Somebody's Calling My Name*; Spencer, *Protest and Praise*; and *Songs of Zion*. Also see Cone, *The Spirituals and the Blues*. Both Cone and Spencer provide helpful discussions of the religious aspects of the blues, which are frequently mistakenly viewed as exclusively secular in their focus.

56. James Baldwin, *The Fire Next Time* (New York: Dial Press, 1963), pp. 47-48.

57. James P. Comer, *Beyond Black and White* (New York: Quadrangle Books, 1972), p. 17.

58. See Spencer, *Protest and Praise*, chap. 9, and Walker, *Somebody's Calling My Name*, chap. 7.

59. Levine, *Black Culture and Black Consciousness*, pp. 174-75.

60. Spencer, *Protest and Praise*, pp. 221-22.

61. Ibid., p. 200.

62. John Storm Roberts, *Black Music of Two Worlds* (New York: Praeger, 1972), p. 171.

63. See Walker, *Somebody's Calling My Name*, especially pp. 180-81.

64. See the helpful discussion of this issue by British Anglican priest Kenneth Leech in *Eye of the Storm: Living Spiritually in the Real World* (San Francisco: HarperCollins, 1992), pp. 62-63.

65. For an in-depth exploration of the general theme of Jung's lifelong attempt to provide "treatment" for a sick Christianity, see Murray Stein, *Jung's Treatment of Christianity* (Wilmette, Illinois: Chiron Publications, 1985). For Jung's personal reflections on his lifelong encounter with religion, see his autobiography, *Memories, Dreams and Reflections* (New York: Vintage Books, 1965). For an interesting comparison of Jung's approach to the spirit with the tenets of traditional Christianity, see Wallace Clift, *Jung and Christianity: The Challenge of Reconciliation* (New York: Crossroad, 1982).

66. See an interesting discussion of such commonalities in Mozella G. Mitchell, *Spiritual Dynamics of Howard Thurman's Theology* (Bristol, Indiana: Wyndham Hall Press, 1985), pp. 159-63.

67. See Buhrmann, *Living in Two Worlds*, which offers a fascinating comparison of the work and training of Jungian analysts and traditional healers among the Xhosa people of South Africa.

68. When the dimension of spirituality is considered at all, it is often, as in the case of Freudian theory, framed in almost exclusively pathological terms.

69. Contemporary Jungians may continue to be influenced, consciously

or unconsciously, by the ambivalent attitudes that Jung himself held concerning African and African American cultures. Regarding images found in the dreams of African Americans collected during his research in the United States, Jung wrote that "it is not a question of a specifically racial heredity, but of a universally human characteristic. . . . This disposition I later called the *archetype*" (*Symbols of Transformation*, p. 153). In this early work Jung clearly believed African Americans to be capable of producing symbolic material rich in "universally human" themes, captured in his concept of the archetype. However, in many of his later writings Jung revealed a great deal of pejorative thinking about black culture. For example, concerning what he perceived as the negative influence on American psychology by blacks, he wrote that "the expression of religious feeling, the revival meeting, the Holy Rollers and other abnormalities are strongly influenced by the Negro, and the famous American naivete, in its charming as well as its unpleasant form, invites comparison with the childlikeness of the Negro" (C. G. Jung, *Civilization in Transition* [Princeton, N.J.: Princeton University Press, 1970], p. 46). The demeaning tone of this passage is typical of Jung's later writing concerning African Americans as well as people of African descent around the world. Continuing the above discussion, for example, Jung wrote that "This infection by the primitive can, of course, be observed just as well in other countries. . . . In Africa, for example, the white man is a diminishing minority and must therefore protect himself from the Negro by observing the most rigorous social forms, otherwise he risks 'going black.' If he succumbs to the primitive influence he is lost" (ibid., p. 47).

It is not surprising that Jung allowed negative racial thinking to contaminate his otherwise extraordinary cross-cultural understanding; racist attitudes were pervasive in the late nineteenth century environment in which he grew up. However, contemporary Jungians and others concerned with inner spirituality have an opportunity to be enriched intellectually and experientially when they are able to transcend these racist limitations to view African and African American cultural symbols in a clear light, a light which Jung, always fascinated by rich symbolic material, would undoubtedly have relished had he not been so blinded by racial prejudice.

Unfortunately, many of the racist ideas prevalent in the culture of Jung's youth persist in more subtle form in today's European-American cultural environments. Such ideas have also occupied a prominent place throughout the history of the social sciences in Europe and America (see Alexander Thomas and Samuel Sillen, *Racism and Psychiatry* [Secaucus, N.J.: The Citadel Press, 1972]). Clearly, social scientists and others who work in earnest to be objective in their understanding of human functioning are not immune from the negative racial influences of the larger society.

70. See, for example, Arnold Mindell, *Dreambody: The Body's Role in Revealing the Self* (Boston: Sigo Press, 1982).

71. Leech, *Eye of the Storm*, pp. 3-4.

72. Ibid., p. 143.

73. Mahalia Jackson, *Gospels, Spirituals, and Hymns* (New York: Columbia

Records, Compact Disc No. C2K 47083, 1991), disc two. The specific site in Chicago of this performance is not designated in the accompanying material for this recording. I have taken the liberty of describing a setting typical of the ones in which Mahalia frequently sang.

5. "Scandalize' My Name"

1. W.E.B. Du Bois, *Prayers for Dark People*, ed. Herbert Aptheker (Amherst, Massachusetts: University of Massachusetts Press, 1980), p. 52. This and other prayers were written by Du Bois for use in his work with the primary, grammar, high school and college students who attended the old Atlanta University, at which Du Bois worked as a professor of economics and sociology from 1897 to 1910. This was a different institution from the current Atlanta University, which functions as the graduate training division of the Atlanta University Center, which was formed in 1929. See Aptheker's introduction to this valuable collection of Du Bois's prayers for the students of the original Atlanta University.

2. See *Songs of Zion*, selection 159.

3. Leech, *Eye of the Storm*, p. 47. The passages Leech is referring to are from Exodus, chapters 7-10, in which God instructs Moses at various points to say to the Pharaoh, "The Lord God of the Hebrews, hath sent me unto thee, saying, Let my people go, that they may serve me in the wilderness (King James Bible).

4. Johnson and Johnson, *American Negro Spirituals*, Book 2, p. 87.

5. Ibid., Book 1, p. 74.

6. Ibid., Book 1, pp. 40-43.

7. *Songs of Zion*, selection 110.

8. Ibid., selection 108.

9. Lovell, *Black Song*, p. 226.

10. See Carawan and Carawan, *Sing for Freedom*, p. 15; Spencer, *Protest & Praise*, pp. 15, 25, 84; Bernice Johnson Reagon, *Songs of the Civil Rights Movement* (Washington, D.C.: Doctoral Dissertation, Department of History, Howard University, 1975), pp. 64-90.

11. *Songs of Zion*, selection 163.

12. Gray, *The Confession, Trial and Execution of Nat Turner*, pp. 234-35.

13. Akbar, *Chains and Images of Psychological Slavery*, p. 2.

14. See Wachtel, *The Poverty of Affluence*.

15. I have described some of my work with such families in "Self-esteem and identity in psychotherapy with adolescents from upwardly mobile middle-class African American families," in Luis Vargas and Joan Koss-Chioino, eds., *Working with Culture: Psychological Interventions with Minority Youth* (San Francisco: Jossey-Bass, 1992).

16. Beverly Daniel Tatum, *Assimilation Blues: Black Families in a White Community* (Northampton, Massachusetts: Hazel-Maxwell, 1987 (originally published by Greenwood Press).

17. Marian Wright Edelman, *The Measure of Our Success: A Letter to My*

Children and Yours (Boston: Beacon Press, 1992), pp. 5-6.

18. Ibid., pp. 17-18.

19. Alice Walker, *Possessing the Secret of Joy* (New York: Harcourt Brace Jovanovich, 1992). This novel explores, in part, the issue of the mutilation of female genitals, which is prevalent in parts of Africa and which has devastating psychological and physical effects on its victims. See the transcript of an interview with Alice Walker in *Emerge* (September, 1992), pp. 9-10.

20. Regardless of what stance one takes theologically on the issue of homosexuality, it is impossible to condone the prevalent climate of hatred and bigotry in our communities directed at homosexual sisters and brothers who have had the courage to announce their identities publicly. One of the most articulate challenges to the African American community's history of ignorance and hypocrisy in this area is found in the transcript of a powerful address by Audre Lorde delivered at Medgar Evers College, "I Am Your Sister: Black Women Organizing Across Sexualities," reprinted in Gloria Anzaldúa, ed., *Making Face, Making Soul: Creative and Critical Perspectives by Women of Color* (San Francisco: Aunt Lute Foundation, 1990), pp. 321-25.

21. Huggins, *Black Odyssey*, p. xvi.

22. Joseph Barndt, *Dismantling Racism: The Continuing Challenge to White America* (Minneapolis: Augsburg Fortress, 1991).

23. U.S. Department of Health and Human Services, Advisory Board on Child Abuse and Neglect, *Creating Caring Communities: Blueprint for an Effective Federal Policy on Child Abuse and Neglect*, September, 1991.

24. Cornel West, "Learning to Talk of Race," *New York Times Magazine* (August 2, 1992), p. 26.

25. See Hayes, *My Songs*, which was published in 1948.

26. Roland Hayes, quoted in MacKinley Helm, *Angel Mo' and Her Son, Roland Hayes* (New York: Greenwood Press, 1942), pp. 110-11.

27. This previously unissued recording of "Scandalize My Name" is included in a Smithsonian Institution Collection entitled *The Art of Roland Hayes* (Washington, D.C.: Smithsonian Institution, Compact Disc No. RD041, 1990). Hayes's infusion of the Judas story into the interpretation of "Scandalize My Name" is reported in the liner notes, p. 21.

6. "There Is a Balm in Gilead"

1. See *Songs of Zion*, selection 123.

2. Jessye Norman, with the Ambrosian Singers and Willis Patterson, conductor, *Spirituals, Philips,* (Compact Disc No. 416 462-2, 1978). See *Songs of Zion*, selection 123.

3. Arna Bontemps, *Chariot in the Sky: A Story of the Jubilee Singers* (Philadelphia: John C. Winston, 1951), pp 182-184. In reference to the Oberlin experience, J.B.T. Marsh's early documentary account of the Fisk tours, *The Story of the Jubilee Singers* (Boston: Houghton, 1880), says simply that "The Council consented to hear a few pieces during a recess in their deliberations" (p. 24). G. D. Pike's documentary account, *The Jubilee Singers and Their Cam-*

paign for Ten Thousand Dollars (Boston: Lee and Shepard, 1873), indicates that "the Council took a recess in an afternoon's session, and listened to a few of their selections. So great was their delight … that nothing which transpired at the Council so interested them as the singing of these ex-slaves" (p. 95). Bontemps, in his semi-fictional story, was attempting to describe from the perspective of the singers what it was actually like that day in Oberlin. Bontemps's story appears to have formed the basis of other accounts of the Fisk singers, such as the one in Langston Hughes's *Famous Negro Music Makers* (New York: Dodd, Mead Co., 1955, pp. 17-26). Regardless of the question of whether the details of Bontemps's novel reflect exactly what happened, it is clear from all of the accounts that Oberlin marked one of the early turning points for the singers, and that their singing of the spirituals from that point on was an important reason for the astounding financial success of their tour. Although the Fisk singers still encountered varied responses after Oberlin, their success was solidified during the New York portion of their tour. See Louis Silveri, "The Singing Tours of the Fisk Jubilee Singers: 1871-1874," in George R. Keck and Sherrill V. Martin, eds., *Feel the Spirit: Studies in Nineteenth-Century Afro-American Music* (New York: Greenwood Press, 1988), pp. 105-16.

4. This story of the experiences of the Jubilee singers is synopsized from the above noted sources and from Lovell, *Black Song*, pp. 402-8.

5. See Lovell, *Black Song*, pp. 408-18. Particularly interesting is Lovell's account of early developments at Howard, where students initially rebelled against singing spirituals. In a student editorial a writer noted that Andrew Carnegie, in a visit to Howard, was more impressed by Howard students' singing of an anthem in Latin than he was by their singing of spirituals. The student went on to ask, "wouldn't it be a wise plan to have one negro college paying especial attention to the study of the great masters?" Fortunately, Howard later became one of the strongest centers of appreciation of the importance of spirituals. See *Black Song*, pp. 416-17. However, the attitudes of the early students at Howard are sadly illustrative of the widespread "miseducation" which led (and leads) to African Americans having an ignorance of their significant cultural roots and a tendency to elevate the importance of European cultural products over their own. See Woodson, *The Mis-Education of the Negro*. In the case of the spirituals, distortions in the history of their origins and meanings have resulted in a particularly strong barrier to their gaining the respect they deserve.

6. Of course, the concert versions of spirituals performed by the Fisk singers were different from the spontaneous singing that had occurred among Africans in slavery. Nonetheless, it is clear that audiences still responded strongly to the melodies and rhythms of these songs. There has been an ongoing debate about what constitutes an "authentic" spiritual. I find myself agreeing with Lovell, who has argued that "there is no such thing as adulterating a spiritual. There is no superstandard to begin with; there are only people creating and singing what is in their hearts, what is on their minds as they survey the living scenes through the eyes and other

senses of their art. . . . As new groups interpret them in new ways, they insure that the spiritual will stay alive. If people were forced to sing the songs the way some arbitrary authority decides . . . the spiritual would quickly die" (*Black Song*, p. 422). I am not swayed by the notion that because a spiritual has been "concertized" it therefore loses its power. For me, the distinguishing issue is whether the singers bring to the song their complete selves, opening themselves to the archetypal power of the song as it moves through their bodies. This can happen in a cappella singing, in "arranged" spirituals, or in spirituals fused with other music forms, as in gospel music.

7. See Lovell, *Black Song*, pp. 471-73 and 544-45, for a description and listing of the most important collections.

8. The long list of distinguished arrangers of spirituals in this genre includes R. Nathaniel Dett, Hall Johnson, Eva Jessye, Edward Boatner, William Grant Still, Frederick J. Work, John Wesley Work II, John W. Work III, Rosamond and James Weldon Johnson, Samuel Coleridge-Taylor, Sylvia Olden Lee, Margaret Bonds, William Levi Dawson, Marylou Jackson, Betty Jackson King, Mary Grissom, Wendell Whalum, Roland Carter, Clarence Cameron White and Jester Hairston. See Lovell, *Black Song*, pp. 425-58; Southern, *Music of Black Americans*, pp. 415-27; Tilford Brooks, *America's Black Musical Heritage* (Englewood Cliffs, New Jersey: Prentice-Hall, 1984), pp. 41-42, 200-226.

With regard to the prevalence in some circles of a strong prejudice against the singing of spirituals by performers trained in the European classical tradition, the issue here is again one of perspective. From one perspective, one could certainly argue that the refined singing style of such singers makes the spirituals very different from the traditional African style in which they were originally sung. However, from another perspective, one that makes more sense to me, one could argue that the persistent tradition of performance of spirituals by classically trained African American singers (begun by such great performers as Hayes, Robeson and Anderson, all thoroughly secure in their identities as African Americans) is a tribute to the robust nature of the African American spirituals tradition, which consistently occupies a salient part of the consciousness of singers whose European training would otherwise provide practically no motivation for such work.

9. Working with "arranged" as well as "original" material, numerous soloists have carried the messages of the spirituals worldwide. These singers have performed in very different styles, ranging from traditional folk to gospel and European classical forms. Nevertheless, all of them, in their unique ways, have had the ability to interpret spirituals in a manner that conveys their deep, archetypally significant meanings. The list of these soloists would include such distinguished artists as Roland Hayes, Marian Anderson, Paul Robeson, Leontyne Price, Mahalia Jackson, Harry Belafonte, Odetta, Sister Rosetta Tharpe, Marie Knight, William Warfield, Kathleen Battle, Joan Baez, Nina Simone, Jessye Norman, Florence Quivar, Barbara Hendricks, Simon Estes, Bernice Johnson Reagon and Roman Catholic Sister Thea Bowman.

Strong communicative integrity has also characterized the singing of spirituals by varied singing groups and ensembles, again very different from each other but equally laudable in their interpretation and communication of the messages of the spirituals. The list of ensembles known for their effective interpretation of spirituals includes the Weavers, the Williams Colored Singers, the Thrasher Wonders, the Hall Johnson and Eva Jessye Choirs, Sweet Honey in the Rock, the Albert MacNeil Jubilee Singers, the Harlem Spiritual Ensemble and countless choirs and ensembles from traditional African American colleges, universities and communities around the country.

10. Consistent with the long history of audience reactions to the spirituals, I have frequently had people attending my own lecture-recital programs make such comments as "This music is so uplifting," "We sure have to make sure we don't lose the spirituals; they are so *healing*," etc.

11. See Harding, *Hope and History*.

12. Thurman, *Deep River*, pp. 59-60.

13. Thea Bowman, "The Gift of African American Sacred Song," in *Lead Me, Guide Me: The African American Catholic Hymnal* (Chicago: G.I.A. Publications, 1987) introductory section.

14. Du Bois, *The Souls of Black Folk*, p. 186.

15. Lovell, *Black Song*, pp. 384-85.

16. In the many lecture-recital programs I have conducted, audience members (African American and non-African American alike) consistently have responded (both on written questionnaires and in comments after the programs) with such comments as, "I had no idea these songs were so complex or that they had so many meanings," "Thank you for this program; I have an appreciation for a part of my culture I had no idea existed," etc. These comments are especially prevalent among people forty years of age and under, suggesting that knowledge of the spirituals, which was previously commonplace, is starting to be lost.

17. Reagon, *The Songs are Free*.

18. See especially Dennison's *Scandalize My Name* for a discussion of the long tradition of co-optation and misrepresentation of African American music that has resulted in the kind of "slavish" images referred to by Lovell. See also Amiri Baraka's excellent essay on the same subject, entitled "The Great Music Robbery," which appears in Amiri Baraka and Amina Baraka, *The Music* (New York: William Morrow and Co., 1987), pp. 328-32.

19. Again, see Woodson, *The Mis-education of the Negro* and the earlier discussion of this issue in Chapter 1.

20. See Walker, *Somebody's Calling My Name*; Spencer, *Protest and Praise*.

21. Walker, *Somebody's Calling My Name*, p. 181.

22. Ibid., p. 187.

23. Ibid., p. 181.

24. Harding, *There Is a River*, p. xxiii.

25. Excerpted from Martin Luther King, Jr., "I Have a Dream," speech delivered on August 28, 1963, in Washington, D.C. Reprinted in Cone, *Martin and Malcolm and America*, pp. 84-85.

26. *Songs of Zion*, selection 80.

27. Not surprisingly, this song was also sung exuberantly at a time of *actual* freedom, the ending of official slavery. See, for example, an account by an ex-slave reported by Hopkins, "Slave Theology," in Hopkins and Cummings, *Cut Loose Your Stammering Tongue*, pp. 44-45.

28. These lyrics are from a rap song by Todd Thomas ("Speech") entitled "Raining Revolution," recorded by the group Arrested Development in an album entitled *Arrested Development: 3 Years, 5 Months and 2 Days in the Life of . . .* (New York: Chrysalis Records [EMI Records Group], Compact Disc No. CDP 21929, 1992).

29. In addition to the creative integration of African American traditions into rap music and other contemporary cultural developments, it is encouraging to witness the appearance recently of collections of traditional spirituals compiled for children and families, signaling a renewed collective recognition of the importance of passing on the voices of the ancestors. Particularly noteworthy are John Langstaff, *What a Morning: The Christmas Story in Black Spirituals* (New York: Margaret K. McElderry Books, 1987); Ashley Bryan, *All Night, All Day: A Child's First Book of African-American Spirituals* (New York: Athenum, 1991); and John Langstaff, *Climbing Jacob's Ladder: Heroes of the Bible in African-American Spirituals* (New York: McElderry Books, 1991).

References

Books and Articles

Abingdon Press. *Songs of Zion*. Nashville: Abingdon, 1981.

Akbar, Na'im. *Chains and Images of Psychological Slavery*. Jersey City, N.J.: New Mind Publications, 1983.

Allen, William Francis, Charles Pickard Ware, and Lucy McKim Garrison. *Slave Songs of the United States*. Reprinted by New York: Peter Smith, 1951, originally published in 1867.

American Psychiatric Association. *The Diagnostic and Statistical Manual of Mental Disorders*. Washington, D.C.: American Psychiatric Association, 1987.

Ames, Russell. *The Story of American Folk Song*. New York: Grosset and Dunlap, 1955.

Appiah, Kwame Anthony. *In My Father's House: Africa in the Philosophy of Culture*. New York: Oxford Press, 1992.

Asante, Molefi Kete. *Afrocentricity*. Trenton, N.J.: Africa World Press, 1988.

———. *The Afrocentric Idea*. Philadelphia: Temple University Press, 1987.

———. *Kemet, Afrocentricity and Knowledge*. Trenton, N.J.: Africa World Press, 1990.

Baldwin, James. *The Fire Next Time*. New York: Dial Press, 1963.

Baraka, Amiri (LeRoi Jones), and Amini Baraka. *The Music*. New York: William Morrow and Co., 1987.

Barndt, Joseph. *Dismantling Racism: The Continuing Challenge to White America*. Minneapolis: Augsburg Fortress, 1991.

Bennett, Jr., Lerone. *Before the Mayflower*, fourth edition. Chicago: Johnson Publishing Co., 1969.

Bennett, Lerone. *The Shaping of Black America*. Chicago: Johnson Publishing Co., 1975.

Blassingame, John W. *The Slave Community: Plantation Life in the Antebellum South*, revised edition. New York: Oxford University Press, 1979.

———, ed. *Slave Testimony*. Baton Rouge: Louisiana State University Press, 1977.

Boatner, Edward. *The Story of the Spirituals*. Miami: Belwin Mills, 1973.

Bontemps, Arna. *Chariot in the Sky: A Story of the Jubilee Singers*. New York: Holt, Rinehart and Winston, 1971, originally published in 1951.

Bowman, Sister Thea. "The Gift of African American Sacred Song." In *Lead Me, Guide Me: The African American Catholic Hymnal*. Chicago: G.I.A. Publications, 1987.

Bradford, Sarah Elizabeth. *Harriet Tubman, the Moses of Her People*. New York: Corinth Books, 1961, originally published in 1886.

Brent, Linda (Harriet Jacobs). "Incidents in the Life of a Slave Girl." In Henry Louis Gates, Jr., ed. *The Classic Slave Narratives*. New York: Penguin Books, 1987.

Brooks, Tilford. *America's Black Musical Heritage*. Englewood Cliffs, N.J.: Prentice-Hall, 1984.

Bryan, Ashley. *All Night, All Day: A Child's First Book of African-American Spirituals*. New York: Athenum, 1991.

Buhrmann, M. Vera. *Living in Two Worlds: Communication Between a White Healer and Her Black Counterparts*. Wilmette, Ill.: Chiron Publications, 1986.

Carawan, Guy, and Candie Carawan. *Sing for Freedom: The Story of the Civil Rights Movement Through Its Songs*. Bethlehem, Penn.: Sing Out Corporation, 1990.

Clift, Wallace. *Jung and Christianity: The Challenge of Reconciliation*. New York: Crossroad, 1982.

Coleman, Will. "Coming Through 'Ligion." In Dwight N. Hopkins and George C.L. Cummings, eds. *Cut Loose Your Stammering Tongue: Black Theology in the Slave Narratives*. Maryknoll, N.Y.: Orbis Books, 1991.

Comer, James P. *Beyond Black and White*. New York: Quadrangle Books, 1972.

Cone, James H. *Martin & Malcolm & America: A Dream or a Nightmare*. Maryknoll, N.Y.: Orbis Books, 1991.

———. *The Spirituals and the Blues: An Interpretation*. Maryknoll, N.Y.: Orbis Books, 1991, originally published in 1972.

Courlander, Harold. *Negro Folk Music, U.S.A.* New York: Columbia University Press, 1963.

Creel, Margaret Washington. *"A Peculiar People": Slave Religion and Community-Culture Among the Gullahs*. New York: New York University Press, 1988.

Cummings, George C.L. "The Slave Narratives as a Source of Black Theological Discourse: The Spirit and Eschatology." In Dwight N. Hopkins and George C. L. Cummings, eds. *Cut Loose Your Stammering Tongue: Black Theology in the Slave Narratives*. Maryknoll, N.Y.: Orbis Books, 1991.

Dennison, Sam. *Scandalize My Name: Black Imagery in American Popular Music*. New York: Garland Publishing, 1982.

Dett, R. Nathaniel, ed. *Religious Folk-Songs of the Negro*. New York: AMS Press, 1972, originally published in 1927.

Dixon, Crista. *Negro Spirituals: From Bible to Folksong*. Philadelphia: Fortress Press, 1976.

Douglass, Frederick. Selection from "My Bondage and My Freedom." In Eileen Southern, ed. *Readings in the Music of Black Americans*. New York: W. W. Norton, 1971.

———. "Narrative in the Life of Frederick Douglass." In Henry Louis Gates, Jr., ed. *The Classic Slave Narratives*. New York: Penguin Books, 1987, originally published in 1845.

Du Bois, W.E.B. *The Souls of Black Folk*. New York: Bantam Books, 1989, originally published in 1903.

————. *Dusk of Dawn*. New York: Harcourt, Brace and Co., 1940.

————. *Prayers for Dark People*. Herbert Aptheker, ed. Amherst: University of Massachussetts Press, 1980.

Edelman, Marian Wright. *The Measure of Our Success: A Letter to My Children and Yours*. Boston: Beacon Press, 1992.

Ferris, Jeri. *Go Free or Die: A Story about Harriet Tubman*. Minneapolis: Carolrhoda Books, 1988.

Fisher, Miles Mark. *Negro Slave Songs in the United States*. New York: Russell and Russell, 1968, originally published in 1953.

Franklin, John Hope. *From Slavery to Freedom*, fourth edition. New York: Alfred A. Knopf, 1974.

Frazier, E. Franklin. *The Negro in the United States*, revised edition. New York: Macmillan, 1957.

G.I.A. Publications. *Lead Me, Guide Me: The African American Catholic Hymnal*. Chicago: G.I.A. Publications, 1987.

Gray, Thomas R. *The Confession, Trial and Execution of Nat Turner*, originally published in 1831. Reprinted in F. Roy Johnson, *The Nat Turner Slave Insurrection*. Murfreesboro, N.C.: Johnson Publishing Co., 1966.

Harding, Vincent. *The Other American Revolution*. Los Angeles: Center for Afro-American Studies, 1980.

————. *There Is a River: The Black Struggle for Freedom in America*. New York: Vintage Books, 1983.

————. *Hope and History: Why We Must Share the Story of the Movement*. Maryknoll, N.Y.: Orbis Books, 1990.

Hayes, Roland. *My Songs*. Boston: Little, Brown and Co., 1948.

Helm, MacKinley. *Angel Mo' and her Son, Roland Hayes*. New York: Greenwood Press, 1942.

Herskovits, Melville. *The Myth of the Negro Past*. Boston: Beacon Press, 1958.

Holloway, Joseph E., ed. *Africanisms in American Culture*. Bloomington: Indiana University Press, 1990.

Hopkins, Dwight N. "Slave Theology in the 'Invisible Institution.' " In Dwight N. Hopkins and George C.L. Cummings, eds. *Cut Loose Your Stammering Tongue: Black Theology in the Slave Narratives*. Maryknoll, N.Y.: Orbis Books, 1991.

Hopkins, Dwight N., and George C.L. Cummings, eds. *Cut Loose Your Stammering Tongue: Black Theology in the Slave Narratives*. Maryknoll, N.Y.: Orbis Books, 1991.

Huggins, Nathan Irvin. *Black Odyssey: The African-American Ordeal in Slavery*. New York: Vintage Books, 1990, originally published in 1977.

Hughes, Langston. *Famous Negro Music Makers*. New York: Dodd, Mead and Co., 1955.

Jackson, George Pullen. *Spiritual Folk-Songs of Early America*. Gloucester, Mass.: Peter Smith, 1975, originally published in New York: J. J. Augustin, 1937.

Jenkins, Adelbert. *The Psychology of the Afro-American: A Humanistic Approach*. New York: Pergamon Press, 1982.

Johnson, James Weldon, and J. Rosamond Johnson. *The Books of American Negro Spirituals.* New York: Da Capo Press, 1973, originally published as two separate volumes in 1925 and 1926.

Jones, Arthur C. "Psychological Functioning in Black Americans: A Conceptual Guide for Use in Psychotherapy." *Psychotherapy,* volume 22 (2S), 1985. Reprinted in Reginald Jones, ed., *Black Psychology,* third edition (Berkeley, Cal.: Cobb and Henry, 1991).

―――. "Psychological Functioning in African American Adults: Some Elaborations on a Model, with Clinical Applications." In Reginald L. Jones, ed. *Black Adult Development and Aging.* Berkeley, Cal.: Cobb and Henry, 1989.

―――. "Self-esteem and Identity in Psychotherapy with Adolescents from Upwardly Mobile Middle-Class African American Families." In Luis Vargas and Joan Koss-Chioino, eds. *Working with Culture: Psychological Interventions with Ethnic Minority Children and Adolescents.* San Francisco: Jossey-Bass, 1992.

Jones, Jr., Ferdinand. "Dancing to the Music in Our Heads." *Brown University Alumni Monthly* 90 (2), October 1989.

Jones, LeRoi (Amiri Baraka). *The Blues People.* New York: William Morrow and Co., 1963.

Jung, C. G. *Psychological Types* (*Collected Works of C. G. Jung,* volume 6). Princeton, N.J.: Princeton University Press, 1971.

―――. *Psychology and Alchemy* (*Collected Works of C. G. Jung,* volume 12). London: Routledge and Kegan Paul, 1953.

―――. *Civilization in Transition* (*Collected Works of C. G. Jung,* second edition, volume 10). Princeton, N.J.: Princeton University Press, 1970. First edition published in 1964.

―――. *Symbols of Transformation* (*Collected Works of C. G. Jung,* second edition, volume 5). Princeton, N.J.: Bollingen Foundation, 1967. First edition published in 1956.

―――. *Memories, Dreams and Reflections.* New York: Vintage Books, 1965.

Katz, Bernard, ed. *The Social Implications of Early Negro Music in the United States.* New York: Arno Press, 1969.

Kovel, Joel. *White Racism: A Psychohistory.* New York: Vintage Books, 1971.

Krehbiel, Henry Edward. *Afro-American Folk-Songs.* New York: Frederick Ungar Publishing Co., 1962, originally published in 1913.

Langstaff, John. *Climbing Jacob's Ladder: Heroes of the Bible in African-American Spirituals.* New York: McElderry Books, 1991.

―――. *What a Morning: The Christmas Story in Black Spirituals.* McElderry Books, 1987.

Leech, Kenneth. *The Eye of the Storm: Living Spiritually in the Real World.* San Francisco: HarperCollins, 1992.

Lester, Julius. *To Be a Slave.* New York: Scholastic, Inc., 1968.

Levine, Lawrence. *Black Culture and Black Consciousness.* New York: Oxford Press, 1977.

Lofton, John. *Denmark Vesey's Revolt.* Kent, Ohio: Kent State University Press, 1983.

Lomax, Alan. *The Folk Songs of North America*. Garden City, N.Y.: Doubleday, 1960.

Lorde, Audre. "I Am Your Sister: Black Women Organizing Across Sexualities." In Gloria Anzaldúa, ed. *Making Face, Making Soul: Creative and Critical Perspectives by Women of Color*. San Francisco: Aunt Lute Foundation, 1990.

Lovell, John Jr. *Black Song: The Forge and the Flame: The Story of How the Afro-American Spiritual Was Hammered Out*. New York: Paragon House Publishers, 1986, originally published in 1972.

————. "The Social Implications of the Negro Spiritual." In Bernard Katz, ed. *The Social Implications of Early Negro Music in the United States*. New York: Arno Press, 1969.

Marsh, J.B.T. *The Story of the Jubilee Singers*. Boston: Houghton, 1880.

Martin, Tony. *African Fundamentalism*. Dover, Mass.: Majority Press, 1983.

————. *Literary Garveyism*. Dover, Mass.: Majority Press, 1983.

McGoldrick, Monica, John K. Pearce and Joseph Giordano, eds. *Ethnicity and Family Therapy*. New York: Guilford Press, 1982.

McKim, James Miller. "Negro Songs." In Bernard Katz, ed. *The Social Implications of Early Negro Music in the United States*. New York: Arno Press, 1969.

Mindell, Arnold. *Dreambody: The Body's Role in Revealing the Self*. Boston: Sigo Press, 1982.

Mitchell, Mozella G. *Spiritual Dynamics of Howard Thurman's Theology*. Bristol, Ind.: Wyndham Hall Press, 1985.

Myers, Linda James. *Understanding an Afrocentric World View: Introduction to an Optimal Psychology*. Dubuque, Iowa: Kendall/Hunt Publishing Co., 1988.

Nobles, Wade W. "African Philosophy: Foundations of Black Psychology." In Reginald L. Jones, ed. *Black Psychology*, third edition. Berkeley, Cal.: Cobb and Henry, 1991.

Oates, Stephen B. *The Fires of Jubilee: Nat Turner's Fierce Rebellion*. New York: Mentor Books, 1975

Parrish, Lydia. *Slave Songs of the Georgia Sea Islands*. Athens, Ga.: University of Georgia Press, 1992, originally published in 1942.

Pike, G. D. *The Jubilee Singers and Their Campaign for Ten Thousand Dollars*. Boston: Lee and Shepard, 1873.

Raboteau, Albert J. *Slave Religion*. New York: Oxford Press, 1978.

Reagon, Bernice Johnson. *Songs of the Civil Rights Movement 1955-1965: A Study in Culture History*. Washington, D.C.: Doctoral Dissertation, Department of History, Howard University, 1975.

Roberts, John Storm. *Black Music of Two Worlds*, New York: Praeger, 1972.

Robeson, Paul. *Here I Stand*, Boston: Beacon Press, 1958.

Scarborough, Dorothy. *On the Trail of Negro Folk-Songs*. Cambridge, Mass.: Harvard University Press, 1925.

Silveri, Louis. "The Singing Tours of the Fisk Jubilee Singers: 1871-1874." In George R. Keck and Sherrill V. Martin, eds. *Feel the Spirit: Studies in Nineteenth-Century Afro-American Music*. New York: Greenwood Press, 1988.

Smith, Jr., Luther E. *Howard Thurman: The Mystic as Prophet*. Washington, D.C.: University Press of America, 1981.

Southern, Eileen. *The Music of Black Americans*, second edition. New York: W. W. Norton, 1983.

Spencer, Jon Michael. *Protest and Praise: Sacred Music of Black Religion*. Minneapolis: Augsburg Fortress, 1990.

Stein, Murray. *Jung's Treatment of Christianity*. Wilmette, Ill.: Chiron Publications, 1985.

Stuckey, Sterling. *Slave Culture*. New York: Oxford Press, 1987.

Tatum, Beverly Daniel. *Assimilation Blues: Black Families in a White Community*. Northampton, Mass.: Hazel-Maxwell, 1987, originally published by Greenwood Press.

Thomas, Alexander and Samuel Sillen. *Racism and Psychiatry*. Secaucus, N.J.: The Citadel Press, 1972.

Thurman, Howard. *Deep River and The Negro Spiritual Speaks of Life and Death*. Richmond, Ind.: Friends United Press, 1975. (Compilation of two separate volumes originally published in 1945 and 1947 respectively.)

———. *With Head and Heart: The Autobiography of Howard Thurman*. New York: Harcourt Brace Jovanovich, 1979.

Unfeker, Robert F., ed. *Music Therapy in the Treatment of Adults with Mental Disorders*. New York: Schirmer Books (Macmillan), 1990.

U.S. Department of Health and Human Services, Office of Human Development Services, Advisory Board on Child Abuse and Neglect, *Child Abuse and Neglect: Critical First Steps in Response to a National Emergency*. Washington, D.C.: U.S. Government Printing Office Document No. 017-092-00104-5, August, 1990.

U.S. Department of Health and Human Services, Advisory Board on Child Abuse and Neglect. *Creating Caring Communities: Blueprint for an Effective Federal Policy on Child Abuse and Neglect*, September, 1991.

Wachtel, Paul. *The Poverty of Affluence: A Psychological Portrait of the American Way of Life*. New York: Free Press, 1983.

Walker, Alice. *Possessing the Secret of Joy*. New York: Harcourt Brace Jovanovich, 1992.

Walker, David. *Walker's Appeal in Four Articles*. Salem, N.H.: Ayer Co., 1989, originally published in 1829.

Walker, Wyatt Tee. *"Somebody's Calling My Name": Black Sacred Music and Social Change*. Valley Forge, Penn.: Judson Press, 1979.

West, Cornel. "Learning to Talk of Race." *New York Times Magazine*, August 2, 1992.

White, Joseph L., and Thomas A. Parham. *Psychology of Blacks*. Englewood Cliffs, N.J.: Prentice-Hall, 1990.

Wilson, August. *Joe Turner's Come and Gone*. New York: NAL Penguin, Inc., 1988.

Woodson, Carter G. *The Mis-education of the Negro*. Trenton, N.J.: Africa World Press, 1990, originally published in 1933.

Work, John W. *American Negro Songs*. New York: Bonanza Books, 1940.

Young, Josiah U. *Black and African Theologies: Siblings or Distant Cousins*. Maryknoll, N.Y.: Orbis Books, 1986.

Recommended Recordings

Marian Anderson. *Marian Anderson*. New York: RCA Victor, 1989.

Marian Anderson. *Marian Anderson: He's Got the Whole World in His Hands*. New York: BMG Music Classics (originally RCA Victor), 1994.

Arrested Development. *Arrested Development: 3 Years, 5 Months and 2 Days in the Life of* . . . . New York: Chrysalis Records (EMI Records Group), 1992.

Kathleen Battle and Jessye Norman. *Spirituals in Concert*. Hamburg, Germany: Deutsche Grammophon, 1991.

Black Christmas: Spirituals in the African-American Tradition. Dobbs Ferry, NY: ESS.A.Y. Recordings, 1990.

Cyrus Chestnut. *Blessed Quietness: A Collection of Hymns, Spirituals and Carols*. New York: Atlantic 1996.

Leland Owen Clarke. *My Lord, What a Morning: African American Spirituals*. Boston: Andell Records, 1998.

Samuel Coleridge-Taylor. *Spirituals*. New York: Koch International, 1992.

Pamela Dillard, Ruth Hamilton, Robert Honeysucker, and Vivian Taylor. *Watch and Pray: Spirituals and Art Songs by African-American Women Composers*. Westbury, NY: Koch International, 1994.

Simon Estes. *Spirituals*. Hanover, West Germany: Philips, 1984.

Aretha Franklin. *Amazing Grace*. New York: Atlantic Recording Company, 1972. Re-released.

Golden Gate Quartet. *The Very Best of the Golden Gate Quartet*. Hollywood, CA: World Pacific, 1997.

Charlie Haden and Hank Jones. *Steal Away*. New York: Verve Records, 1995.

Harlem Spiritual Ensemble. *The Harlem Spiritual Ensemble, in Concert*. New York: Arcadia Records, 1991.

Harlem Spiritual Ensemble. *Free at Last*. New York: Arcadia Records, 1992.

Kim Harris and Reggie Harris. *Steal Away: Songs of the Underground Railroad*. Appleseed, 1998.

Roland Hayes. *The Art of Roland Hayes*. Washington, D.C.: Smithsonian Institution, 1990.

Roland Hayes. *Favorite Spirituals*. New York: Vanguard Classics, 1995.

Mahalia Jackson. *Best Loved Spirituals*. New York: Sony, 1993.

Mahalia Jackson. *Gospels, Spirituals and Hymns*. New York: Columbia Records, 1991.

McIntosh County Shouters. *The McIntosh County Shouters: Slave Shout Songs from the Coast of Georgia*. Washington, D.C.: Smithsonian/Folkways Recordings, 1984.

Albert McNeil. *"They've Got the Whole World in Their Hands": Spirituals, Gospel and African-American Folksongs by the Albert McNeil Jubilee Singers*. Hermosa Beach, CA: Golden Jubilee Records, 1991.

Jessye Norman, with the Ambrosian Singers and Willis Patterson, conductor. *Spirituals*. Phillips, 1978.

Index of Spirituals

Index of Names